ESSENTIAL WINES AND WINERIES
OF THE PACIFIC NORTHWEST

ESSENTIAL WINES AND WINERIES

OF THE PACIFIC NORTHWEST

A Guide to the Wine Countries
of Washington, Oregon,
British Columbia, and Idaho

COLE DANEHOWER

Photography by Andrea Johnson

TIMBER PRESS
Portland ∗ London

FRONTISPIECE: One important advantage to wine grape growing in the Northwest is the extra hours of sunlight the grapes receive. TITLE PAGE: The tasting room at Januik Winery in Woodinville, Washington.

Maps by Allan Cartography, Medford, Oregon

Published in 2010 by Timber Press, Inc.

The Haseltine Building
133 S.W. Second Avenue, Suite 450
Portland, Oregon 97204-3527
www.timberpress.com

2 The Quadrant
135 Salusbury Road
London NW6 6RJ
www.timberpress.co.uk

ISBN-13: 978-0-88192-966-9

Printed in China

Library of Congress Cataloging-in-Publication Data

Danehower, Cole.
  Essential wines and wineries of the Pacific Northwest : a guide to the wine countries of Washington, Oregon, British Columbia, and Idaho / Cole Danehower ; photography by Andrea Johnson.
     p. cm.
  Includes bibliographical references and index.
  ISBN 978-0-88192-966-9
  1. Wine and wine making—Northwest, Pacific—Guidebooks. 2. Wineries—Northwest, Pacific—Guidebooks. 3. Northwest, Pacific—Guidebooks. I. Title.
  TP557.D357 2010
  641.2´209795—dc22   2010005073

A catalog record for this book is also available from the British Library.

To Andrea and Heidi

CONTENTS

PREFACE

When I moved to rural Oregon from California many years ago, I brought with me a typical American wine bias: California was the only real wine country in North America, and anywhere else that made its own local wine was . . . quaint. So I reacted with skepticism when my sister and brother-in-law, who owned a restaurant on the Oregon coast, served me my first bottle of Pacific Northwest wine. It was a pinot gris, a grape I had never encountered in California, from a winery called The Eyrie Vineyards, a name that was also unknown to me.

To my surprise, I liked the wine. Even more surprising, I found I liked a lot of the wines I began tasting from my new Pacific Northwest home. And I quickly developed an acute curiosity about the wines of the region, from Oregon, Washington, British Columbia, and even Idaho. A long story later, including meeting my wife over a bottle of Oregon wine, I have become intimately familiar with, and infinitely respectful of, wines made in the Northwest.

Since 1999, I have been making my living writing about Pacific Northwest wines and the region. I've had the pleasure of visiting all the wine-producing areas of the Northwest, from Kelowna, British Columbia, in the north to Cave Junction, Oregon, in the south; from Vancouver Island in the northwest to Boise, Idaho, in the southeast; and all the places in between. From these experiences, I have developed tremendous admiration for the people who have created this world-class wine region, and my esteem for

the splendid range and quality of the wines they produce grows with each new vintage.

In this book, I want to share my enthusiasm for these wines and discuss exactly why I think the Pacific Northwest is such an exciting wine region. This book is not a typical wine book. It's not a winery-by-winery touring guide, though in its pages you'll find discussion of plenty of outstanding wineries you should visit. Likewise, it's not a bottle-by-bottle guide to the best wine buys from the Pacific Northwest, though you'll find mention of all manner of great regional wines to seek out and try. And, this is not a coffee table wine book, filled mainly with alluringly romantic photographs of the wine country idyll, though the images created by expert Northwest photographer Andrea Johnson will surely entice you to tour the Pacific Northwest's wine regions.

Over the years I've come to favor Pacific Northwest wines. There is, I believe, a broad stylistic signature to these wines, which, while it varies significantly within the region, distinguishes Northwest wines from those of other places. On average, I prefer an Oregon pinot noir wine to a California one, a Washington syrah to an Australian shiraz, and a British Columbia riesling to most of what I taste made anywhere else in North America.

In this book, I explain what makes the Pacific Northwest a special wine region. My Northwest wine preference is rooted in the realities of how wines are grown and made here. The region's geography, geolo-gy, and climate combine with the visions and actions of dedicated winegrowers and winemakers to create a regional wine identity that is truly distinctive.

Illustrating that identity, I knew, would be crucial so that readers could fully appreciate the Pacific Northwest's wine regions. It was vital to me that the photographs accompanying the text be as expressive of place as possible. Photographer Andrea Johnson's informed eye and close connection to the wine regions of the Pacific Northwest made her a perfect collaborator. Throughout the writing of the manuscript, Andrea and I met often to work on ideas for images. Then she would go off to capture the best images, often at absurdly early hours to obtain optimum light. Upon returning from her journeys, we studied and selected the results of each expedition. The power of her photographs is apparent throughout the book.

If I've done my job properly, in these pages you'll find Northwest wine places you're inspired to visit and wines you can't wait to taste. And I hope this book will start you on a lifelong love affair with the wine countries of the Pacific Northwest.

ACKNOWLEDGMENTS

In writing this book I have incurred many debts of gratitude and been the object of much generosity. I take great joy in expressing my appreciation to so many wonderful people.

Foremost, I give my ardent thanks to my wife, Andrea Danehower, for her help, support, and companionship, not only through innumerable glasses of Northwest wine and pleasurable wine country jaunts, but also through the writing of many, sometimes painful, pages of text.

Two other Andreas were intimately involved with this book, and their contributions were invaluable. From the earliest days of this project, I have been privileged to work with an unusually fine photographer, Andrea Johnson. The acuity of her eye and the richness of her images bring an aesthetic verve to the natural beauty of the Pacific Northwest's wine regions. I am grateful for her partnership and patience.

Andrea Slonecker, my research assistant, has been indispensable to me in completing this book. She has doggedly gathered winery information for the gazetteer, helped with the bibliography, and in countless ways made the work easier.

Enthusiastic thanks are owed for the forbearance of my business partner, Cameron Nagel, whose review of much of the work has been a tremendous contribution. I also thank the expert staff at *Northwest Palate* magazine, particularly Peter Szymczak and Sarah Bagley, who patiently nursed the magazine while I worked on the book.

Many other people helped in different ways. Dick Boushey generously shared his Washington winegrowing wisdom and knowledge of Yakima Valley, and helped Andrea Johnson to get photographs. Master of Wine Bob Betz kindly answered my questions about wine and grapes in Washington. Tremendous appreciation goes to John Schreiner, who shared his unparalleled knowledge of British Columbia wines and supplied intriguing insight for this exciting region. Lisa Cameron, general manager of the British Columbia Wine Institute, and John H. Nixon, general manager of the British Columbia Wine Authority, were gracious in answering questions and supplying data. Much appreciation goes to Harry Hertscheg, executive director of the Vancouver Playhouse International Wine Festival, for his detailed review of the British Columbia section. Special appreciation goes to Ted Farthing, executive director of the Oregon Wine Board, who reviewed the Oregon sections of the manuscript and offered valuable pointers. Also, I thank Susan Horstmann, executive director of Oregon Pinot Camp, who shared the superbly crafted educational material that OPC presents to trade people at each year's Pinot Camp. I am grateful to sommelier Erica Landon who graciously reviewed the manuscript and provided valuable input. Ryan Pennington at the Washington Wine Commission and Moya Shatz of the Idaho Grape Growers and Wine Producers Commission were both generous in providing information.

I am greatly indebted to Gregory V. Jones, associate professor in the geography department at Southern Oregon University, for allowing me to use some of his research on the climate of the wine appellations of the Pacific Northwest. Greg's studies of climate and climate change in the world's winegrowing regions are remarkable, and have deeply influenced perceptions of many winegrowers and winemakers internationally about the impacts of climate change on viticulture.

I especially thank Heidi Yorkshire, who first approached me with the idea of writing this book and helped make it possible, and Lisa Donoughe who thought of me when the book idea came up. Thanks to Lisa Shara Hall who has been an inspiration and mentor in my wine writing. Others important in helping me finish this project include Kelley Swenson, Daniel Shoemaker, and David Shenault.

I want to express my admiration for the patience of my editor, Tom Fischer, which knows no bounds, and my appreciation for the temperate, helpful comments of Eve Goodman, both of which have surely enhanced the book. Special thanks go to Ellen Wheat, whose sensitive yet pointed editing has been thorough and even inspirational.

Significantly, I owe infinite gratitude to all the winemakers, vineyard managers, and tasting room and cellar staffs I've met over the years of writing about Northwest wines. It doesn't matter how remote the wine country, how grand the winery, or how humble the vineyard, I have never met a more helpful, congenial group of people than those in the Northwest's wine industry. My thanks to them all.

GETTING TO KNOW THE PACIFIC NORTHWEST WINE REGIONS

Blue Mountain Vineyard and Cellars in British Columbia's Okanagan Valley is an example of how beautiful the wine countries of the Pacific Northwest can be.

(*opposite*) Officially designated wine countries of the Pacific Northwest.

THE PACIFIC NORTHWEST is a young wine region still developing its character on the world's wine stage, but how fast it has grown. In less than a single generation, Washington state has blossomed into the second largest wine-producing region in North America, Oregon has gained a global reputation as the New World's answer to Burgundy, British Columbia has burst onto the scene by winning impressive international wine awards, and Idaho has become the virtual Wild West of North American wine experimentation.

From only about a dozen fine wine producers in 1970, the Pacific Northwest has grown to approximately 1200 wineries, with a combined economic impact on the region of $6.67 billon. One Northwest wine producer ranks in the top 10 largest by volume in North America, and the region's best small wineries get critical acclaim from even the most demanding of global wine critics. By nearly any measure, Pacific Northwest wine has arrived.

Yet for all its successes, the Pacific Northwest is not well understood by many wine consumers and critics, and its wines seem lamentably underappreciated. There are many reasons for this. For one thing, California sets the standard for what most wine lovers expect from North American wine. Plus, the irresistible vineyard images from the Golden State have come to embody our collective ideal of what wine country should look like. Since the Pacific Northwest has less than half the number of wineries and its geography doesn't always conform to the California stereotype of wine country, many people haven't made the effort to get to know the region's wines.

Even the concept of the Pacific Northwest as a definable region is unfamiliar to many. The states in the upper left corner of the country—Washington, Oregon, and Idaho—don't have large populations and aren't generally perceived outside the region as possessing a specific cultural identity, at least not in the same way that people understand the South or New England. Add British Columbia to the geographic mix and regional identity becomes even more confused. Since it's in another country, how can we consider it as part of the Pacific Northwest? And the concept of Pacific Northwest wine countries? That's a vague notion to most.

The images most frequently conjured up by the term Pacific Northwest—crab fishermen, plaid-shirted lumberjacks, baristas, software developers, tree-huggers, aerospace engineers, caffeine-gulping grunge hipsters—don't include wine. Coffee? Of course. Beer? Absolutely. But wine? Not so much.

And yet wine from the Pacific Northwest, often great wine, is an integral and thriving part of the North American epicurean scene. The region's many wine countries are growing, prosperous agricultural areas that increasingly attract wine and culinary tourists eager to experience wines and wine cultures that are different in character from anywhere else. More and more, people around the globe are coming to respect the developing importance and distinctive qualities of wine grown in Washington, Oregon, British Columbia, and Idaho.

I wrote this book for wine-curious consumers who want to understand what makes the Pacific Northwest one of the most exciting wine regions in the world. Wines come from, and reflect, specific places. To appreciate the character of Northwest wines, we need to understand the nature of the places—the wine countries—they come from.

Throughout the history of wine, some places have proven themselves consistently capable of producing wines of great character and quality. Such places have been set apart from surrounding lands as special wine territories. In France, they are called appellations, and are governed by strict winegrowing and winemaking rules. The American analog is the American Viticultural Area (AVA), which defines the sources of domestic wine grapes but not wine processes or quality. British Columbia wine-producing regions are called Designated Viticultural Areas (DVAs). Both these titles, despite their differences, do one thing: they define wine countries. By whatever other name—appellation, AVA, or DVA—wine countries are designated places where distinctive wine is grown and made, and where the wine lover can visit to see and sample what regional wines are all about.

I begin the book with a look at the broad environmental factors that unify the Pacific Northwest from a viticultural standpoint, to clarify how and why the region is distinct from other North American wine areas. I explain how the geography, geology, and climate of the Northwest contribute to the nature of the region's wines, and I introduce you to some his-

tory and to some of the people who have built the Northwest wine world.

In the Pacific Northwest Wine Countries Gazetteer, proceeding by state or province, I examine every designated wine country in the region and define what makes each special. The wine countries form the organizing principle in this book. An area's physical characteristics have a vital influence on the varieties of grapes that can be grown and the styles of wine that can be made within each wine country.

Following each wine country description, I offer profiles of representative wineries under the heading "Wineries to Visit and Wines to Try," with a discussion of what makes each of them distinctive. These wineries, which are just a small selection of the total Northwest winery population, were chosen based on their history and impact on the appellation's character or renown, the sustained quality of their wines,

Oregon winemaker Lynn Penner-Ash tastes fresh juice from fermenting grapes.

Winemaker Christophe Baron of Cayuse Vineyards had the insight to plant syrah grapes in the unusual cobblestone ground of the Walla Walla Valley, and produces some of the most sought-after wines in the Northwest.

Dedicated Northwest winegrowers treat vines individually to get grapes of the best quality.

and, in the case of new or small wineries, the brightness of their promise.

For a deeper appreciation of what distinguishes the Pacific Northwest as a winegrowing region, it is important to understand the interplay between three vital wine variables: place, plant, and people. I like to express it as a formula: Great Wine = (Place + Plant) × People.

The story of any wine region must explain how place, plant, and people interrelate to produce fine wine. After all, great wine is the result of human intention playing across the potential of the land, climate, and plants. Every wine region has its own set of place, plant, and people variables. Match a wine grape variety to a vineyard location whose climate and soils fulfill the specific growing and ripening requirements for that individual grape, and you have a base for successfully growing and making wine from that grape at that vineyard. But to be able to make really great wine, you must multiply the place-plus-plant factor by the leveraging power of knowledgeable, skillful, dedicated people.

In the Pacific Northwest, this formula for great wine operates differently than in other areas because of the region's unique geography, climate, and people. Understanding those differences helps explain the character of Northwest wine and the wine countries that grow it. After all, wine did not arise naturally in the Northwest; there were no native grapes to work with. It took people with vision and imagination to see the geography's latent advantages for viticulture, and it took drive and creativity to develop and realize the potential they saw.

Today, that potential is only beginning to be realized. While the great European wine regions have traditions that go back centuries, in the Pacific Northwest we've been making fine wine for barely 50 years. We've only just begun to explore the region's vast territory for its wine prospects. The sense of discovery and experimentation throughout the Northwest is exciting to behold—and taste—and is what makes this wine region so compelling.

THE IMPORTANCE OF PLACE TO PACIFIC NORTHWEST WINE

The Pacific Northwest does not immediately appear to be hospitable wine country. When we envision the western edge of the region, we typically see lush conifer forests, towering snow-capped mountains, remote rocky coastlines, and rain-sodden cities—not vineyards. And when we think of the eastern part of the Northwest, we see tumbleweed deserts, sweeping wheat fields, hydroelectric-dammed rivers, and seemingly unending tracts of hot, dry, vacant scrubland. Indeed, until the 1960s, viticulture was considered impractical in much of the region. Conventional wisdom held that Oregon was unsuitable because it was too cold and wet, and Washington couldn't support quality winegrowing because severe winters would kill vines. Back then, Idaho and British Columbia barely merited consideration.

Though these notions were simplistic and uninformed, they drove perceptions of the Northwest's viticultural potential for a long time. Vestiges of that attitude linger today in the surprise often expressed that British Columbia has such a high-quality wine community or that Idaho produces award-winning wines. Yet grapes of all kinds, including wine grapes, had been planted throughout the Northwest, albeit in small quantities, since the earliest settling of the region. The European wine grape species that produces all the great wines, *Vitis vinifera*, could in fact be grown successfully here, and small starts at a regional wine industry sprouted all around the Northwest in the second half of the nineteenth century and into the early 1900s.

The early beginnings of viticulture in the United States were unceremoniously uprooted by the strictures of Prohibition. That disastrous social experiment, which banned the production and sale of alcoholic beverages from 1919 to 1933, devastated what had once been a thriving winemaking industry in California and, to a lesser extent, in the Northwest. So widespread were Prohibition's effects that

Vitis vinifera
THE VINE THAT MAKES THE WINE

About 60 species of vines make up the genus *Vitis*, but only one species produces what wine authority Jancis Robinson has estimated to be 99.998 percent of the world's wines: *Vitis vinifera*. Native to Europe and parts of Asia, *V. vinifera* may have been cultivated as early as from 7000 to 8000 BCE, and wine was systematically made from such vines perhaps as far back as 3500 BCE. Most of the other species of genus *Vitis* are native to North America and Asia, and though prolific, they account for a microscopic amount of wine that is deemed lesser in quality than wine produced from the vinifera species.

Genetically precocious, the grapevine mutates easily. The earliest vine tenders no doubt learned to pick out the best vines for their needs—the sweetest berries, the hardiest plants. By the time of the ancient Greeks, specific grape varieties were commonly recognized for making a superior quality of wine. Today's vinifera species may have originated from the selection of wild vines, but thousands of years of both husbandry and natural mutations have resulted in approximately 10,000 different varieties of vinifera. And from these varieties, only a limited number produce what we consider to be fine wine. All the currently familiar wine grape varieties, from arneis to zinfandel, are *Vitis vinifera*, and throughout this book we will be discussing primarily vinifera grapes, with a few hybrid grapes mentioned.

When the first settlers arrived in North America, they found grapevines but none that could produce fine wine. The native North American species, primarily *Vitis labrusca*, *V. riparia*, *V. rupestris*, *V. rotundifolia*, *V. aestivalis*, and *V. cinerea*, produced wine with a strong, unpleasing, so-called foxy quality, though some species produced good table grapes. Early attempts to create a winegrowing industry in America proved infertile. Imported vinifera vines did not flourish anywhere in eastern America because of climate and disease, despite well-intentioned efforts ranging from Thomas Jefferson's plantings at Monticello to ambitious efforts in Ohio in the 1830s. Because early attempts with vinifera were unsuccessful, a variety of hybrids were created with parents of both native and European species, some of which are still used today to produce small quantities of North American wines, most often where the climate is too harsh for vinifera to flourish.

The earliest viticulture in the Pacific Northwest was likely with native species brought to the region from back east and used for table grapes, though there are scattered records of *Vitis vinifera* importations from Europe in the mid-nineteenth century. Similarly, the earliest wine production in the Northwest was likely from other fruits or perhaps some nonvinifera grapes. Nineteenth-century records rarely indicate the actual kinds of grapes used in winemaking.

very little dedicated winegrowing or fine winemaking took place anywhere in the United States until the 1950s, and it wasn't until the 1960s that a serious fine wine industry really began to develop.

The modern wine development of the Northwest was begun by a handful of individuals who saw beyond the orthodoxy of the day and found within the Northwest a home where great wine grapes could be grown. Whether in the cool Willamette Valley, the warm Rogue Valley, the arid Columbia Valley, the dramatic Okanagan Valley, or the barren Snake River Valley, these early modern winegrowers understood that the region's geography offered unique climate variances that were ideal for viticulture. They saw qualities of place that inspired them to plant their wine roots here.

Wine knows no human-made boundaries; the vine follows the dictates of climate and terrain. So when we look at the wine countries of the Pacific Northwest, we can ignore the lines on the map that divide countries, states, and provinces, and instead, pay attention to the natural landforms, the broad climate patterns, and even the cultural conditions that combine to create a common growing range for wine grapes. First, we must comprehend the geography and climate of the region, if we are to understand the wine countries of the Northwest.

The Significance of Latitude

In the northern hemisphere, *Vitis vinifera* grows well within a band between latitude 32°N and 51°N. Within this range, the climate offers enough overall warmth for wine grapes to ripen properly. Though not every location within this band of land is suitable for wine grapes, grape growing is broadly feasible. At higher latitudes outside this range, the climate is too cold for grapes to ripen reliably, and at lower latitudes the climate is too warm and humid. The Pacific Northwest's wine countries are within the upper 10° of the wine-growing latitude in the northern hemisphere. The northernmost wineries in British

The pinot noir harvest at Archery Summit in Oregon's Dundee Hills is done by hand.

19

THE MYTH OF THE 45TH PARALLEL

Oregon wineries, and to a lesser extent Washington wineries as well, like to boast that their vineyards lie on the same latitude as the two most famous wine regions of France: Bordeaux and Burgundy. Much marketing verbiage and many miniature maps on wine labels and winery brochures proclaim this geographical circumstance. But is it important? Not very. While a particular latitude does confer some broad climatic characteristics, latitude alone does not a wine country make. Regional and local geographic and climate conditions are much more important in determining whether a specific area will prove conducive to quality winegrowing.

Nevertheless, Northwest wineries are often so enamored of the romance of latitudinal parallelism that they like to tout it. Some Oregon wineries have proudly drawn a line connecting the Willamette Valley and Burgundy. But in fact, the Willamette Valley's 45°N parallel goes through Bordeaux, not Burgundy. And the town of McMinnville, in the heart of Oregon's pinot noir country, is on the same latitude as Pauillac, famed French cabernet territory.

Washington's wineries also sometimes claim the latitude connection. Yet the town of Sunnyside, in the center of the Yakima Valley, so famous for its Bordelaise varieties, is on the same parallel as the French town of Mâcon, which is in Burgundy, pinot noir's home. If latitude alone determined which grapes grow best in a place, then Yakima Valley should be growing pinot noir and Willamette Valley cabernet sauvignon. Clearly, local conditions determine what grapes grow best.

Columbia lie a little above 50°N latitude—equivalent to the most northerly of Europe's ancient wine regions—while the southern boundary of Northwest wine countries is at 42°N.

When the modern era's early winegrowers looked at a map, they were impressed by the fact that the Northwest places they saw as potential vineyard land lay roughly on the same latitudes as the great French wine regions of Bordeaux and Burgundy. Surely that was a portent of good potential, they thought. But California, the most successful wine region in North America, is located at relatively low latitudes, from Mendocino in the north at around 39°N, to Santa Barbara in the south at about 34°N. Were these latitudes better for grape growing? The Northwest's pioneers thought not. They saw their region's location at the northern edge of viticultural viability as offering important winegrowing advantages. Ultimately, the latitudinal similarity to the great wine regions of France was a circumstance that offered more marketing beneficence than viticultural relevance.

What is significant is that the Northwest's northerly latitude delivers two critical benefits to winemakers: more sunlight and more coolness. Vineyards in the Northwest receive distinctly more sunlight hours per day during the average growing season than vineyards farther south. Oregon's wine countries receive a little over one hour more sunlight than California's key wine regions, while Washington's vineyards experience approximately two hours more sunlight than Napa Valley. And Sumac Ridge, a winery in

One important advantage to wine grape growing in the Northwest is the extra hours of sunlight the grapes receive.

(*opposite*) Vineyards thrive at the northerly latitudes of the Pacific Northwest.

British Columbia, claims its Black Sage Vineyard receives more sunlight hours than any other vineyard in North America and has the most sunlight intensity of any vineyard in the world.

For winegrowing, the extra sunlight hours mean flexibility: potentially more grape varieties can be optimally ripened in Northwest wine countries. At any point in the growing season, Northwest grapevines receive more solar energy for photosynthesis than the same plant would, at the same time in the season, at a more southerly latitude. The Northwest's extra sunlight hours act like an extended season, giving grapevines an extra boost to power ripening of their fruit. In cooler Northwest wine countries, the extra sunlight helps grapes ripen even when temperatures are relatively low. In the warmer parts of the Northwest, winegrowers have the best of both worlds: plenty of air temperature warmth for vine growth and an extra measure of sunlight to fuel fruit ripening.

The northern latitude offers another, seemingly paradoxical benefit: true cool-climate growing conditions. In some Northwest wine countries, especially those impacted by marine air, the latitude means average daytime temperatures in the summer can be viticulturally cool. The cool climate is naturally suited for those grape varieties that are adapted to the earlier ripening pattern that lower growing season temperatures require—pinot noir and pinot gris are two examples. Though cool-climate wine countries often aren't warm enough to ripen warm-adapted grapes such as cabernet sauvignon or merlot, their coolness means that the Northwest can easily match cool-climate grapes to legitimately cool-climate wine countries for more even fruit ripening.

A northern latitude also means well-defined seasons and cold winters, two underappreciated viticultural advantages. Wine grapevines require a dormant period in the winter months as part of their natural life cycle. Vines must fully shut down their metabolism as part of a renewal process before being reawakened in the spring. Dormancy is triggered by

the onset of colder weather as the seasons change from fall to winter. In the Northwest, this transition is distinct and usually rapid. Once accomplished, the winters are reliably cold, and grapevines easily reach the full dormancy that can be difficult to achieve in the milder winters at lower latitudes. There is a dark side, though, to the higher latitude. In some Northwest wine countries, the winters can get too cold, and winter vine damage can be a significant risk.

Winemaker Anna Matzinger tests a wine sample for sugar, acidity, and other compounds at Oregon's Archery Summit Winery.

(*opposite*) Cold winters in the Northwest provide a viticultural advantage by ensuring full dormancy of grapevines.

These weather conditions are discussed in the book's sections on individual wine countries where harsh winters can be an issue.

A final, and crucial, implication of winegrowing in the Northwest's higher latitude is its effect on the development of acidity in the grapes. Acidity is a necessary balancing element in wine, imparting a desirable quality of crisp freshness and vitality to a wine's flavors. As grapes ripen, they lose acidity. The amount of acidity retained in grapes is affected by their respiration, which is influenced by temperature: warmth increases respiration and the loss of acidity, and coolness increases the retention of acidity. In the cool-climate areas of the Northwest, lower average daytime temperatures help grapes retain acidity as they ripen, reinforced by even cooler nighttime temperatures. Even in the warmest Northwest wine countries, very cool night temperatures create a wide diurnal swing (the difference between daytime and nighttime temperatures), which enables warm-climate grapes to keep their acid levels naturally high throughout the fruit ripening period, even though daytime temperatures can be very warm.

The geology and climate of the vast drainage basin of the Columbia River, seen here at Cave B Winery in Washington, is a unifying factor in Northwest winegrowing.

One common signature to Pacific Northwest wine is its pleasingly high levels of brisk natural acidity, thanks in part to the cool temperatures of the northerly latitude. This acidity gives Northwest wines a lively, mouthwatering character that imparts a pleasing definition to the fruit flavors of the region's wines. Natural acidity is a tastable point of differentiation between Northwest wines and those from lower latitudes.

The Effects of Ocean and Mountains

In the Northwest, the two geographic features most salient to winegrowing are the waters of the Pacific Ocean and the mountains of the Cascade Range. The way in which landforms block and channel the eastward movement of marine air in the Northwest is one of the prime determinants of what grapes the region's wine countries can grow best. Prevailing westerly winds constantly push relatively cool, moisture-rich marine air from the ocean toward the coasts of Oregon, Washington, and British Columbia. As this air moves eastward, it meets coastal mountains that inhibit its movement landward. In Oregon it first encounters the Coast Range, in Washington it hits the Olympic Mountains, and in British Columbia it meets the Vancouver Island Ranges.

These coastal mountains act as a rain barrier, a critical geographic theme in the Northwest. The lower lying land on the lee side of these mountains is in a rain shadow, and the weather here is consequently drier and warmer than the ocean air. The interior valleys on the eastern slopes of the coastal mountains, generally located 40–50 mi (60.4–80.4 km) from the ocean, form one important class of Northwest wine country: the marine-influenced, cool-climate winegrowing regions. Throughout the growing season, warm air builds during the daytime in the interior valleys, creating high-pressure zones that keep the denser marine air backed up against the coast mountains. This warm air provides enough daytime heat to ripen wine grapes that require generally cooler temperatures to thrive. At the end of the day, the valley air cools enough to let pent-up up marine breezes escape through mountain passes, providing a cooling affect.

In Oregon, the Willamette Valley wine country is on the lee side of the Coast Range, in Washington the Puget Sound area is in the shadow of the Olympic Mountains, and in British Columbia the eastern slopes of Vancouver Island, the neighboring Gulf Islands, and Fraser Valley are in the rain shadow of the Vancouver Island Ranges. These cool-climate wine countries are characterized by warm (though to a grape, relatively cool), dry summers and mild, wet winters, which are best suited for grapes that ripen early in the season.

Farther inland, a second, greater rain barrier is formed by the majestic Cascade Range from 5000 to 14,000 ft. (1524–4267 m) high and extending from southern British Columbia to southern Oregon. Higher altitude marine air can push past the coastal barriers and continue eastward, but it eventually meets the Cascades. As it rises against the westward slopes, the air cools and drops its moisture as rain in the warmer months and snow in the winter. Because of the height of the peaks, storms wring out all their moisture on the west side, leaving the lands to the east literally high and dry.

On the eastern side of the Cascades, the Northwest's second kind of wine-growing area is found: the continental-influenced, warm-climate wine coun-

tries. The climate of these regions during the growing season is dictated by the hot, windy, semi-arid landmass of the interior. Summers deliver very warm to intense daytime heat with dramatically cooler nights and almost no precipitation. Winters are very cold, sometimes damagingly so. The Northwest's warm-climate wine countries support a wide range of later ripening grape varieties that simply can't mature properly in the cool-climate wine countries.

The Unifying Effect of the Columbia River Watershed

With the Pacific Northwest's geography creating such starkly different types of wine countries, it might seem a stretch to think of the region as a single wine producing area having an identity of its own—but it is. The unifying factor is a vast common geographical feature: the 258,000-square-mile (668,216.9-km2) watershed of the mighty Columbia River. Beginning at Columbia Lake in British Columbia at an altitude of 2650 ft. (809 m), the Columbia River flows 1270 mi (2043.8 km) toward the ocean. Along its length, the great river is swelled by the flows of tributaries with names familiar to Northwest wine lovers: the Willamette, Yakima, Snake, Okanagan, and Similkameen Rivers, among many others. Approximately 80 percent of the Pacific Northwest's vineyards are located along the hillsides, valleys, and slopes that dot the Columbia River drainage. The only Northwest wine countries that aren't located within the Columbia River watershed are Southern Oregon, Puget Sound, Vancouver Island, Fraser Valley, and the Gulf Islands.

Momentous geologic events shaped much of the Pacific Northwest's best-known wine countries. Approximately 15 million years ago, huge fissures many miles long opened in the earth's surface in what is now eastern Washington and Oregon, emitting massive flows of lava that swept across the land. Hundreds of flows of liquid rock oozed from huge cracks in the earth, and these shield volcanoes continuously inundated the land with lava for millions of years.

Eventually, these basaltic floods covered about 63,000 square miles (160,000 km2) of the Pacific Northwest to a depth of 8,000 ft. (2438 m). The molten rock followed the contour of the land, filling lower elevations and tracing the ancient course of the Columbia River, finally spilling into the Pacific Ocean. Eventually these gigantic basalt flows reached to the north in central Washington, southeastward along the Snake River toward Boise, westward through what is now the Columbia Gorge, and down into the Willamette Valley.

Over time, the flooding subsided and the lava cooled into today's basalt bedrock, which underlies much of the Northwest's vineyards. The sheer weight of this immense mass caused the area to fold and warp as it sank little by little into the crust. Over millennia, this region, now called the Columbia Basin, tipped gently to the south and dropped lower in elevation than the surrounding territories. It is into this vast catch basin that much of the Columbia River's watershed flows today.

But that's not the end of the relevant, and stupendous, geologic story of the Northwest's wine countries. During the last Ice Age, between roughly 18,000 and 13,000 years ago, part of the Cordilleran ice sheet, a virtual ocean of frozen water that covered much of Canadian North America, crept into northern Washington and Idaho. One arm of the ice sheet formed an ice dam along the Clark Fork River, causing water to back up about 200 mi (321.8 km) behind the dam into what is now Montana. The ice dam was gargantuan, approximately 30 miles (48.2 km) wide and rising to a staggering height of 2000 ft. (609.6 m). The lake that formed behind the ice dam, called Glacial Lake Missoula, grew to contain approximately 500 cubic miles (2084 cubic km) of water with a surface area estimated at 2900 square miles (7510 km2), about the size of Lake Erie and Lake Ontario combined.

At some point, the dam failed catastrophically, and with instantaneous and monstrous violence, the largest floodwaters ever experienced in earth's geologic history exploded westward through the Columbia River drainage. The scale of this glacial outburst flood (technically called a jökulhlaup) is difficult to imagine. A wall of water 2000 ft. (609.6 m) high, with a volume as big as two of the Great Lakes, spewed toward the Pacific Ocean at around 65 miles per hour, taking with it roughly 50 cubic miles (208.4 cubic km) of sediment ranging from suspended dirt to 200-ton boulders. To visualize the size of this flood, consider that the flow rate of the Missoula Flood has been estimated to equal the combined flow of all the rivers of the world, times 10. And it didn't just happen once: it happened again and again, perhaps as many as a few dozen times, for the next 2000 years.

Each of these floods scoured the land down to the basalt bedrock, obliterating ancient soils. In their place, the Missoula Floods deposited mammoth quantities of gravels, rocks, and boulders, left behind as succeeding floods swirled, slowed, and receded. In some places, they deposited gravel bars that are miles long and hundreds of feet deep. Left behind by these titanic floods are the substrates upon which the topsoils of today's Northwest vineyards later formed. The wine countries of south-central Washington, such as the Wahluke Slope, Yakima Valley, and Walla Walla Valley, are deeply influenced by the structures of the land left behind by the Missoula Floods. Even Oregon's Willamette Valley was dramatically impacted by the floods.

THE IMPORTANCE OF PLANTS TO PACIFIC NORTHWEST WINES

Different wine grape plants require different growing conditions to properly ripen their fruit. Put a grapevine into the ground wherever other fruiting plants

(opposite) *Terroir* is the idea that all the elements of a specific place—the nature of the soil and the weather—are eventually expressed through the vine and into the wines made from that place.

Terroir
THE TASTE OF PLACE

It is perhaps sobering to realize that when we open a bottle of Northwest wine, we are tasting the results of millions of years of cataclysmic geologic forces. While this may seem like wine-speak puffery, there is a controversial, though in many places well-accepted, school of thought that says you can literally taste the sense of a place in a wine—the *goût de terroir*, as the French put it.

Terroir is a key concept in wine, and is particularly important in the Pacific Northwest. *Terroir* is an idea that is difficult to translate: it tries to encompass the totality of influences that go into creating the character of a wine. *Terroir* holds that each spot where a grapevine grows has its own special variables—like soil type, exposure, elevation, temperature, sunlight, wind, moisture, microbial life in the soil—that are unique to that place. Over the course of many years, as a grapevine becomes more balanced with, and rooted to, the particular combination of conditions that make up that place, those qualities get passed on to the wine made from that vine's grapes. The features of that place can be detected in the smell and taste of the wines from that place: its *terroir*.

Part of *terroir* comes from the geology where the grapevine is planted. As the vine matures, its roots drive downward in search of moisture, through the topsoil, penetrating the subsoil, and sometimes deep enough to abut the bedrock.

These roots are chemical receptors that, in ways not well understood, draw from the soil and rocks the nutrients and minerals that both sustain the plant and help fuel the ripening of its fruit.

But *terroir* is more than just the soil. While plants are rooted in a singular place, the engine of their growth is the leaves above the ground, nakedly exposed to the unique climate conditions of its particular place. This, too, is a part of *terroir*. The warmth of the weather, the force of the winds, the angle of the sunlight, the coolness of the night, the moisture in the air—all impact the plant's ability to conduct photosynthesis, to metabolize the nutrients it draws from the soil, and to ripen its fruit. Northwest wines made from the same grape grown in different places can taste quite different. The nature of the soil surrounding the vine's roots and the atmosphere enveloping its leaves must surely influence the character of its wine.

While there is no scientific verification of *terroir*, it is clear that some places are more desirable for certain kinds of grapes than others. Oregon and Burgundy winemaker Véronique Drouhin-Boss once said to me, "Every place has its own *terroir*, but not every *terroir* is good *terroir*." When *terroir* is good—when the character of wines from specific places display similar desirable traits over the years—we come to value these wines highly.

prosper in the Northwest, and chances are it will grow successfully. But for fine winemaking, proper ripening of grapes is all important, and that isn't possible just anywhere.

As place is determined by geology, the places where grape plants prosper is determined by climate—plant and climate are inseparable. More than geology, climate often distinguishes one wine country from another, especially in the Northwest, where climate variances can be significant.

Grapevines are essentially sugar-creating machines—there is no plant better at producing and storing sugar (glucose and fructose) than *Vitis vinifera*. The grapevine's entire growing cycle has evolved to ensure the development of ripe grapes, helped along by generations of human selection for sweetness of fruit, both to eat and to convert into wine. But ripe grapes require the right climate.

The winegrower's responsibility is to nurture and protect the grapevine's ability to ripen fruit; every vineyard task is designed to optimize the quality of the fruit. The most important vineyard requirement, then, is to choose a place to plant the vines that offers an environment best suited for ripening the fruit

Grapevine cuttings ready to be planted.

of each wine grape variety. Today, the mantra of Northwest winegrowing is to plant each variety only where the climate best matches its natural growing needs.

As we have seen, wine grapes fall into two broad classes: those that ripen best with less growing season heat and those that ripen best with more. Early ripening grapes are best suited for cool-climate growing regions. Popular varieties such as pinot noir, pinot gris, riesling, gewürztaminer, and chardonnay have a natural ripening pattern that more closely matches the climate of cooler Northwest wine countries. Later ripening grapes, including such well-known varieties as cabernet sauvignon, merlot, and syrah, need more seasonal warmth to achieve complete and balanced ripening, and they find good homes in the Northwest's warm-climate wine countries.

In the Northwest especially, it is convenient to think of wine countries as being differentiated by the amount of beneficial growing heat the appellation experiences. If you know the amount of growing heat, or heat accumulation, a wine country generally experiences during the growing season, you can easily deduce what wines that appellation is most likely to excel at growing. There is an easy tool to help wine lovers understand the viticultural character of Northwest wine countries: it is called growing degree days (GDD). Growing degree days, also called heat summation, are calculated by taking the average of the daily maximum and minimum temperatures and then subtracting it from the minimum temperature required for growth—for grapes it is 50°F (10°C)—for every day of the growing season, from April 1 to October 31. The higher the GDD number, the more potential growing heat there is to ripen grapes. Winegrowers use GDD as a tool to help determine which grape varieties to plant in what region. Wine consumers can also use GDD as a convenient way to understand the differences among the wine countries of the Pacific Northwest.

Gregory V. Jones, associate professor in Southern Oregon University's department of geography, has

(*right*) Northwest wine-growers are meticulous in their winegrowing so that the vines they tend ripen fruit of optimum quality.

(*bottom left*) At Venturi-Schulze Vineyards, on Vancouver Island, British Columbia, winegrowers carefully cut out individual bad berries from ripe clusters to ensure only the best fruit is fermented.

(*bottom right*) Winemakers strive to retain all the natural character inherent in their grapes. In Oregon, Stoller Vineyards' winemaker, Melissa Burr, monitors an automated punchdown device.

NORTHWEST CLIMATE ZONES FOR WINE GRAPE GROWING

Climate	Growing Degree Days (GDD) in °F (°C)	Ripening Period	Important Northwest Wine Grape Varieties
Very cool	<1800 (982)	Very early	pinot noir, pinot gris, gewürztraminer, and some hybrid varieties
Cool	1800–2200 (982–1204)	Early	pinot noir, pinot gris, gewürztraminer, riesling, pinot blanc, chardonnay, müller-thurgau
Warm	2200–2600 (1204–1426)	Early-to-middle	riesling, chardonnay, sauvignon blanc, sémillon, cabernet franc, tempranillo, merlot, syrah
Very warm	2600–3000 (1426–1648)	Middle-to-late	merlot, malbec, syrah, sangiovese, tempranillo, cabernet franc, viognier, cabernet sauvignon, grenache, sangiovese, zinfandel
Hot	3000–3400 (1648–1871)	Late	cabernet sauvignon, grenache, zinfandel, petite verdot, nebbiolo, sangiovese

Source: Gregory V. Jones, Pacific Northwest American Viticultural Area 1971–2000 Growing Degree Days (Base 50°F), map

done extensive climatological research on Pacific Northwest wine countries. Using national climate data and a rigorous climate model, he has compiled representative GDD data for each Northwest appellation in the United States. His data are exclusively used here with permission. The accompanying table presents Professor Jones's classification of GDD ranges and representative wine grape varieties whose ripening pattern best matches each range. I have added qualitative labels to each GDD range along a continuum from "very cool" to "hot." By using the GDD ranges in conjunction with each Northwest wine country description, you'll be able to judge what kinds of wines each Northwest wine country is likely to produce well.

Because the Northwest has such distinctly different climate zones, it is important to take care in deciding where to grow particular grapes. For instance, warm-climate grapes generally can't achieve optimum ripeness and full varietal flavor when they are grown in a cool-climate wine country. It would be unreasonable to expect a syrah wine from the cool Willamette Valley (and there are some) to have the same character as one grown in the very warm Wahluke Slope. But almost any cool-climate grape can be grown in the Northwest's warmer appellations. When cool-adapted grapes are grown in warmer climates, however, they can ripen too quickly and, unless carefully managed, can ripen unevenly. For instance, pinot noir grown in a warm-climate wine country can reach sugar ripeness and be ready to pick well before the development of mature flavors. The resulting wine cannot show the same varietal character as a pinot noir ripened more slowly in the cool climate for which the grape has evolved.

THE IMPORTANCE OF PEOPLE TO PACIFIC NORTHWEST WINES

Choose the right place, plant the right grape variety, and you're still only part way toward the goal of

Grapevines flourish and produce the best wine when they are properly matched to the right climate, like these still-productive old pinot noir vines at Ponzi Vineyards in Oregon's Willamette Valley.

(*opposite*) Each grape variety requires a different amount of growing heat to properly ripen. At Garry Oaks Winery on Vancouver Island, British Columbia, these pinot noir grapes have achieved veraison, the point at which color and sugar begin to develop.

Despite the romantic aura surrounding it, winegrowing is farming. Vineyard manager Mark Gould, at Oregon's Ken Wright Cellars, typifies the Northwest's commitment to growing the best possible fruit for making wine.

producing fine wine. The missing link is the leveraging power of human endeavor. To reliably make truly fine wine, wine that turns on critics' scores and turns up sales, you need people of passion, commitment, knowledge, and drive. In these attributes, the vignerons of the Pacific Northwest have always been abundant.

Wherever people move, they seem to take grapes with them to plant. As the pioneers pushed past the prairies and on toward the Pacific Ocean, they brought with them a technology long mastered by their European forebears: viticulture. The earliest grape plantings in the Northwest are generally assumed to have been at Fort Vancouver, Washington, on the northern bank of the Columbia River, opposite present-day Portland. Records show grape vineyards, apparently planted from seed, at the Hudson's Bay Company's outpost there as early as 1825. It is not known what the grape variety was or if wine was made from the fruit. But since the seeds came from Europe, we suspect they were for vinifera vines. And we know there was a taste for wine in the early Northwest. European wine bottles and barrels were shipped to Fort Vancouver, and bottle shards from France's Château Margaux have been found at Fort Nisqually, another Hudson's Bay Company encampment on Puget Sound.

Other early immigrants sporadically planted grapes in the Northwest. During the 1820s and 1830s, French Canadian trappers who had worked at Fort Vancouver settled in an area of the north Willamette Valley that came to be called French Prairie. They established Oregon's first farms and are thought to have planted vineyards. There is no specific record of grape types or of wine, though in 1835 a distilling business there apparently offered to make brandy from wine.

In 1848, Henderson Luelling brought to Oregon 700 grafted fruit trees and grape plants—which may have included *vinifera* though we don't know for sure—from Iowa by way of ox cart, and established the area's first commercial nursery near what is now the town of Milwaukie. By the 1850s, Luelling had

supplied many fruit cuttings, including grapevines, to other nursery outlets in the Puget Sound region and western Washington, as well as to French Canadian settlers and other immigrants to the Walla Walla Valley in southeastern Washington.

In 1854, pioneering horticulturalist and artist Peter Britt planted southern Oregon's first vineyard near Jacksonville, which four years later became the state's first known commercial winery under the Valley View Winery name. By the 1860s, Britt was ordering cooperage and cuttings from California, expanding his vineyards, and selling well-regarded wines such as "Claret, Zinfandel, Muscat, Gutedel, and Cabernet."

Oregon pioneer settler Jessie Applegate planted 40 vineyard acres (16 ha) near the southern Oregon town of Yoncalla in 1876, and in the next decade, Edward and John Von Pessl planted one of the earliest vinifera vineyards in southern Oregon to zinfan-

del, riesling, and sauvignon blanc. In 1888, Adam Doerner came to the region after having worked harvest with the Beringer brothers in California. Also a cooper, he brought some degree of sophistication to his task: he made a point of not including grape stems in his fermentations, and he aged his wines in the barrels he carefully crafted.

By the 1860s, the Walla Walla Valley was also becoming a growing grape center. Two nurseries were importing grape cuttings from the Willamette Valley, California, and Europe, likely including vinifera varieties. Contemporary newspaper accounts indicate that by the 1870s, at least two people were making what seem to be commercial quantities of

Tasting in the barrel room at Mission Hill Family Estate Winery in British Columbia's Okanagan Valley. Wine is ultimately about pleasure.

wine, which may have been Washington's first winery businesses.

Farther north, in the Okanagan Valley of British Columbia, there was talk of the possibility of grape growing as early as 1859. After having been one of the first two ordained Catholic priests in what is now Washington and having done religious work in Oregon, Father Charles John Felex Adolphe Marie Pandosy arrived in Kelowna to establish an Oblate mission. In an 1859 letter, Pandosy referred to the place of his mission as a "valley situated on the left bank of the great Lake Okanagan and rather near the middle of the Lake." He goes on to say that if a fellow Oblate priest in Oregon would send "some vine cuttings, we shall be able to start a plantation," probably for sacramental wine.

These early attempts to establish grapevines in the Pacific Northwest were adventurous and experimental. Vine growing success here was rarely assured, partly because the Northwest's climate was

Northwest wineries, like Penner-Ash Wine Cellars, apply technology as well as craft to create high-quality wines.

not as easygoing for grape growing as it was in California—which was famed for its grapes even in the nineteenth century, and then the only place in the United States capable of consistently growing vinifera vines—and partly because growers lacked real knowledge about what made particular grape varieties prosper. What knowledge was gained ultimately came to naught. Though winegrowing had a foothold in the Northwest by the dawn of the twentieth century, it was dealt a fatal blow by Prohibition.

It took decades for the Northwest to recover and begin building a modern winegrowing culture. While today's Northwest viticulture is not an exact science, we know much more about what climate each vinifera variety requires to deliver the best possible fruit for making wine. But that knowledge is relatively recent and it has been hard won. In Oregon, for instance, the modern idea of matching grape variety to climate and place reached early fulfillment in the late 1960s, by a few dogged individualists such as Richard Sommer, David Lett, Charles Coury, Dick Erath, and Dick Ponzi. Pursuing individual visions, they planted the first post-Prohibition wine grapes in Oregon after analyzing climate data and grape variety ripening patterns. Sommer planted cabernet sauvignon and riesling in the warmer Umpqua Valley region, where he felt they best matched the climate. The others planted pinot noir in the Willamette Valley because that variety best matched that region's growing season. Today the roots planted by the state's first generation of modern winemakers not only support the continued existence of nearly all the wineries they created, but they also provided the foundation upon which has been built one of the most highly respected wine regions in North America.

In Washington, vinifera winegrowing was pushed forward by men like William Bridgeman, who established some of the earliest wine grape vineyards in the state before Prohibition, as well as Washington's first modern vinifera winery after Repeal, Upland Vineyards. Beginning in the late 1930s, a scientific approach to winegrowing was provided by Walter J.

Clore, whose decades of work at Washington State University's Irrigation Experiment Station at Prosser (known today as the Irrigated Agriculture Research and Extension Center) immeasurably improved the quality of winegrowing in Washington, and earned for him the accolade Father of Washington Wine.

Washington winegrowing proceeded into the modern era because of the entrepreneurial sense of two groups of dedicated people. In 1954, a company called American Wine Growers was created out of the merger of two fruit wineries, and it began buying up the few scattered vinifera vineyards in eastern Washington. Through many transformations, the firm eventually evolved into what is today Ste. Michelle Wine Estates, the largest wine producer in the Northwest.

In 1962, a band of dedicated amateur Seattle-area winemakers led by Lloyd Woodburne formed the Associated Vintners with the goal of making the best possible vinifera wines. Today, the company continues as Columbia Winery, one of the most important wineries in Washington's history.

The agricultural potential of British Columbia's Okanagan Valley was realized early in its history, but it wasn't until the 1920s that viticulture really took root, though it was at first for table grapes, not *Vitis vinifera*. In 1976, Helmut Becker of the Geisenheim Research Institute in the Rheingau, Germany, visited the Okanagan Valley and became convinced that the area could support vinifera grapes. After eight years of trials, several varieties were identified that could ripen well in the region. Even so, by the 1980s, British Columbia's wine industry was almost exclusively based on nonvinifera grapes.

A major change occurred in 1988 with the passage of the Canada–U.S. Free Trade Agreement. Suddenly, the British Columbia wine industry had to compete on an international level. To help, the provincial government created a program to pay vineyard owners to pull up their hybrid grapes. Some vineyard owners took the money and ran; others took the challenge and competed. Harry McWat-

ters of Sumac Ridge, for instance, focused on making high-quality vinifera wines, and helped build the province's fine wine industry with enhanced quality designations and vine health screening.

Quickly, throughout the Okanagan Valley, new plantings of higher quality vinifera grapes began to drastically change the face of British Columbia wine. Those changes continue today. For an industry just a little over 20 years old, British Columbia's wines have become a showcase of viticultural excellence, and the wine countries of the province are among the most satisfying to visit in the Northwest.

Though Idaho's wine industry can be traced back to vineyards as early as 1872, it wasn't until 1971 that the first modern wine vineyards were planted in the state. In 1976, William Broich founded Ste. Chapelle Winery, which is still the largest wine producer in Idaho. Today Idaho's small wine industry is rapidly expanding, and hearty individuals are creating a fine wine tradition for the state.

Part of the fun and challenge of the Pacific Northwest wine region is that winegrowing here is not yet a fully defined activity. There is still an exciting attitude of exploration and experimentation. Even though much is known today that the earliest pioneers could never have imagined, there is still much to discover.

As Northwest wine countries mature—as winegrowing knowledge in the region advances—new growing potentials will be discovered and better matches of variety to site will evolve. Even as this book was being written, new appellations were awaiting approval and new wine varieties were being released. The Northwest is continually learning how wine grapevines adapt to local climates and local places. And if the past is any example, the focused intention of passionate people, matching plant to place, promises a bright future for Pacific Northwest winegrowing.

GLOSSARY

Here are definitions for some important wine terms to help in our exploration of Pacific Northwest wines and wine countries.

Ageable, aging: Wine is a living thing and, as with people, it can mature and decline in quality over time. Depending on its style, a wine can be aged in oak barrels or stainless steel tanks for many months prior to bottling so that the various elements—acids, tannins, flavors—have time to integrate. Once in the bottle, well-made wines can continue to age, acquiring more complex character. Estimating the maturity curve of a wine is an inexact science: it depends on many factors and cannot be predicted with certainty.

Appellation: In North America, the term appellation is often used to identify an officially recognized wine grape growing region. In North American usage, it is synonymous with AVA or DVA. In Europe, particularly in France, the term appellation has a more specific meaning, referring to a defined region as well the related regulations concerning viticulture and enology.

AVA: American Viticultural Area, the designation, by the Alcohol and Tobacco Tax and Trade Bureau of the U.S. Department of the Treasury, of a specific area within the United States as a recognized wine grape growing region.

Biodynamic winegrowing: Biodynamics is a controversial approach to farming that views the farm as a self-sustaining living entity. Sometimes viewed as an extreme form of organic farming, biodynamics employ a variety of techniques designed to improve the health of the soil and the farm system, often applied in concert with lunar and solar cycles. While still considered a fringe approach to winegrowing, biodynamics is becoming more popular in Europe, particularly in Burgundy, as well as on the west coast of the United States, particularly in Oregon and California.

Bordeaux-style blend: A wine blended in the style of Bordeaux, France, using any combination of the grapes traditionally grown there. For red blends, this includes cabernet sauvignon, cabernet franc, merlot, malbec, petit verdot, and carmenère. For whites, it includes sauvignon blanc and sémillon.

Canopy management: Techniques used to prune and tend the grapevines in order to influence fruit ripening, for example, removing leaves to expose the fruit to more sunlight.

Cellar: General term used for the place where winemaking processes take place once grapes have arrived from the vineyard.

Clone: A genetic duplicate of a mother plant, produced by growing a new plant from a cutting of the old.

Cuvée: A commonly used French term to denote a specific blend of wine or an individual batch of wine.

Diurnal variance: The daily difference between the maximum daytime and minimum nighttime temperatures. Wider diurnal swings help retain acidity in wine grapes.

Dry farmed: Vineyards that are farmed without artificial irrigation, so they are reliant on what moisture nature delivers.

DVA: Designated Viticultural Area; the designation by the British Columbia Wine Authority, Canada, of a specific area within the province as a recognized wine grape growing region.

Enology: The study and practice of making wine.

Estate vineyard: A vineyard that is owned by a winery. The winery is not always located at the vineyard, but the designation "estate" indicates that the winery owns the vineyard.

Extraction: A term referring to the amount of color and flavor density that is taken out of the grape skins and retained in the juice during winemaking.

Fermentation: The winemaking process of converting sugar into alcohol by the action of yeast, whether naturally occurring or induced by the winemaker.

Fermenter: The vessel in which fermentation takes place. In the Northwest, fermenters are most often made of oak, stainless steel, or food-grade plastic.

Gravity flow: The movement of must, juice, or wine through gravity, without the use of mechanical pumping.

Growing degree days (GDD): A measurement of the amount of growing heat that a plant receives. For grapes, GDD is the number of degrees per day that the average temperature is above 50°F (10°C).

Lees: The accumulated grape skins, grape flesh, expired yeast cells, and natural residue that results from fermentation and settles out of suspension in barrels or tanks as the wine is left to naturally clarify.

Malolactic fermentation (ML, sometimes malo): A secondary fermentation that wine undergoes after the initial fermentation converts sugar to alcohol. The process makes a wine feel softer by converting malic acid in the grape must into lactic acid. Most red wines go through ML, either naturally or induced by the winemaker. White wines can undergo ML to make them softer, or can be prevented from doing so to retain crisp, fruity flavors.

Master of Wine: A prestigious title conferred by the Institute of Masters of Wine, in England, earned after extensive study and rigorous testing on all aspects of wine theory and practice. There are only about 250 in the world.

Méthode champenoise: The traditional method of Champagne, France, to make sparkling wine, including most importantly a second fermentation that takes place in the bottle and produces the carbon dioxide bubbles that are the signature of the style.

Must: The combined juice, skins, seeds, and crushed grape flesh that is the raw material for fermentation.

Native yeast (also, indigenous yeast, or wild yeast): Naturally occurring yeasts from the vineyard and within the winery that can spontaneously begin fermentation of the must. Some winemakers prefer that fermentation proceed with this naturally occurring yeast, believing that it creates a finished wine more characteristic of its place and vintage, while others like the control that commercial yeast strains can provide.

Oak aging: Many types of wine are matured in oak barrels to both add wood-influenced flavors and protect the wine from exposure to air as it ages. Some winemakers also feel that the wine benefits from exposure to minute amounts of oxygen that may seep through the pores in the wood.

Off-dry: The perception of light sweetness in a wine. The sweetness is the result of a small amount of unfermented sugars left in the wine.

Old-vine wine: An imprecise term, most often used in marketing to indicate a wine made from the grapes of particularly old vines, implying that the wine will have higher quality.

Own-rooted: The grapevine is not grafted, but instead is planted to grow on its own roots.

pH: A chemical measurement of the amount of active acidity in solutions, including the juice of grapes. The lower the pH, the higher the acidity.

Phylloxera: A vine-killing pest that feeds on the roots of vinifera vines. Often, vinifera vines are grafted to native American rootstocks, which are resistant to phylloxera.

Punchdown: The process, manual or machine-driven, of pushing down into the grape must the accumulated seeds and skins that float to the top of the fermentation vessel in order to expose them to the juice.

GLOSSARY

Raisining: At the end of the growing season, grapes left hanging on the vine can lose water and begin developing shriveled, raisinlike skins.

Reserve wine: Wineries use this term on their wine labels to indicate a wine they feel to be of superior quality.

Rootstock: *Vitis vinifera* vines are often grafted to a root and stem of a different species of grapevine. The vine grows as it would normally, but is influenced by the growing cycle of the rootstock. The most important reason for grafting to rootstock is to provide resistance to phylloxera. But grafting can also be used to alter the growth cycle, and therefore ripening time, of the grapes.

Single-vineyard wine: Wine only made from grapes that were grown on an individual, named vineyard.

Sparkling wine: Wine that, when opened, releases carbon dioxide in the form of bubbles. Sparkling wine is also the term for a wine of this style that does not come from Champagne, France, but is made in the manner of champagne. The sparking wine called Champagne only comes from France's Champagne district.

Structure: Usually refers to the degree of tannin and acid in a wine. Structure can mean the elements of a wine that contribute to texture and mouth-feel, but which are separate from the actual fruit flavors of the wine.

Subappellation: When one appellation is located entirely within the boundaries of a larger appellation, it is often referred to as a subappellation. But the term does not imply subordination: every appellation stands on its own, without a hierarchy of importance or value.

***Sur-lie* aging:** The process of letting wine rest for a period of time on the dead yeast cells that remain after fermentation is complete.

***Terroir*:** A French term that describes the influence that a specific place has on the style of wine produced from that place.

Veraison: The point at which grape ripening begins, as signaled by a change in color from green to various shades of yellow or pink, depending on the type of grape.

Variety: There are many varieties of wine grape belonging to the species *Vitis vinifera*, and each variety has a distinct flavor and growing pattern. Pinot noir and merlot are examples of two different red grape varieties, chardonnay and riesling are two white varieties. Wines made from particular varieties of grapes are sometimes called varietal wines.

Vintage: Most widely used to mean the year or growing season in which a wine was made. Also sometimes used as a term to describe the physical process of harvesting grapes.

Viticulture: The study and practice of growing grapes.

***Vitis vinifera*:** The species of grape plant whose fruit is most widely used for wine.

Wine country: A winegrowing region, synonymous with appellation, AVA, and DVA.

Yeast: Single-celled organisms that perform fermentation by converting the sugars in grape juice to alcohol.

Yield: The amount of grapes that are harvested, usually in tons per acre. Yield is variable depending on the number of vines planted per acre (density) and the amount of fruit on each vine. Low yields (generally under 3 tons per acre) are considered to produce finer wines than high yields because they deliver more concentrated flavors.

PACIFIC NORTHWEST WINE COUNTRIES GAZETTEER

WINE IS PERHAPS the only agricultural product that displays such a wide variation of expression depending on where the wine grapes were grown. Hence, the concept of wine countries, or defined geographic areas where wine character is deemed distinctive. Defining a wine country is as old as wine itself.

The classical Greeks prized wines from the islands of Thasos, Lesvos, and Chios over wines from the mainland regions of Thessaly or the Peleponnese. The Romans defined different growing zones along the slopes of Mount Falernus for their favored Falernian wine. In 1756, the prime minister of Portugal established legally defined geographic boundaries to protect the authenticity of port wines. And in the nineteenth century, France famously created its *appellation d'origine contrôlée* system to define the borders of its wine districts as well as to regulate winegrowing and winemaking standards.

Today, nearly all the world's wine-producing countries have some sort of winegrowing designation system based on geography, usually derived to some degree from the French appellation model. In fact, the French word appellation has become universally synonymous with the term wine country. In the Pacific Northwest, there are 29 designated wine grape growing regions, or wine countries. In this section, I offer detailed descriptions of every officially designated Northwest wine appellation as of the end of 2009.

Many people misunderstand what North American appellations actually are. The U.S. appellations, officially called American Viticultural Areas (AVAs),

and the British Columbia appellations, known as Designated Viticultural Areas (DVAs), provide labels that are used interchangeably in this book with the informal synonyms wine country and appellation. The U.S. AVA system is administered by the Alcohol and Tobacco Tax and Trade Bureau (TTB) of the U.S. Department of the Treasury. According to the TTB, AVAs define "a viticultural area for American wine as a delimited grape-growing region distinguishable by geographic features, the boundaries of which have been recognized and defined." Declaring an AVA "allows vintners and consumers to attribute a given quality, reputation, or other characteristic of a wine made from grapes grown in an area to its geographical origin." The fundamental purpose of an AVA is to allow "vintners to describe more accurately the origin of their wines to consumers and helps consumers to identify wines they may purchase."

American AVA designations have historically had nothing to do with wine itself. This confuses many wine lovers who are familiar with the French *appellation d'origine contrôlée* system, which regulates winegrowing and winemaking practices that influence the character, quality, extent, or viability of wine production within a defined appellation.

French appellations are as much about wine character as they are about grape source. As the TTB has frequently declared, in the United States, "the regulations pertaining to the establishment of viticultural areas do not require the existence of a substantial viticultural history, a production of unique wines, or a demand for wines originating in the proposed viticultural area." An AVA name on a wine label only means that 85 percent of the grapes in that wine were grown in that AVA; it says nothing about the quality or winemaking style of the wine in the bottle. Even though limited in scope, American AVAs are important precisely because they are based on geography. If we accept that Great Wine = (Place + Plant) × People, then the starting point for great wine is necessarily place, or geography.

In British Columbia, the appellation system is similar in effect but different in process. Under legislation called the Wines of Marked Quality Regulation, the British Columbia Wine Authority was given the responsibility to administer the regulation, including the province's Vintners Quality Alliance program (BC VQA). Though complex and evolving, the BC VQA is described as an "appellation of origin system that guarantees authenticity of origin and stipulates minimum quality standards." To earn the BC VQA stamp, wineries submit their wines to an expert tasting panel that certifies the wine is free of specific faults. The regulation specifies how certain wines can be made and prescribes limits on winemaking practices, which the American AVA system does not do. The regulation also defines Designated Viticultural Areas within the province—analogous to American AVAs—which appear on the labels of BC VQA wines when 100 percent of the grapes were grown in British Columbia and 95 percent came from the DVA.

Most of the Pacific Northwest's earliest wine countries were defined as large areas that encompassed broad viticultural potential. In recent years, those broader appellations have been subdivided into more specific wine countries. In most cases,

these new AVAs and DVAs have been created with careful consideration to the viticultural distinctions of each defined region. This is a blessing for wine lovers, because it means they should be able to appreciate the unique identity of each Northwest wine country, based on real distinctions among each geography and the wines produced.

In the pages that follow, the wine countries of the Pacific Northwest—in Washington, Oregon, British Columbia, and Idaho—are described in detail. Within a state or province, each wine country is presented, including parts of the wine country that may overlap political borders. Each wine country is introduced by a sidebar summarizing the basic facts of that wine-producing region, followed by a discussion of the key factors that influence the wines made there, including topography, geology, climate, and history. Appellations that are located within the boundaries of a larger AVA are commonly referred to as subappellations and are listed in alphabetical order, but each appellation or subappellation is independent and is not subordinate to another.

In the summary sidebars, the numbers of wineries given for each wine country are estimates compiled from regional winery and winegrowers' organizations, state and province wine associations, and other sources. There is no single source for a precise accounting of wineries; the numbers are subject to constant change as new wineries are born and others close. The same goes for the approximate vineyard acreage within each wine country. Both the total acreage and vineyard growing degree day numbers are from the work of Gregory V. Jones. The total acreage figures are rounded to the nearest 10 acres/hectares. The GDD ranges represent heat accumulation at elevations within an AVA where vineyards would normally be planted; GDD numbers appear first in degrees Fahrenheit, followed by the equivalent number in Celsius in parentheses.

For each wine country, I provide a rounded picture of its geographic and climatic qualities, its wine-growing and winemaking approaches, and a sense of its styles and kinds of wines produced. I also offer profiles of representative wineries in the wine country to which they are most closely associated. Generally, either the winery has estate vineyards in the wine country, or its tasting rooms or winery headquarters (when they are not at the same location) are within the wine country. In the case of wineries located in a subappellation within a larger wine country, which produce wines from grapes grown in multiple appellations, thereby having no specific identification with one locality, I list them in the largest appellation that reasonably fits.

For the winery profiles, I have selected Northwest wineries that I feel represent important aspects of each wine country. These may include legacy wineries that helped build a wine country's reputation, prestige wineries with a national presence for the wine country, under-the-radar artisan wineries that embody the spirit of the wine country, or newly hatched wineries showing a promise of furthering the reputation of the wine country. The wineries referenced here are less than 10 percent of the Northwest's winery population. I have met with the winemakers, visited the wineries, or extensively tasted the wines of each listed winery.

For each winery, I include the address and contact information of the winery or tasting rooms, and I list the history, scale, and representative wines and prices; in the British Columbia section, prices listed are in Canadian dollars (C$). I also include a brief description of each winery, along with my personal evaluation of its importance and wines, to give you a sense of its style and approach. Prices of individual wines are given on a scale, since actual individual prices are subject to change and can vary across the country:

$	=	under $15
$$	=	$16 to $30
$$$	=	$31 to $50
$$$$	=	$51 to $100
$$$$+	=	above $100

Wineries generally release many different kinds of wine for each vintage. Some Northwest wineries produce as many as 28 different wines each year. For each winery, I list three kinds of wines: the signature wine, the wine I consider to be the winery's best-known release; the premium wine, the winery's most expensive wine, and often the wine the winery considers to be its best release; and the value wine, the winery's least expensive and often its most widely available wine. Sometimes the same wine appears in more than one of the three categories; often a winery's premium wine is also its signature wine. These listings give you a sampling of the kinds of wines each winery produces, and guide you to the release that may best meet your interests and budget.

Regarding winery visiting hours, many Northwest wineries are small outfits without formal tasting rooms or regular opening hours. So for each winery, I indicate the general policy of accepting visitors. When the entry indicates "open during the season," that means approximately from May through October. When it says "limited hours," that may mean the winery is only open on weekends, or only from noon to 4 p.m. on certain days. Contact the winery or visit its Web site to confirm visiting hours.

Wine preferences are purely personal. Don't ever let someone tell you what you should or should not like in a wine: always follow your own taste. To discover what kinds of Northwest wines you like best, it is important that you taste as widely as possible. Visit winery tasting rooms, pay attention to what you taste, and try to identify what it is about a wine you like or dislike. When you find a wine you like, look on the label to understand the wine. Then, do some research to find similar styles of wine. It won't do to simply read the winery's notes on a wine: they are based on someone else's palate and are designed to sell the wine. Read books, visit Web sites, and above all, taste around—it is the only way you'll learn about your own Northwest wine palate.

WASHINGTON

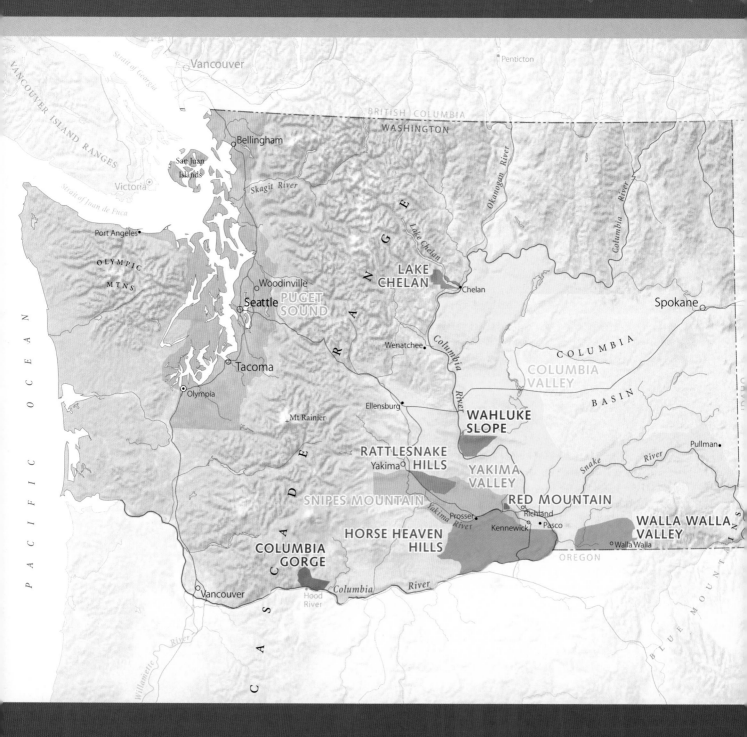

WASHINGTON'S WINE COUNTRIES AT A GLANCE

Vineyard acreage:	36,000 acres (14,568 ha)
Number of wineries:	650+
Annual cases produced:	8.47 million
Economic impact of wine:	$4.7 billion

Most important grape varieties
riesling, chardonnay, cabernet sauvignon, merlot, syrah, sauvignon blanc, pinot gris, gewürztraminer, cabernet franc, viognier.

Wine countries (AVAs)
Puget Sound
Columbia Valley*
    Yakima Valley
        Rattlesnake Hills
        Red Mountain
        Snipes Mountain
    Walla Walla Valley*
    Horse Heaven Hills
    Wahluke Slope
    Lake Chelan
Columbia Gorge*

*Shared with Oregon.

Washington's large vineyards enable economies of scale that deliver high quality grapes both for high-volume, value-priced wines and for high-end craft-made wines.

WASHINGTON is a proud model of Northwest wine success. Smart, sophisticated, and successful, Washington state's wine industry is the largest and fastest growing in the Pacific Northwest. More than anywhere else in the region, the state's wine industry has achieved the seemingly opposite goals of being large and lucrative as well as individualistic and boutique-y, and is widely envied by its neighbors for its accomplishments. But Washington's wine success has not come easily. Growing grapes in the state has never been simple, and marketing its wines beyond the Northwest has been a challenge only recently overcome.

Wine lovers familiar with California's Napa and Sonoma Valleys as the North American archetype of wine country—verdant vales with posh wineries posted every quarter mile or so on a charming rural road, with tasting rooms nestled neatly among trellised estate vineyards—can be disoriented when confronting Washington's distinctly different geography. Washington is not a simple wine region to understand. It is a wine region of contrasts, not conformity. Consider a few of the state's wine dichotomies:

Overleaf: Number of wineries based on Washington Wine Commission data. Economic impact as reported by Washington Wine Commission, based on Economic Impact Study performed by MKF Research using 2006 data. Annual case production volume calculated from 20.073 million gal. (in 2006) reported by Washington Wine Commission from the same Economic Impact Study. Grape varieties listed in order of tons harvested, 2008 Washington Wine Grape Harvest Report, U.S. Department of Agriculture, National Agricultural Statistics Service.

❧ The tasting rooms of many of Washington's most prestigious wineries are located in the leafy but nearly vineyard-free suburb of Woodinville, which is easily accessible to crowds of wine tourists stepping out from Seattle's vibrant city center. Yet all the grapes for these wineries are grown on the sparse, windswept steppes of the Columbia Basin, hundreds of miles away in the rustic reaches of south-central eastern Washington.

❧ Washington offers wine aficionados amenities that include architect-designed tasting rooms, European-inspired winery buildings, luxe boutique hotels and spas, and nationally acclaimed restaurants. Yet accommodations in the rural heart of wine-growing eastern Washington are more basic. Tasting rooms are often utilitarian, divorced from vineyards, and range in form from converted homes to numbered bays in industrial parks on the fringes of rural towns like Prosser or Walla Walla.

Washington is home to behemoth wineries with powerhouse, nationally recognized wine brands, yet the state also possesses more individual wineries, more acres of vineyards, and each year makes more vinifera wine than any other place in North America except California. Despite a few large producers, most of Washington's wineries are modest, individually and family-owned enterprises whose small-lot independent wines are often available only at their tasting rooms, often far from any population center.

Washington wineries offer the connoisseur all the cachet of cult, small-batch, top-scoring prestige wines that are only available to privileged cognoscenti on an annually vetted mailing list. Yet at the same time, Washington also delivers droves of outstanding quality wines in the $10 to $15 range, and in sufficient quantity to ensure availability at nearly any wine shop or grocery store wine shelf across the continent.

This yin-yang character of Washington's wine world has been both a blessing and an affliction. On the one hand, Washington has achieved spectacular success in both wine quality and wine value, proving that it has earned a top spot on the world's wine stage. Yet Washington's wine reputation hasn't caught up with this success and is frequently ob-scured by the shadow of California's wine prestige. Washington winemakers, wine marketers, and wine writers protest that the state is not properly appreciated as a world-class wine region.

The state's wine geography and history have resulted in a wine culture that is different from anywhere else. This wine culture combines a pragmatic attitude toward all aspects of the wine profession, from the hard science of agriculture and fermentation to the business economics of production and distribution, while maintaining respect for the romantic disciplines of craft and creative expression. This combination creates a duality that tensions Washington's wine culture: the push of industrially produced, mass wine quantities from a few large companies versus the pull of craft-created, small-batch bottlings that reflect the personal vision of individual winemakers. Approximately 80 percent of Washington's wine production comes from about 20 large wineries, and hundreds of small producers make the state's remaining volume.

Washington has managed to successfully evolve a symbiotic relationship that supports and capitalizes

Washington's vineyards are planted in dry, hot, remote country where the climate gives winegrowers greater control over their vines and the potential to grow all kinds of wine grape varieties.

Washington's tasting room experience can be smart and sophisticated, like this one at Januik Winery (*top*), or intimate and casual, like the personal treatment that winemaker Kay Simon offers at Chinook Wines (*bottom*).

on this uneven distribution of wine production. The prosperity of large wineries, such as Ste. Michelle Wine Estates, Hogue Cellars, and Precept Brands, instead of squashing smaller wineries, creates an infrastructure for the success of all the smaller enterprises. A rising wine tide, as it were, lifts all barrels, and in Washington's case, expanding sales of the state's biggest producers helps stimulate growth for its smaller producers.

Many are the winemakers, vineyardists, and marketing people who, having built experience within the security of one of the state's large wine companies, have left to establish their own small Washington winery. Applying what they learned in the corporate incubator, they've created individual and family-owned wine brands and earned their own independent reputations and economic success. This mutually beneficial process continuously populates the state with new vineyards, wineries, and wine sales, far beyond what the behemoth companies could do entirely on their own and more than the tiny ones could achieve without the support of the larger brands.

Another unusual characteristic of Washington's wine industry is the overabundance of winemakers in relation to winegrowers. In 2009, the Washington Wine Commission reported almost twice as many wineries (650) as wine grape growers (350). Oregon is the reverse case, with 400 wineries and 850 vineyards; British Columbia has approximately 540 growers for 170 wineries. Washington's wine culture hews closer to a winemaking spirit than a winegrowing ethos. There are many winemakers-for-hire in the state, but few consulting vineyard managers; indeed there is a shortage of them.

Most Washington wineries do not own their own vineyards: it requires less capital, experience, and time to start a winery than it does to start a vineyard. The majority of Washington's wineries contract to purchase fruit from those relative few who own their own vineyards. There are far fewer estate vineyards in the Washington than elsewhere in the Northwest.

WINE STYLES: THE RESULT OF THE LAND OR THE HAND?

Wine can be made in many styles. A cabernet sauvignon may be dense and lush, or bright and fruity; a riesling may be bone dry and austere, or thick and sweet. While the climatic conditions that prevail in a wine region (the influence of the land) provide broad boundaries for the kinds of wines that can be made from the area, it is the decisions made by individual winemakers (the influence of the hand) that determine the final style of a wine.

Within the climate-influenced framework of a wine country, a winemaker can easily alter a wine's natural style. For instance, a normally light-bodied wine from a cooler climate region can be made more substantial by bleeding off some juice to concentrate flavor and body, or by giving it longer aging time in oak barrels. A soft, supple wine from a warm-climate region might be made more fresh by the addition of extra acidity.

No one in the wine world disputes the importance of place in influencing a fine wine's character; but equally, no one dismisses the power of the winemaker to dampen or accentuate what nature provides. The style of a wine, therefore, is an amalgam of nature and nurture.

Washington's large wineries, like Chateau Ste. Michelle, have been instrumental in fostering the state's wine growth.

Yakima Valley winegrower Dick Boushey is the prototype Washington vineyardist who manages his own vineyard and consults for other wineries.

This circumstance has brought prominence to a tiny group of smaller scale vineyards that are more personally farmed. These vineyards have earned reputations for fruit excellence thanks to hand-farming techniques and low yields for fruit concentration. Quality-focused winemakers often prefer to buy from such vineyards, especially when they are allowed the chance to help determine how the grapes from these sources are grown. Some of Washington's best-known wine names—Boushey, Klipsun, Ciel du Cheval, Champoux, Seven Hills, Pepper Bridge, Celilo, Cold Creek, Red Willow—are vineyards.

The essence of Washington's wine character comes from its unique geography, distinctive climate, sparse soils, and commitment of people like Jim Holmes, winegrower and owner of Ciel du Cheval Vineyards in the Red Mountain AVA.

Since most of Washington's grapes are sourced from the state's larger population of sizeable, mechanically farmed vineyards that deliver higher yields and more formula farming, does that mean their fruit is of lesser quality? Not necessarily. Many of Washington's large vineyards were planted by local farming families with multigenerational agricultural histories and holdings. Vinifera grapes are an important crop for them, and they have every economic incentive to grow quality fruit. Because of the high number of winemakers chasing grapes from a lesser number of sources, to prosper a vineyard must grow the best possible fruit.

Fortunately for everyone—grower, winemaker, wine lover—economies of scale apply in Washington more efficiently than anywhere else in the Northwest. With plenty of gently rolling vineyard land and an amenable climate, large vineyards can grow quality fruit at reasonably high yields and have

it cost-effectively harvested by machine. These large crop quantities are easily absorbed into the expansive production capacity of the state's wineries. The happy result for consumers is plenty of inexpensive, well-made wines. This important marketing advantage also helps spread the Washington wine gospel. When consumers taste a $10 Washington cabernet sauvignon wine that's *this* good, they become interested in exploring what the more expensive boutique wineries can do.

And, the boutique wineries deliver. Washington's premium-priced, smaller edition wines regularly receive critical plaudits in the national wine press, right next to the "best buy" recommendations for mass-produced inexpensive wine from a larger Washington producer.

It seems that the state's future belongs to the boutiques. Washington wine is hipper than ever to locals, so new investment money is pouring into the state's wine industry—from local sports stars and celebrities to financial managers and multigeneration farming families looking to diversify. Increasingly

in Washington, it takes cash, flash, and panache to make a lasting mark in the market.

At a peak rate of a new winery a week in 2008, the state's winery population has exploded. Young winemakers drawn to the glamour are skipping over the concept of a corporate apprenticeship and finding immediate homes as winemakers in new small, well-funded enterprises. Conscious of the importance of their marketing image, these wineries emphasize well-crafted stories and compellingly designed labels, their tasting rooms are staffed with fully coached salespeople, and the wines are invariably well made.

As the second largest wine producer in America, Washington is having a growing impact on the larger wine market. In the summer of 2009, in the midst of a recession, Washington wine sales grew over 19 percent by value over the previous year and nearly 10 percent by volume, nearly twice the rate of the na-

Visitors to Lake Chelan, Washington, enjoy both fine wines and views at the wine country's small wineries.

tional market's growth. But the market for sales is different from the market for respect. Washington wine advocates are still dogged by the idea that the world perceives Washington as an also-ran, not a gold-medalist, in the race for wine prestige. But there is a proud undercurrent of independence among Washington's winemakers. They simply believe that if they continue to make good wine, and more of it, eventually the world will catch on to Washington. The state's wine industry is perfectly content to continue its growth by making great wines that people want, even without the rest of the wine world cheering.

WASHINGTON'S WINE GEOGRAPHY

The common image of Washington is of a state filled with snow-capped mountains, lush conifer forests, and lots and lots of rain. While not inaccurate—Washington, after all, is nicknamed the Evergreen State—this image is incomplete.

The dual nature of Washington's wine culture reflects geographic and demographic splits within the state itself. The third of the state west of the Cascade Range is a marine-influenced climate zone of minimal viticultural significance. Yet this area is home to the majority of Washington's population and economic activity, as well as a raft of important wineries. With Seattle as its center, a dense welt of development swells around the city's Puget Sound satellites of Everett, Bellevue, Tacoma, and Olympia. Here is the economic engine that drives regional demand for Washington wines.

While the wet weather of Washington's west creates the common image of the Evergreen State, the source of its wine is in the arid eastern two-thirds of the state. Ninety-nine percent of Washington's vineyards are planted in the dusty ground of the Columbia River Basin, a viticulturally fecund region of continental climate–influenced weather deep within the parched rain shadow of the Cascade Range. Hot, dry, and sparsely populated, this south-central sec-

tion of Washington is a huge geography of naturally desiccated rolling hills, dusty river valleys, and barren small mountain ranges. The geologic formation of the Columbia Basin fundamentally influences the character of Washington's wines. Soils are varied in structure, but share characteristics that make them favorable for winegrowing. They are well-drained, so vine roots grow deep in search of water; they lack much organic matter, so vines put more energy into fruit ripening than vegetative growth; and they often have an alkaline composition that is thought to encourage greater fruit intensity. Intersecting the Columbia Basin's geology, three important climatic elements—dryness, heat, and light—help give the state's wines their unique character.

A vital viticultural reality of south-central and eastern Washington is that it is almost completely dry. While Seattle can average 38 in. (96.5 cm) annual precipitation, the heart of Washington's wine country averages between 7 and 12 in. (17.7–30.4 cm), most of which falls in winter, with only a few spots getting as much as 20 in. (50.8 cm). This aridity is an important winegrowing advantage: it gives winegrowers more control over the growth of their vines. Since the weather is reliably dry, winegrowers are rarely at the mercy of unpredictable or damaging weather events during the growing season. With careful application of irrigation, they can manage how their vines grow. While irrigation may on the surface seem a costly disadvantage—and it is true that water rights and irrigation systems are a significant expense and a limiting factor in vineyard expansion—irrigation is a key tool in managing the quality of fruit grown here.

An important additional benefit to the region's dryness is that it discourages pests and disease. The arid atmosphere inhibits the infestation of bugs and the formation of fungus. The vine-killing pest phylloxera, for instance, is almost unknown in Washington, and the dry climate and sandy soils may be two reasons why. Related to dryness is the factor of wind in many Washington vineyards. Thanks to locations

Southeastern Washington's climate delivers consistently dry, warm weather, making the region ideal for winegrowing.

(*left*) By carefully controlling the application of water to individual vines, Washington's vineyard managers can better manage the grapevine's growth.

near the Columbia River, many of the state's wine countries get plenty of persistent wind. Not only does this also help reduce the incidence of disease and pests, but it also provides a natural check on vine growth, resulting in shorter shoot length, smaller berries, and more concentrated fruit.

Complementing eastern Washington's aridity is the reliable warmth of the growing season. In Prosser, the heart of the Yakima Valley wine country, summer maximum temperatures average 88°F–90°F (31.1°C–32.2°C), beneficial for warm-climate grapes. Growing degree days vary from a low of around 2025 (1107) in parts of the Rattlesnake Hills to 3200 (1760) at spots in the Columbia Valley. This wide spectrum allows eastern Washington to successfully grow most all vinifera varieties within its wine countries.

Also, the difference between daytime and nighttime heat—the diurnal swing—helps make the region such a good wine-growing area. While daytime temperatures can average in the high 80s°F (20s°C), nighttime temperatures in the Columbia Basin can easily drop to the 40s°F or 50s°F (4°C–10°C). This wide diurnal range has a direct impact on the character of Washington wines. The desertlike warmth of the daytime develops full, ripe flavors in the grapes, which are then balanced by cooler nighttime temperatures that allow for the retention of acidity. This results in the combination of fresh fruit flavors and the bright crisp acidity that is a hallmark of Washington's wine character.

Sunlight provides the third key factor in Washington's wine personality. Eastern Washington's vine-

SURVIVING DISASTER TOGETHER

An unsung aspect of Washington's wine culture is the cooperative nature of wineries that might normally be considered competitors. When a severe winter freeze in 2004 attacked vineyards in the Columbia Valley wine country, a number of small wineries were devastated, particularly in the Walla Walla Valley area. In some cases, estate vineyards were almost completely wiped out, and in others, fruit that had been contracted for purchase was simply gone. The potential loss of a complete vintage, an entire growing season's crop, not only threatened the livelihood of many smaller vintners, but it severely reduced the output of an entire appellation.

Concerned over the impact of the freeze, Ted Baseler, President and CEO of Ste. Michelle Wine Estates, Washington's largest vineyard owner, decided to offer fruit from Ste. Michelle's vineyards—including their prestigious Cold Creek and Canoe Ridge Estate Vineyards—to affected smaller wineries. With about 3500 acres (1416 ha) of vineyards, Ste. Michelle was geographically diversified enough that a large part of their production was not damaged by the cold snap.

The result was that many wineries potentially facing ruin were able to secure fruit and stay in business with wine to sell from the 2004 vintage, thanks to Ste. Michelle Wine Estates. It was a remarkable gesture that benefited the entire industry.

"We didn't do it for publicity," says Baseler (and the story has not been widely reported). "We did it because it benefited Washington wine. Relative to the great wine regions of the world, we're just babies. In other places, things can be quite different; over the years rivalries build up and there's not as much cooperation. We still have youthful exuberance. We all understand that when we work together, we'll all be more successful. It's part of the Washington character."

yards receive about 17.4 hours of daily sunlight during the growing season—2 hours more than in California's prime growing regions. Plus, the region's clear skies—little cloud cover, no industrial air pollution, and lots of wind to remove particulates in the atmosphere—mean the grapes receive a full measure of intensity from all that additional light. The additional light acts as a substitute for extra ripening time on the vine at the end of the growing season: Washington's grapes can be harvested off the vine sooner yet still achieve balanced ripeness and mature flavor.

These climatic conditions are great benefits for winegrowing, prompting the Washington Wine Commission in 2005 to launch a marketing initiative promoting the state as "the Perfect Climate for Wine." But there is one important drawback: winter cold. Average winter temperatures in Columbia Valley wine countries of 20°F–25°F (−6.6°C to −3.8°C) do not pose significant threats to grapevines. But not all eastern Washington winters are average. Roughly every four to eight years, the norm is shattered by arctic blasts blowing down from Canada that can bring sustained temperatures as low as −20°F (−28.8°C), which can seriously damage or kill vines. It happened in 1996, again in 2004, and to a lesser extent in 2008. Extremely cold air masses descended on eastern Washington and lingered, damaging some vineyards and significantly reducing yields. In 2004 it was estimated that as much as 80 percent of the vines in the Walla Walla Valley were damaged.

For a long time, people thought that the threat of extreme winters was too great a danger to the growth of the wine industry in eastern Washington. But with increased experience and viticultural knowledge, much of the risks from winter damage have been reduced. New vineyards are planted with more attention to air drainage, more modern frost

To help protect against frost, huge fans help circulate air in many of Washington's vineyards.

mitigation techniques are employed, greater care is taken to properly prepare vines for dormancy, and the increased age of the area's vineyards means that the vines themselves are more hardy, have deeper roots, and are better able to survive extreme weather conditions.

Cold temperatures pose another winegrowing risk, though one not quite so damaging: frost. At the start of the growing year, a late spring frost can damage vulnerable young shoots and buds, potentially reducing the crop and perhaps its quality. Similarly, early fall frosts can damage vines that haven't yet naturally hardened off for winter dormancy, leading to reduced yields in the following year.

Washington's winter cold is not entirely an unfriendly circumstance. For instance, the average winter's cold temperatures allow vines to go into deep dormancy, which is healthy and encourages long life. Winter cold also reduces threats from pests. Many potentially damaging insects cannot survive the temperatures of eastern Washington's winters, and the coldness of the soil in winter is thought to be a factor in keeping phylloxera at bay in Washington.

THE GRAPES AND STYLES OF WASHINGTON'S WINES

So what kind of wine is Washington best known for? If you answered big red wines, you are partially correct. Washington's national wine reputation centers on the high-scoring glamour of its expensive, small-production red wines. Yet, more white grapes are grown in the state: the 2009 ratio was 52 percent white to 48 percent red. This fact is another dimension in Washington's duality: Washington makes more white wines, although it is better known for its reds. To some, this situation means that Washington does not have a unified market position as a wine-producing region. Many Washington wine insiders lament that the state is not known for its mastery of a dominant grape variety. Consumers are

surprised when they learn that riesling is Washington's most widely planted grape when perhaps they were expecting merlot, or that the state produces more chardonnay than the cabernet sauvignon that has achieved critical accolades. Everyone knows that California's Napa Valley means cabernet sauvignon, and in the Northwest, Oregon's Willamette Valley is synonymous with pinot noir. Why doesn't Washington have a preeminent grape variety it can hang its marketing hat on?

This concern is a simply an illusion. Washington's wine industry has done just fine without a killer reputation for a single grape variety. Blessed with a much-vaunted perfect climate for wine, it makes sense that Washington would grow many grape varieties well. And having a signature grape is no marketing panacea. Just talk to Oregon's warm-climate

winemakers, who've struggled to explain to consumers why their nonpinot Oregon-made wines are *also* great. Washington's future success simply requires a broader awareness of all the grapes that Washington grows so well. So let's look at the state's top five wine grapes, ranked by the number of tons harvested in 2009.

(*left*) Every bottle of wine begins with a single drop of juice from ripe grapes.

(*right*) Washington grows more white grape varieties than red.

Riesling

Riesling is the most widely harvested wine grape in Washington. The state is home to the largest producer of riesling wines in the world: Ste. Michelle Wine Estates makes over 800,000 cases of it each year under its various brands. If there is to ever be a signature Washington grape, riesling will be a strong contender.

Sadly, riesling has not always enjoyed widespread market respect in North America, partly because too many domestic growers have too often treated the grape with less respect than is deserving of one of the world's greatest wine grapes. Some producers farm for higher yields or apply only basic winemaking, resulting in plenty of simplistic, often overtly sweet, riesling wines that, while enjoyable and inexpensive, don't get the best from the grape's potential. Consequently, many consumers have only known riesling as a cheap, sugary wine of no particular interest. Thankfully, this is changing.

Riesling was one of the earliest wine grapes grown in Washington, mostly because people felt Washington was too far north for success with any but cool-climate grapes, which riesling definitely is. So why does it thrive in Washington's warm-climate wine countries? Washington's unique growing conditions allow the grape to express both the rich fruit flavors produced by abundant daytime heat, and still display crisp acid resulting from cool nights. When grown with care and appropriate yields, riesling ripens slowly and gains full varietal character yet retains excellent acidity for balanced freshness.

Riesling produces very aromatic wines, and the best Washington examples display a myriad of fragrant tones. Often an appealing sense of dried flower blossoms and fresh straw are the first things smelled in the wine, followed by touches of dried herbs, slate, and minerals. Sometimes the fruit in the aromas can be overwhelmed by a sense of riesling's varietal spice—a distinctive aroma difficult to describe but often called petrol or diesel. More appealing than it sounds, this aroma isn't generally strong in a young wine, and its presence or absence isn't necessarily an indicator of quality.

My tasting experience of Washington riesling reveals two general styles. One mode emphasizes rich, warm, naturally fruit-sweet riesling flavors, particularly of peach and apricot, with tropical undertones like pineapple or mango. The other expression stresses a lean, tart approach, with flavors reminiscent of green apples, pears, and citrus fruits. In both cases, accents of honey and minerality can lend complexity to the fruit center.

If there is a single stylistic stamp to Washington's riesling wines it would be residual sugar. Few are truly dry. Sweetness is not an indicator of quality, only of style. Regardless of the level of sugar, what makes a Washington riesling compelling is the degree of balancing acidity, something the state's wines naturally achieve. When good acidity is present, it dampens the sense of sweetness on the palate, allowing the fruit to taste bright and fresh rather than simply sappy or sweet. Acidity also helps highlight the additional layers of complexity—minerality and spice, for instance—that riesling grapes can give wine.

The best Washington riesling wines, regardless of their degree of sweetness, have a ripe fruity character that sets them apart from Old World rieslings, which tend to be more austere and less fruity. At the same time, the generally high acidity in Washington rieslings contrasts with many other warm-climate wines, whose emphasis on fruit can be overly lush.

Well-made riesling wines tend to be very long-lived. North Americans are not in the habit of aging white wines; most Washington rieslings are consumed early. But when allowed some bottle age, they can take on impressive weight and depth. If you find a well-balanced Washington riesling that you love, put some bottles in the cellar for a few years. You may be surprised at how well they develop.

One rare class of riesling that is made extremely well in Washington is the late-harvest style. To make this wine, riesling grapes are left hanging on the vine well after the normal harvest, often deep into the colder months of late autumn and early winter. These grapes ripen additional sugars and flavors, developing concentrated juice; they can sometimes be arduously picked by the individual berry, and the winemaking process is long and messy. When pressed and fermented, they make unctuous, nectarlike wine that is expensive and rare. Washington only produces a small amount, but when done well, the wines are highly prized, and consumed with relish by aficionados.

Chardonnay

Chardonnay is a workhorse white grape in many wine regions, and Washington is no exception. Chardonnay is the second most harvested grape in the state, but not by much; for many years it beat out riesling. While there is a lot of Washington chardonnay available to slake the seemingly insatiable taste for this wine, there's not really a distinctive style to Washington chardonnay. Chardonnay is sometimes called a blank slate grape that doesn't have a strongly characteristic flavor of its own. Whether that saying is true or not, winemakers have lots of latitude in shaping chardonnay grapes to the style of wine they wish to create. In Washington, as in other North American winegrowing regions, two basic styles of chardonnay have resulted.

For a long time, the predominant chardonnay style in America has been a weighty, lush, tropical-fruit, butter-and-oak-influenced, vaguely sweet-seeming wine that came to be popularly referred to as a California chard. This type of chardonnay is usually first fermented in oak barrels, goes through a secondary fermentation that softens the wine through converting malic acids into lactic acids, and is aged on its lees, or the remains of dead yeast cells, in oak barrels. Chardonnay created in this manner is popular because it delivers a richly textured wine with plenty of intermingling tastes. A number of Washington producers make fine chardonnays in this manner.

In reaction to the dominance of this chardonnay mode, many producers are now also making an opposite style of wine. Sometimes referred to as unoaked or stainless steel chardonnay, this style is fermented in steel tanks, does not go through malolactic fermentation, and does not undergo significant barrel aging. These chardonnay wines emphasize clean fruit flavors, are lighter bodied, are higher in acidity, and often have green apple, kiwi, and tart citrus notes.

Each chardonnay style has its proponents, and each is well made in Washington. Increasingly, however, Washington's winemakers are finding a middle path to chardonnay success. By combining winemaking components from both styles, a number of Washington wineries are producing a more balanced, broadly satisfying chardonnay that can be enjoyed by adherents of either stylistic pole. But how do you know what style of chardonnay is in the bottle? If you like plush, creamy-textured chardonnay, look for back labels that use terms like malolactic fermentation, *sur-lie* aging (indicating it was aged on its lees), or barrel fermented. If you prefer crisp, fresh, sleek flavors, seek wines whose labels indicate an "unoaked," steel, or tank-fermented background, with no malolactic fermentation.

Cabernet Sauvignon

Washington is famous for so-called "big reds," and many of the best are made from cabernet sauvignon grapes. It was a Washington cabernet sauvignon that earned the first 100-point score for a Northwest wine from Robert M. Parker Jr.'s *The Wine Advocate*, and it has been cabernet sauvignon that many critics see as the state's wine variety most competitive with California.

The first commercial planting of cabernet sauvignon in Washington took place in 1957, at what is now Otis Vineyard near Grandview in the Yakima Valley, using plant material that came from the University of California, Davis. Those 52-plus-year-old vines are not only the oldest cabernet sauvignon plants in the Northwest, they are some of the oldest in North America, and they still produce fruit for wine.

Cabernet sauvignon is a late-ripening grape that requires ample time on the vine and plenty of uni-

Cabernet sauvignon, like these vines at Klipsun Vineyards, is the grape most wine lovers associate with Washington's wine countries.

(*inset, right*) The 2002 Quilceda Creek Cabernet Sauvignon from Washington was the first Northwest wine to earn a coveted 100-point score from the famed wine critic Robert M. Parker Jr.'s publication, *The Wine Advocate*.

form heat to develop full varietal flavors. In eastern Washington, cabernet sauvignon can be reliably ripened in many locations without risking overripeness and raisining, or dehydration. By the time of an October harvest when nights are getting quite cool, plenty of acid is retained in the grapes to balance the sugars and help showcase the varietal character.

Washington's cabernets are sometimes said to occupy a middle ground in style between the rich, fruit-forward, soft, succulent California cabernet, and the lean, more assertively tannic, taut, herbaceous young Bordeaux cabernets. For a while it seemed that Washington cabernet producers were striving to create a style of wine that could be considered clearly Washingtonian. Such cabernets emphasized the naturally high acidity and the fresh, vibrant cassis, cherry, and

THE PERFECT WASHINGTON CABERNET SAUVIGNON

For many, Washington came of age as a wine region when one of the state's cabernet sauvignon wines earned a perfect 100-point rating from wine critic Robert M. Parker Jr. The Quilceda Creek Vintners, of Snohomish, Washington, received this cherished accolade for their 2002 Quilceda Creek Cabernet Sauvignon, and they repeated the performance for their 2003 and 2005 vintages. If there is a holy grail for winemakers, it may be achieving a perfect Parker score.

As the world's most influential wine critic, Parker doles out scores in *The Wine Advocate* that are closely watched by winemakers and consumers alike. A score between 90 and 95 means the wine is "an outstanding wine of exceptional complexity and character," and wines between 96 and 100 points are "of profound and complex character displaying all the attributes expected of a classic wine of its variety."

In awarding its first 100-point score to a Northwest wine, *The Wine Advocate* described the 2002 Quilceda Creek Cabernet's nose as having aromas "of violets, sweet blueberries, dark cherries, and slight undertones of asphalt." It remarked on the "concentrated layers of cassis, blackberries, red cherries, raspberries, violets, spices, and touches of candied plums" on the palate. In summation, they described the wine as "rich, exquisitely balanced, sweet, and broad" as well as being "harmonious, graceful, and awesomely long." High praise indeed.

The Wine Advocate's reviewer for Washington state, Jay Miller, wrote in 2008, after the wine's third 100-point award, that "Quilceda Creek's Cabernet Sauvignon remains the benchmark for what can be achieved in Washington and the United States."

raspberry flavors of the fruit without drifting into either high-alcohol, super-concentrated "fruit bombs," or tannic monsters that take decades to soften.

Would that this continued to be the case. For my taste, too many of the state's winemakers are opting for a more region-generic style of cabernet sauvignon wines, one that emphasizes extremely ripe, soft-bordering-on-gooey-sweet fruit, lavish doses of barrel-induced vanilla and chocolate, high alcohol potency, and chunky, chewy tannins. This style scores well with critics, and undeniably is a popular seller.

But perhaps some of the distinctive Washington character of these wines has been sacrificed in favor of market plaudits. When cabernets are made with excessive barrel influence, rough tannins, alcoholic sweetness, and overripe fruit flavors, there is not much room left to display Washington *terroir*. Fortunately, there are the beginnings of a backlash

Ripe grapes fresh off the vine in Washington's Red Mountain wine country.

to these heavy approaches to cabernet sauvignon, and the diligent seeker can find leaner, cleaner, and fresher styles that better show the native qualities of Washington cabernet.

Merlot

Merlot was long considered Washington's great red hope. Some of the first Washington wines to attract national critical attention were merlots, and enough merlot is produced in the state to make well-crafted, tasty, and affordable merlot wines accessible to anyone. But here's the rub: merlot from anywhere is just about everywhere in the market these days, and consequently respect for the variety has declined. California has 10 times more planted acres of merlot than Washington, and merlot is often the most popular red wine in consumer surveys, but even given these facts, merlot simply doesn't have the cachet it used to have, no matter how good it is. Which is unfortunate, because Washington merlot wines can be among the best in the world.

Merlot is one of the earliest grapes to be annually harvested in the Columbia Valley. Though a warm-climate grape variety, it prefers relatively cooler vineyard sites. Determining the right time to pick is vital, because merlot has a tendency to lose acidity quickly once physiological ripeness is reached; there is not much margin for extra time on the vine. But when grown well and picked right, merlot achieves fully ripened flavors and wondrous complexity in Washington.

Merlot is amenable to winemaking manipulation, so it can be molded into a variety of styles, from light-bodied and quaffable to profound and ageable. Perhaps because of its reputation as the easy-drinking cousin of cabernet, much of the merlot in today's marketplace is made simply. But in Washington, the grape is given due winegrowing respect, and is made with care and consideration, even when inexpensively priced.

Restraint is a quality often associated with Washington merlot, meaning that while the wines display rich, full flavors, they are rarely soft and overblown. Food-friendly is also a frequently cited attribute. The state's famous acidity gives definition and verve to the intense, complex flavors produced by the climate's dry heat, but without the high-alcohol, flabby, overextracted qualities that so often mar the food-pairing capacity of many merlot wines from other regions. The best Washington merlots are aromatic, with wafts of spice and floral notes reminiscent of violets, roses, sandalwood, and mint. The rich core of cherry flavors often evolve into darker black currant and blackberry notes on the palate, with an appealing earthiness not readily found in merlot from other growing regions.

Many Washington merlot wines are really merlot-based blends, with no more than 25 percent other grapes added, which is a little unusual. In most places, it is more common for merlot to be added as an accent to cabernet sauvignon, but in Washington, merlot is more frequently the dominant base of a blend.

Washington merlots come in a variety of styles, some tending toward more oak, others more fruit. Many are made for current consumption, others for cellaring. As with cabernet sauvignon, there has been a recent tendency for many Washington merlot wines to be made in a blowzy, high-alcohol, overblown style. The back labels and winery descriptions can provide some guidance in selecting a merlot, but since there are no standard definitions for descriptions like "gobs of ripe fruit," you must take a buyer-beware stance until you've had a chance to taste the wine.

Syrah

In recent years, syrah has become the glamour grape of Washington. With laudatory national press, plenty of craft producers, and growing acreage planted with the variety, there's no denying syrah's impact on the state's wine scene. But syrah is still a young red grape in Washington, and its ultimate role in the pantheon of the state's varieties is yet to be settled.

Syrah was first planted in Washington in 1986 at the Red Willow Vineyard in Yakima Valley, the result of a collaboration between Red Willow's owner, Mike Sauer, and the late David Lake, then winemaker for Columbia Winery and one of the few certified Masters of Wine in the Northwest. Lake was convinced that Washington's climate was close enough to syrah's home in France's Rhône region that it was worth experimenting with. They obtained cuttings from California, planted them in the spring of 1986, and made Washington's first commercial syrah wine in 1988. The theory was that since the greatest of French syrah wines came from the hot, steep, south-facing slopes of the Côte Rotie in the northern Rhône region, a similar site in Washington's distinctly continental climate might prove conducive to the vine. It did. Today syrah is planted all over eastern Washington.

Before syrah could become accepted in Washington, it had to prove itself on two fronts. Did it make good wine here, and could it survive a hard Washington winter? David Lake proved the case on both accounts. He released Washington's first commercial syrah wine, the 1988 vintage grown at Red Willow Vineyard, at a Rhône conference in California in 1991. Even the French winemakers in attendance were impressed. The first Washington syrah showed potential. In 1996, when a devastating frost damaged vines throughout eastern Washington, the syrah at Red Willow survived. Syrah was off to the races.

From my tasting experience, Washington's syrah wines fall into three stylistic camps: the lean and fruity, the plush and plump, and the herby and mineral rich. Each style is partly dependent on the nature of the soil and climate where the fruit is grown, and partly the result of explicit winemaking decisions. Lean and fruity syrah wines come from grapes grown in the cooler parts of the Columbia Valley AVA, particularly in the mid-Yakima Valley. Here, syrah easily achieves full ripeness, and the cooler temperatures allow for more acidity, longer time on the vine, and more complex flavors. This style of syrah displays the trademark plum, blackberry, black pepper, and spice characteristics of the variety, but with an added freshness.

style of syrah emphasizes layers of different flavors, and sometimes the fruitiness takes second position. Ample notes of minerals and earth, cinnamon, sage, fresh-ground white pepper, and broiled meat are other prominent sensations, with lurking blackberry, raspberry, or plum fruitiness. These terms describe broad stylistic families, but a single syrah can display any combination of these characteristics, especially when the grapes are blended from different vineyards.

As is the case with many Washington red wines, some winemakers are lunging toward an ever bigger and plumper style of syrah wine. Picking syrah grapes when extremely ripe for higher extraction and alcohol and adding voluminous amounts of oak are part of this trend. While a few years ago Washington's syrah fame was for its leaner, more structured, elegant wines, today's bigger-than-thou, fruit-bomb syrahs risk becoming indistinguishable from syrahs made elsewhere in the world.

Other Important Grapes

In terms of production, the next most important grapes in Washington are sauvignon blanc, pinot gris, gewürztraminer, cabernet franc, and viognier. All are made well into wine in the state, but few have achieved the same level of prominence as the top five varieties.

Washington's "perfect climate for wine" means that over 30 different varieties of wine grapes are grown in the state, though many only in boutique-scale quantities as yet. Lurking in some obscure vine row today may be the one or two grape varieties that will someday emerge as a new generation of leading wines for the state. For instance, tempranillo is a fast-rising variety in Washington. Though the quantities planted are as yet miniscule, early wines show a rich meaty quality that distinguishes them from the more familiar red grapes in the state. Likewise, sangiovese, barbera, and nebbiolo are red varieties gaining a foothold in Washington. Though there is still too little experience with these grapes to know just what

The plush and plump versions of syrah come from warmer precincts such as Red Mountain and the Wahluke Slope. The added heat imparts a deeper richness of dense, pure fruitiness, almost with a sweet bent, and frequently higher alcohol. The mouth feel of this style is supple, leaning to unctuous, with thick fruitiness that can border on being jammy. While the spicy qualities of the fruit are not lost, the sometimes over-the-top fruitiness of the style can dampen the variety's pepper, earthy, and herbal nuances.

When grown in rocky or calcareous soils (which are claylike, containing calcium carbonate or chalk), especially in parts of the Walla Walla Valley, some of the most interesting syrahs display complex shadings of dried herbs, minerality, and a rich meatiness sometimes described as a sense of bacon fat. This

Syrah is rapidly becoming one of Washington's most important grape varieties.

their future may be, the intriguing early wines merit following.

Grenache (also known as garnacha) is a Spanish red grape variety that has a small community of advocates paying it renewed attention—renewed because some of the earliest vinifera grapes planted in Washington were grenache vines. This variety does not tolerate cold winters well, but new plantings that have the benefit of modern viticultural knowledge have shown great promise. Washington grenache can be sumptuously delicious, with bright fresh fruitiness that also has weight and character. I expect it to be a grape with a big future in Washington.

There are others as well. The Rhône counoise, mourvèdre, marsanne, and roussanne grapes are made into tiny quantities of very good wine. The lesser Bordeaux malbec, petit verdot, and carmenère grapes are increasing in popularity, though they are made only in small amounts. More obscure French grapes, such as cinsault, aligoté, chenin blanc, and the somewhat better known gamay, have small plantings. A range of internationally eclectic grapes can be found across the state including muscat, dolcetto, albariño, lemberger, zinfandel, primitivo, and grüner veltliner. The adventurous wine lover will always find something to like in Washington's diversity of wines.

Blends

America's obsession with wine labeled by grape variety does a disservice to what is often the best embodiment of a winemaker's skill: the blended wine. Washington in particular is home to master wine blenders. Amid the clamor for a signature Washington grape, we may all be missing blended wines as the state's most impressive wine style. Federal regulations require that a wine labeled as a single variety be composed of a minimum of 75 percent of that grape. Some wines labeled as a merlot, for instance, may contain as much as 25 percent of other grapes. In practice, most Washington wineries give their own proprietary name to wines they consider to be blends, even if the wine qualifies to be labeled as a varietal wine.

Washington's blends are often artful mixtures of the different characteristics of each grape in the blend. Blended wines can also be a deft way for a winemaker to express the character of a vintage rather than the expression of any one grape. With a blend, the winemaker can pick and choose differently ripening grapes of a vintage to offer what he or she feels are the best grape characteristics of the year, unrestricted by the need to keep to the flavor of a single grape.

When visiting Washington tasting rooms, don't shy away from a blended wine simply because you are more familiar with named grape varieties or are unsure of what it might taste like. The best Washington blends present a wine experience that is greater than the sum of its grapes. Winemakers apply their best skills to crafting their leading blends, and often take more pride in their blended wines than they do the single-variety wines.

Winemakers, like these at Ste. Michelle Wine Estates in Washington, constantly taste wines to keep their palates sharp and to help them assemble their own blended wines.

WASHINGTON'S WINE COUNTRIES

Puget Sound Wine Country

From a purely winegrowing perspective, there's not a lot to the Puget Sound appellation. But for wine touring, tasting, and buying, the Puget Sound region is in some ways Washington's most important wine country—another of the state's quirky wine polarities. Established in 1995, the Puget Sound appellation is an anomaly. The only appellation in western Washington, the only certifiably cool-climate appellation in Washington, and the Washington appellation with the fewest vineyard acres, this wine country is held up by some as an example of AVAs gone wild.

It is true that the amount of wine grapes grown in the region is negligible, that the varieties grown here are mostly out of the mainstream, that the wines produced here are not among those that have made Washington famous. But the region's climate is amenable to cool-climate winegrowing, with plenty of daylight hours and sufficient warmth for early ripening grapes. And the area is home to some of Washington's largest and most prestigious wineries. It is the place most people come to experience the big names in Washington wine. And it is home to a number of small vineyards and wineries with dedicated owners who, however unconventionally, are making passionately produced wines.

The Puget Sound AVA extends from the United States–Canada border south along the east side of Puget Sound to below the state capital of Olympia. The western portion of the AVA reaches northward along the rim of the Sound and the eastern coast of the Olympic Peninsula, and turns west to follow the peninsula's north coast to Port Angeles. Vineyards and wineries of the appellation are concentrated in three general regions: the islands of the Sound, the Skagit Valley area, and the north coast of the Olympic Peninsula.

Exposed to a temperate marine climate, the region's summers are rarely hot and winters are rarely cold. Vineyards on Vashon Island, for instance, experience average high summer temperatures of 75°F (23.8°C) and minimum winter temperatures just above freezing. Vineyard growing degree days range between 1661 and 2002 (905–1094), making the Sound viable only for the most cool-adapted grape varieties.

The Puget Sound wine country gets plenty of rain, from 30 to 60 in. (762–1524 mm) annually, but little of it falls during the summer months. The Olympic Mountains are a sizable rain barrier that keeps summer storms from reaching much of the Puget Sound region. Vineyards in the appellation are dry by the middle of the summer, and the temperate climate plus long sunny days make for extended and even ripening of grapes.

The only viable vinifera varieties for Puget Sound are early ripening grapes such as pinot noir, pinot gris, and gewürztraminer, though little of these grapes are grown here. Hybrid grapes seem to do best, and are more widely planted, the most popular of which are müller-thurgau, madeline angevine, and siegerrebe.

Some of Washington state's earliest attempts to grow grapes took place within the Puget Sound region, but today the combination of a borderline climate for the most popular wine varieties and a dense population occupying much of the region's potential vineyard land has limited wine grape growing to a little over a dozen hearty entities. Most Puget Sound–based wineries import grapes from eastern Washington for at least some of their wines, even if they also locally grow their own grapes.

While Puget Sound–grown wines and their associated wineries can be an interesting diversion for the wine tourist seeking a more adventurous tasting experience, those who wish to sample some of the most notable Washington wine brands will find resources within ready reach of Seattle. Seventeen miles east of the city, in the green vale of the Sammamish River Valley near the town of Woodinville, is a concentration of some of the best wine names in the state. Without a doubt, the countryside around Woodin-

PUGET SOUND WINE COUNTRY AT A GLANCE

Year established: 1995

Number of wineries: 15*

Total acreage: 2,879,800 acres (1,165,400 ha)

Approximate vineyard acreage:
    100 acres (40 ha)

Predominant soil types: glacial till

Vineyard growing degree days:
    1413–2002 (767–1094)

Most important grape varieties

madeline angevin, müller-thurgau, siegerrebe

*Approximate number of wineries growing or sourcing grapes from within the Puget Sound AVA. Does not include wineries whose tasting rooms or business offices are located within the appellation but do not source grapes from the appellation.

Most wine visitors come to Washington's Puget Sound wine country to visit tasting rooms in Woodinville, like this one at Chateau Ste. Michelle.

ville is the most wine-populated and significant area of the Puget Sound appellation, even though it is distinctly not grape-growing country; there is only one operating vineyard in the area. Here, an exploding population of wineries has transformed this suburb into a locus of tasting rooms and has become one of the most visited wine centers in the Northwest. In fact, for many wine lovers, their only experience of Washington wine comes from visiting one of the Woodinville-area tasting rooms. There is even a marketing group branding the area as Woodinville Wine Country.

The emergence of a wine tasting center in Woodinville is a testimony to the business savvy of Washington's wine industry. Many of the state's best known wineries understand that it makes better economic sense to locate their tasting rooms close to their best market of buyers, with Seattle only 30 driving minutes away, than it is to be nearer their source of grapes, 350 mi (563 km) distant in eastern Washington.

Château Ste. Michelle led the way. By far the largest wine company in the Northwest, Ste. Michelle Wine Estates' corporate headquarters are deliberately located in easy-to-visit Woodinville. Opened in 1976, the tasting room is one of the most visited and photographed in the Northwest. It delivers the kind of romanticized vision of wine country elegance that most people expect: a chateau-style building surrounded by landscaped grounds that include demonstration vines, even though the company's vineyards and much of its winemaking are three driving hours away.

Capitalizing on Ste. Michelle's magnetic draw, many small wineries, including prestige favorites, have created a critical mass of tasting rooms in Woodinville that attracts more wine tourists each year. The wineries are here for the business climate, not the growing climate. The fact that they are in the Puget Sound appellation is also unimportant—none of their wines carry the AVA name. Yet they are an essential part of Puget Sound wine country, attracting scads of wine-thirsty visitors, some of who also find their way out to estate wineries of the larger Puget Sound wine country.

The Woodinville, Washington, corporate headquarters of Ste. Michelle Wine Estates is one of the most visited winery tasting rooms in the Northwest.

WINERIES AND WINES TO SAMPLE

ANDREW WILL WINERY

12526 SW Bank Road, Vashon Island, WA
206-463-9227; www.andrewwill.com
Not open.

Year founded:	1989
Annual production:	4500 cases
Signature wine:	Sorella ($$$$)
Premium wine:	Sorella ($$$$)
Value wine:	Sangiovese ($$)
Estate vineyards:	Two Blondes, Champoux

Owner and winemaker Chris Camarda was one of the earliest Washington advocates of making wines all sourced from the grapes of single vineyards, and he has been a key force behind the growing fame of the state's wines. By applying a rigorously consistent winemaking procedure to grapes sourced from multiple eastern Washington vineyards, he has been able to clearly show the individual taste of place inherent in each vineyard. He was an early buyer of grapes from vineyards that today are tops in the state: Ciel du Cheval, Klipsun, Pepper Bridge, Seven Hills, Champoux, and Sheridan.

In more recent years, Camarda has moved to making blends as well, represented by his highly respected Sorella Bordeaux-style red blend. In his Andrew Will wines, named for his son and nephew, Camarda feels enabled to express both the appealing complexity of blends and the special character of each vineyard. He is respected for his winemaking adroitness and integrity, and has crafted some of the best quality wine Washington can produce.

BETZ FAMILY WINERY

13244 Woodinville-Redmond Road NE, Redmond, WA
425-861-9823; www.betzfamilywinery.com
Not open.

Year founded:	1997
Annual production:	3500 cases
Signature wine:	Père de Famille Cabernet Sauvignon ($$$$)
Premium wine:	Père de Famille Cabernet Sauvignon ($$$$)
Value wine:	Clos de Betz ($$$)
Estate vineyards:	uses purchased fruit

Master of Wine Bob Betz is an undisputed leader of the Northwest wine scene. The embodiment of the gentleman-and-a-scholar ethos, Betz's incomparable knowledge of viticulture and enology has helped propel Washington into the world's wine limelight, and his winery into cult status. After 28 years working for what is now Ste. Michelle Wine Estates, Betz left to create his own personal expression of Washington wine, focusing exclusively on red wines.

Using fruit sourced from Washington's elite vineyards, he blends his grapes into consistently compelling wines of both Bordeaux- and Rhône-inspired styles that express both his craft and the individual vineyards that grew the grapes—a rare accomplishment. His winemaking prowess produces bottles that deftly balance big, ripe, fruit flavors with taut acidity and structure. Betz's wines are enjoyable in the near term, yet able to add character with age, and they are always great accompaniment to food.

BRIAN CARTER CELLARS

14419 Woodinville-Redmond Road NE, Woodinville, WA
425-806-9463; www.briancartercellars.com
Open all year; limited hours.

Year founded:	1997
Annual production:	6500 cases
Signature wine:	Solesce ($$$$)
Premium wine:	Solesce ($$$$)
Value wine:	Abracadabra ($$)
Estate vineyards	uses purchased fruit

Brian Carter has been influential in Washington's wine world for many years, having consulted with some of the state's best-known wineries. He began making his own blended wines in 1997 while still consulting, and incorporated Brian Carter Cellars in 2004 as the first Washington winery to focus exclusively on blended wines.

Ranging across Europe for his wines' models, Carter produces red blends in a super Tuscan-style (called Tuttorosso), a signature Bordeaux-style (Solesce), a tasty southern Rhône-style (Byzance), and an intriguing white blend of roussanne, riesling, and viognier (Oriana). He has recently added a Spanish-style blend (Corrida), and each year he makes his Abracadabra red blend, depending on what he feels the vintage delivers. His wines are always beautifully balanced, with rich and complex flavors that admirably display the blender's art.

CAMARADERIE CELLARS

334 Benson Road, Port Angeles, WA
360-417-3564; www.camaraderiecellars.com
Open during the season; limited hours.

Year founded:	1992
Annual production:	5000 cases
Signature wine:	Grâce ($$$)
Premium wine:	Elégance ($$$)
Value wine:	Storm King Red ($$)
Estate vineyards:	uses purchased fruit

A prime example of Washington's you-can-live-any-where-and-still-make-wine mentality, Don and Vicki Corson are happily ensconced in their Olympic Peninsula winery, about 300 miles away from the vineyards where they purchase their trucked-in grapes.

Don Corson's engaging personality is reflected in his wines: elegant and supple, forward and fresh, possessing pleasing sophistication without being ponderous. Known best for his Grâce Bordeaux-style red blend, and his cabernet franc and cabernet sauvignon varietal wines, he also produces a range of additional wines, including merlot, malbec, tempranillo, syrah, viognier, and a white blend.

CHATEAU STE. MICHELLE

14111 NE 145th Street, Woodinville, WA
425-415-3300; www.ste-michelle.com
Open all year.

Year founded:	1934
Annual production:	1,952,800 cases
Signature wine:	Chateau Ste. Michelle Columbia Valley Riesling ($)
Premium wine:	Eroica Single Berry Select ($$$$+, 375ml)
Value wine:	Chateau Ste. Michelle Columbia Valley Dry Riesling ($)
Estate vineyards:	Canoe Ridge Estate, Cold Creek, Horse Heaven

Ste. Michelle Wine Estates, the corporate string of which Chateau Ste. Michelle is one of the pearls, is Washington's preeminent wine brand. One of the largest wine companies in North America and a foundational Washington winery whose roots go back 75 years, Ste. Michelle is also the largest vineyard owner in the state.

Ste. Michelle produces superb wines across the board under the direction of head winemaker Bob Bertheau, and many at extremely reasonable prices. The Chateau Ste. Michelle brand includes a number of product lines: best-of-vintage blends under the Ethos Reserve name, single-variety wines from single vineyards (Cold Creek, Canoe Ridge Estate, Horse Heaven), the Indian Wells series of varietal wines blended from grapes from different vineyards, and the Columbia Valley series of varietal wines. Also of note is the Eroica line of rieslings.

The other Northwest pearls in the Ste. Michelle Wine Estates necklace, some of which are discussed as individual winery listings, are Col Solare, Columbia Crest, Domaine Ste. Michelle, Northstar, Red Diamond, Snoqualmie, Spring Valley Vineyard, 14 Hands, Stimson Estate Cellars, and Erath.

CHATTER CREEK

18658 142nd Avenue NE, Woodinville, WA
425-485-3864; www.chattercreek.com
Open all year; Saturdays only.

Year founded:	1996
Annual production:	3000 cases
Signature wine:	Syrah, Clifton Hill Vineyard ($$$$)
Premium wine:	Nebbiolo, Clifton Hill Vineyard ($$$)
Value wine:	Pinot Gris ($)
Estate vineyards:	uses purchased fruit

Owner, winemaker, and cellar rat Gordon Rawson has been making wine since 1996, and opened Chatter Creek in 2000 after working for Columbia Winery under David Lake. Chatter Creek is a fine example of an artisan winery driven by the passion of the owner. Rawson makes pinot gris, viognier, grenache, syrah, cabernet franc, cabernet sauvignon, a red blend, and, unusually for the Northwest, a nebbiolo from the Wahluke Slope.

Chatter Creek's pinot gris is quite tasty, and the syrahs are very well made. The nebbiolo is a red wine made in extremely small quantities, following the traditions for Barolo production, the classic Italian expression of the grape, including aging three years in barrel. This Northwest nebbiolo is a true rarity, and worth seeking out.

COLUMBIA WINERY

14030 NE 145th Street, Woodinville, WA
425-482-7490; www.columbiawinery.com
Open all year.

Year founded:	1962
Annual production:	160,000 cases
Signature wine:	Otis Vineyard Cabernet Sauvignon ($$$)
Premium wine:	Peninsula ($$$)
Value wine:	Cellarmaster's Riesling ($)
Estate vineyards:	uses purchased fruit

Columbia Winery is the direct descendant of Associated Vintners, one of the two founding wineries of Washington's fine wine industry, and has been producing vinifera wines since the 1967 vintage. For much of its history, Master of Wine David Lake not only ensured the quality of Columbia's wines, but introduced new varieties to Washington, such as syrah, that helped define the state's wine character.

Today, Director of Winemaking Kerry Norton shepherds Columbia's wine portfolio, continuing to use fruit from legendary vineyards like Otis (planted in 1957), Red Willow (cabernet sauvignon going back to 1973), and Wyckoff (chardonnay planted in 1977). Norton also makes an intriguing series of small lot wines from grapes such as barbera, malbec, and viognier.

The styles of Columbia's wines are a bit atypical for Washington. The whites are more crisp, lean, and taut than the average, and the reds can be tight, initially tannic, also lean, and often closed up when young. These wines are more broadly European in tenor, and not quite as overtly fruity as the typical Washington wine. But they are very well made and have proven to age extremely well.

DELILLE CELLARS

14208 Woodinville-Redmond Road NE, Redmond, WA
425-489-0544; www.delillecellars.com
Open by appointment only.

Year founded:	1992
Annual production:	4500 cases
Signature wine:	Chaleur Estate Red Wine ($$$$)
Premium wine:	Grand Ciel Cabernet Sauvignon ($$$$+)
Value wine:	Chaleur Estate Blanc ($$$)
Estate vineyards:	Grand Ciel

DeLille Cellars is one of Washington's premier wineries, with a special emphasis on Bordeaux-style wines. They also produce Rhône-style wines under the Doyenne label. Winemaker Chris Upchurch is a deft blender. His Chaleur Estate Red and Chaleur Estate Blanc are two of the best examples of New World interpretations of classic French blends that you'll find anywhere.

DeLille sources grapes from leading vineyards including Klipsun, Ciel du Cheval, Boushey, Sagemoor Farm, and Red Willow, and makes a cabernet sauvignon wine from the state's second oldest plantings of the grape at Harrison Hill Vineyard. In 2004, the winery released its first wine from its new estate vineyard on Red Mountain, Grand Ciel Estate Vineyard. DeLille's wines are dense, succulent, full of fruit and spice, yet remarkably polished, stylish, and elegant. In many ways, DeLille wines represent the epitome of Washington's wine character: powerful and bold, without being aggressive.

McCREA CELLARS

11515 Eagleview Lane, Rainer, WA
360-446-8466; www.mccreacellars.com
Open by appointment only.

Year founded:	1988
Annual production:	4000 cases
Signature wine:	Cuvée Orleans Syrah ($$$)
Premium wine:	Cuvée Orleans Syrah ($$$)
Value wine:	Columbia Valley Red Wine ($$)
Estate vineyards:	uses purchased fruit

Doug McCrea has been ahead of the curve for about 20 years. He caught on to the potential of Rhône varieties, including syrah, long before they became some of the hottest grapes for the state's warmest sites. McCrea made the second syrah wine in Washington, the first Rhône-style blend, the first viognier, and the first counoise wines in the state.

Collaborating closely with elite vineyards, Mc-Crae now works with roughly 10 Rhône grape varieties, including the picpoul and grenache blanc, which are almost unheard of in this country. From these, he produces multiple versions of succulent syrah wines, plus a meaty and deliciously different mourvèdre and a ripe roussanne. His Washington versions of Châteauneuf du Pape–style blends, called Sirocco and Sirocco Blanc, are full of finesse and fine flavors not found in traditional Washington blends.

OLYMPIC CELLARS WINERY

255410 Highway 101, Port Angeles, WA
360-452-0160; www.olympiccellars.com
Open all year.

Year founded:	1979
Annual production:	10,000 cases
Signature wine:	La Dolce Vida Syrah ($$)
Premium wine:	La Dolce Vida Petit Verdot ($$$)
Value wine:	Dungeness White Riesling ($)
Estate vineyards:	uses purchased fruit

Olympic Cellars is woman-owned and operated proudly applying a playful style to the marketing of their wine. Grapes are sourced from eastern Washington and made into three product tiers: Premium La Dolce Vida wines, which feature clean, bright varietal flavors with a touch of oak; Working Girl wines, which are more casual (Rosé the Riveter is an example of their lighthearted style); and the value-oriented Dungeness wines. The tasting room, located in a picturesque barn, is crammed with merchandise and always buzzing with activity.

Kathy Charlton is the owner and dynamic public face of Olympic Cellars, and the force that successfully settled an unbelievable suit brought by the U.S. Olympic committee, which wanted the winery to cease using the word Olympic—which refers to the mountains, not the games—in its brand name. Olympic Cellars also has a unique donation program that helps support women's and family health and sustainable community causes.

QUILCEDA CREEK VINTNERS

PO Box 1562, Snohomish, WA
360-568-2389; www.quilcedacreek.com
Not open.

Year founded:	1978
Annual production:	not available
Signature wine:	Columbia Valley Cabernet Sauvignon ($$$$+)
Premium wine:	Columbia Valley Cabernet Sauvignon ($$$$+)
Value wine:	Columbia Valley Red Wine ($$)
Estate vineyards:	Galitzine, Palengat, Champoux

With no less than three perfect Parker scores (tied only by Château Margaux, Château Haut-Brion, and Châteaux Latour), Quilceda Creek is the elite of Washington's wineries and its wines the epitome of cult cuvées. Even though it makes substantially more wine than many other cult brands, access to its top releases is only through a usually closed mailing list.

The Golitzin family has taken a deliberate approach to their craft, meticulously working for decades on every aspect of winegrowing and winemaking. Alex and Jeannette Golitzin began the winery, and today son Paul is winemaker, continuing to work with his father. In 2004, they built a new winery, and have since added new estate vineyards to their arsenal of winemaking weapons.

Taut when young, with a profusion of polished tannins framing the laser-focused fruit, Quilceda Creek's cabernet sauvignon wines open and broaden with age, allowing for the maturation of a deep, layered complexity not equaled elsewhere in the Northwest, or indeed on the West Coast. The merlot wines are similarly tight when young, but more approachable. They, too, age with remarkable grace to deliver a pure fruitiness after a few years in the bottle, which makes it difficult to save them for the future. Immensely gratifying as they mature, Quilceda Creek's wines are the definition of greatness, and a benchmark for any Northwest Bordeaux-style winery.

SOOS CREEK WINE CELLARS

24012 172nd Avenue SE, Kent, WA
253-631-8775; www.sooscreekwine.com
Not open except for annual open house.

Year founded:	1989
Annual production:	1650 cases
Signature wine:	Ciel du Cheval Vineyard Bordeaux Blend ($$$)
Premium wine:	Champoux Vineyards Cabernet Sauvignon ($$$)
Value wine:	Sundance Red Wine ($$)
Estate vineyards:	uses purchased fruit

Soos Creek doesn't get the publicity that some larger producers garner, yet its wines exemplify fine hand-crafted winemaking, top vineyard sources, and superb overall quality. Dave Larsen uses a personal style of winemaking, employing small open-top fermenters, hand punchdowns, minimal pumping, limited use of new oak, and a confidant reliance on his own palate.

Larsen likes to blend in the Bordeaux tradition, feeling that it can produce a more balanced and complex wine. In some vintages, however, he also opts for a single-vineyard bottling when he believes the fruit merits it. He also makes an Artist Series that features cabernet franc as an important component, and the Sundance blend, representing a softer, more easily quaffable wine. The Bordeaux-style wines of Soos Creek are a testament to what can be done when a winemaker sticks to the grapes he knows and loves best.

Columbia Valley Wine Country

The Columbia Valley AVA is a large appellation that encompasses all of Washington state's wine countries except Puget Sound and the Columbia Gorge. Within its boundaries, 99 percent of the state's grapes are grown. It is a mammoth appellation that is truly too big and diverse to describe in any but the broadest terms. Its size is both its biggest strength as a wine country and its greatest weakness.

On the plus side, the generous borders of the Columbia Valley AVA were deliberately drawn to encompass as much legitimately potential vineyard land as possible. The huge drainage basin of the Columbia River and its tributaries share broad geologic and climatic conditions that are favorable to wine grape growing and present immeasurable viticultural opportunities. Within this vast geography, a multitude of potential vineyard sites await discovery for generations to come.

But the sweeping size of the Columbia Valley AVA has its drawbacks. It is not possible, for instance, to meaningfully describe the viticultural character of an area that takes up fully a third of the state's area. Putting Columbia Valley on the label of a wine bottle does not tell a consumer very much about the wine inside, except that the grapes were grown in a warm, dry, northerly climate, anywhere from Lyle in the southwest, to the confluence of the Columbia and Spokane Rivers in the northeast, or from Ellensburg in the west to the Idaho border in the east, an area of some 18,000 square mi (46,619 km2). It is no wonder, then, that the Columbia Valley is progressively being divided into discrete appellations.

Today, the largest concentration of wineries and vineyards are in the Yakima Valley, extending southeast from the town of Yakima to Richland, and in the Walla Walla Valley. In 2009, Lake Chelan received official AVA status, adding a more northerly compo-

CAVE B ESTATE WINERY

348 Silica Road NW, Quincy, WA
509-785-3500; www.caveb.com
Open all year; limited hours.

Year founded:	2001
Annual production:	5200 cases
Signature wine:	Syrah ($$$)
Premium wine:	Cuvée du Soleil ($$$)
Value wine:	Riesling ($$)
Estate vineyards:	Cave B

Cave B Winery is perched on steep slopes above the Columbia River in Washington.

With vines dramatically terraced down the steep slopes that side the Columbia River, grape growing at Cave B Estate Vineyard is literally a beautiful challenge, and one that winemaker Alfredo "Freddy" Arredondo relishes. Arredondo selects carefully grown grapes and treats them with minimal processing. The Cave B wines are best known for the force of the reds, particularly the Bordeaux-style blend Cuvée du Soleil, a ripe and spicy wine that shows leather, tobacco, and cocoa in combination with a core of sweet blackberry and plum fruit.

With careful handling, attentive winemaking, and a commitment to natural viticulture, Arredondo and his team strive to make wines that match the magnificence of their site. Located in the Columbia Cascades area, the winery and the architecturally stunning Cave B Inn at SageCliffe are surrounded by the vineyards.

FIELDING HILLS WINERY

1401 Fielding Hills Drive, East Wenatchee, WA
509-884-2221; www.fieldinghills.com
Not open.

Year founded:	2000
Annual production:	850 cases
Signature wine:	Tribute ($$$)
Premium wine:	Syrah ($$$)
Value wine:	Cabernet Franc ($$)
Estate vineyards:	RiverBend

Fielding Hills is an artisan winery making wonderful wines in miniscule quantities. Mike and Karen Wade began their wine adventure in 1998 by planting grapes at their RiverBend Vineyard on the Wahluke Slope near Mattawa, Washington, and two years later they went commercial with their first vintage. Their winery is in an orchard workshop on the property where they live, and the process is entirely hands-on for the owners. While their operation is on a small scale, their wines are impressive to taste.

Fielding Hills wines are exceptionally polished, layered with flavors, and sophisticated. The cabernet sauvignon is silky and very approachable when young, and the syrah is expansively fruity yet contained by great acidity and spicy accents. The Tribute blend is composed of cabernet sauvignon, cabernet franc, merlot, and syrah, and ably combines raspberry and boysenberry flavors with great structure and elegance. Fielding Hills is one of Washington's quintessential artisan wine crafters.

PACIFIC RIM WINEMAKERS

8111 Keene Road, West Richland, WA
800-818-7979; www.rieslingrules.com
Open by appointment only.

Year founded:	2006
Annual production:	120,000 cases
Signature wine:	Dry Riesling ($)
Premium wine:	Solstice Vineyard Riesling ($$)
Value wine:	Sweet Riesling ($)
Estate vineyards:	Wallulla, Solstice, Selenium

Pacific Rim's roots go back to famed winemaker Randall Graham and Bonny Doon Winery in California, where the Pacific Rim Dry Riesling was a best-seller. Branching off from Bonny Doon, in 2006, Pacific Rim became its own brand, complete with one of the largest riesling vineyards in Washington and a portfolio that includes many single-vineyard rieslings, a chenin blanc, a white blend and red blend, and a most delightful sparkling riesling.

A self-confessed riesling zealot, winemaker and general manager Nicholas Quillé crafts Pacific Rim wines under the belief that riesling is the most versatile, complex, and food friendly of all the vinifera grapes. For the grape to show its best, Pacific Rim is committed to sustainable farming, even sourcing riesling from Washington's first certified biodynamic vineyard. Various single-vineyard bottlings from Washington and Oregon vineyards show different dimensions of the grape, from bone dry to a delicious dessert wine. An additional appeal is that Pacific Rim wines are inexpensively priced, at no sacrifice of wine quality.

Boushey Vineyard is a valued Yakima Valley vineyard source in one of Washington's most important wine countries.

Freshly picked grape clusters await the journey to the winery.

Even as a subappellation, the Yakima Valley is too diverse a wine country to easily describe. There are so many landforms and mesoclimates that almost any generalization can be contradicted by a difference in one spot or another. Most of Yakima Valley's vineyards are planted along the south slopes of the Rattlesnake Hills in a band between 800 and 2000 ft. elevation (243.8–609.6 m). The slopes help gather additional sunlight and expose the grapes to the wind that courses through the valleys at higher elevations, helping reduce risks from disease and frost. The ground here is composed of thin layers of silty loam and windblown loess on top of basalt bedrock. There are also isolated pockets of larger glacial rock, which are sought out for their capacity to retain extra heat. The climate is consistent with the Columbia Valley rubric: warm dry summers with long, high-sunlight days and wide diurnal swings, plus cold winters and the threat of periodic damaging low temperatures.

While the range of Yakima Valley's growing degree days is broad throughout the appellation, GDD numbers show consistent warmth. Depending on the site, growing degree days can be as low as 2200 (1204), while in other places they can approach 2900 (1593). So, much of the Yakima Valley is cooler than the nearby Horse Heaven Hills and Wahluke Slope wine countries as well as Yakima Valley's own hot subappellation Red Mountain. The coolest parts of the Yakima Valley are in the mid-valley areas and the Rattlesnake Hills wine country, with mean growing degree days of 2169 (1187), a low number for most of south-central Washington. But it must be emphasized that Yakima Valley is not a cool-climate growing region. When you sometimes hear about cool-climate wines from Yakima Valley, the use of the term cool in this context is purely relative to the warmer wine countries in the state.

Still, the lower growing degree days in the Yakima Valley distinguish the area from surrounding regions. The fruit here matures more slowly and can hang on the vine longer. Often Yakima Valley vineyards will harvest up to three weeks after Red Mountain and other warmer wine countries. This longer ripening cycle gives Yakima Valley wines bright flavors and elegance, while the nearby warmer regions are characterized by greater power and concentration.

At the west and east edges of the appellation, the growing conditions are generally the warmest. Red Willow Vineyard, the highest, most westerly vineyard in the Yakima Valley, has experienced an average of 2796 (1478) GDD since 2003, and Olsen Estate Vineyards in the eastern part of the appellation experienced around 2800 (1537) GDD in 2007 and 2008. In the center of the valley, where the well-respected Boushey Vineyards resides, heat accumulation can be closer to 2700 (1482) GDD. The fruit from these different parts of the Yakima Valley is grown in essentially the same soil families, but the vineyards differ in elevations and exposures. Local variations in temperature mean the fruit character, and therefore the wine character, can be different. Fruit from the center, cooler, areas of the appellation is often harvested one to three weeks after fruit from the warmer ends.

Chardonnay and merlot are two of the most widely planted grapes in the Yakima Valley. There is no predominant chardonnay style in this wine country. The grapes ripen extremely well and retain good acidity. Merlot is also made in many styles here, and is known for displaying good fruit richness with crisply defined flavors. Riesling is also widely grown, but the vines are often cropped for high yields that are made into pleasing, if perhaps not profound, off-dry wines.

Cabernet sauvignon grapes perform well in the Yakima Valley, where they can take their time to ripen. In the less warm temperatures of the Yakima Valley, the grapes yield wines that are usually less fruit forward and intense than cabernet sauvignon grown in warmer nearby appellations, and they have extra complexity and finesse. Syrah, cabernet franc, gewürztraminer, sémillon, and sauvignon blanc are also popular grapes in the valley, but increasingly vintners are experimenting with other, less well-known grapes. Small plantings of Spanish, Italian, and Portuguese grapes are becoming productive, and in coming years the varietal complexion of the valley will be more diverse and no doubt interesting to taste.

WINERIES AND WINES TO SAMPLE

CHINOOK WINES

220 Wittkopf Loop, Prosser, WA
509-786-2725; www.chinookwines.com
Open during the season; limited hours.

Year founded:	1983
Annual production:	3500 cases
Signature wine:	Yakima Valley Cabernet Franc ($$)
Premium wine:	Cabernet Sauvignon ($$)
Value wine:	Yakima Valley White Wine ($)
Estate vineyards:	Chinook

Husband and wife team Clay Mackey and Kay Simon are among the most respected names in the Washington wine industry: Simon for her winemaking acumen and Mackey for his viticultural prowess. Chinook Wines has almost single handedly made cabernet franc a prominent variety in the state, thanks to its ability to make plushly textured versions that deliver peak cherry, raspberry, blueberry, and floral notes without overoaking. The same qualities appear in the cabernet sauvignon and merlot releases, all made from Yakima Valley fruit. Chinook's chardonnay is particularly fine, with a remarkable combination of plump flavors on a lean frame. Both the Yakima Valley White Wine and Red Wine are deft blends that provide excellent value. Chinook Wines embody the full character of Yakima Valley fruit: strong varietal character, fresh berry flavors, and ample but constrained structure.

DESERT WIND WINERY

2258 Wine Country Road, Prosser, WA
509-786-7277; www.desertwindwinery.net
Open all year; limited hours.

Year founded:	2001
Annual production:	50,000 cases
Signature wine:	Ruah ($$)
Premium wine:	Late Harvest Gewürztraminer ($$$)
Value wine:	Chardonnay Bare Naked ($)
Estate vineyards:	Desert Wind

Desert Wind has both an impressive winery, tasting room, and lodging facility, and a large 540-acre (218.5-ha) vineyard that is the source for its luscious, supple wines. Owned by the same family that owns Duck Pond Cellars in Oregon, this Washington winery produces well-crafted, texturally thick red wines and plush, full-of-fruit whites. The Ruah blend combines merlot, cabernet sauvignon, and cabernet franc into a polished though dense, blackberry-focused wine. While rich and weighty, it shows the characteristic Washington acidity. As does Desert Wind's line of Bare Naked (no wood treatment) white wines—crisply styled, clean fruitiness in a bottle.

HOGUE CELLARS

2800 Lee Road, Prosser, WA
509-786-4557; www.hoguecellars.com
Open all year; limited hours.

Year founded:	1982
Annual production:	600,000 cases
Signature wine:	Riesling ($)
Premium wine:	Reserve Cabernet Sauvignon ($$$)
Value wine:	Pinot Grigio ($)
Estate vineyards:	uses purchased fruit

Winemaker Co Dinn has the enviable job of selecting prime fruit, making gobs of top-notch wines, and then selling them at appealing prices. Hogue's beginnings go back to 1974, when Mike Hogue planted 6 acres (2.4 ha) of riesling. In 1982, brothers Gary and Mike opened Hogue Cellars, which is today owned by Constellation Brands.

Inside Chinook Wines, Washington.

Desert Wind Winery, Washington.

Hogue wines come in three tiers: affordable, fruit-forward Hogue-branded wines; Genesis by Hogue wines that focus on pure varietal flavors from premium vineyard sources; and Hogue Reserve wines, made with extra care, oak aging, and complexity. A fourth tier, the Terroir series, offers unusual grape varieties; those wines are only available the Hogue Cellars tasting room. At all levels, Hogue's wines are value priced, beautifully made, and widely available throughout the United States.

MERCER ESTATES WINERY

3100 Lee Road, Prosser, WA
509-786-2097; www.mercerwine.com
Open all year; limited hours.

Year founded:	2008
Annual production:	30,000 cases
Signature wine:	Cabernet Sauvignon ($$)
Premium wine:	Merlot ($$)
Value wine:	Sauvignon Blanc ($)
Estate vineyards:	Mercer, Dead Canyon

Mercer Estates is both brand new and time tested. Two of Washington's most respected growers, the Mercer family and Gary Hogue (no longer part of Hogue Cellars), have teamed to deliver remarkably fresh, clean wines that embody the qualities of the wine countries where the grapes are grown. Winemaker David Forsyth, formerly of Hogue Cellars, is an experienced, skillful craftsman; few know their way around the Washington wine world as well as he does.

The product plan of Mercer Estates is, like the wines, clean and straightforward. They make pure varietal wines from cabernet sauvignon, chardonnay, merlot, pinot gris, riesling, and sauvignon blanc grapes. The focus is first on the vineyard, to get quality-grown, fully ripe grapes, and then in the cellar to produce faithful expressions of varietal accuracy at a reasonable price.

SNOQUALMIE WINERY

660 Frontier Road, Prosser, WA
509-786-5558; www.snoqualmie.com
Open all year.

Year founded:	1984
Annual production:	50,000 cases
Signature wine:	Winemaker's Select Riesling ($)
Premium wine:	Reserve Syrah ($$)
Value wine:	Sauvignon Blanc ($)
Estate vineyards:	in Yakima Valley, Columbia Valley, and Horse Heaven Hills

Winemaker Joy Anderson is one of the most experienced in Washington. She regularly produces excellent wines that consistently deliver higher quality than their low prices would indicate. Snoqualmie was one of the earliest Washington wineries to focus on organics, and today farms some of the largest organic vineyards in the state.

Snoqualmie's wines start with a Columbia Valley range of wines, offering concentrated flavors that reflect the pure varietal character of the fruit. The range of Naked-label wines, meaning grown in certified organic vineyards and made in a certified organic facility, are made from 100 percent organic grapes and deliver remarkably clean, fresh flavors. The Reserve wines come from hand-harvested fruit that is individually managed throughout the winemaking process for greater depth and complexity.

THURSTON WOLFE

588 Cabernet Court, Prosser, WA
509-786-3313; www.thurstonwolfe.com
Open during the season; limited hours.

Year founded:	1987
Annual production:	6000 cases
Signature wine:	Zephyr Ridge Petit Sirah ($$)
Premium wine:	Primitivo ($$)
Value wine:	PGV ($$)
Estate vineyards:	uses purchased fruit

Wade Wolfe has long been a fixture in the Yakima Valley. Wolfe, who has a PhD in grape genetics, has spent time managing vineyards for Chateau Ste. Michelle and as general manager of Hogue Cellars. In 1987, Wade and partner Rebecca Yeaman started Thurston Wolfe to focus on small lots of grape varieties not widely planted in Washington: primitivo, for example. Thurston Wolfe was the first in Washington to plant this Italian variety of zinfandel in 1997, and one of the very few to bottle this variety. Petit sirah and lemberger are two other examples of unusual grapes turned into great wine. The wines of Thurston Wolfe are distinctive examples of the diversity of grapes that can be successfully grown in the Yakima Valley.

The tasting room at Thurston Wolfe, Washington.

Rattlesnake Hills Wine Country

The marketing materials for the wineries of the Rattlesnake Hills wine country often take pains to inform prospective visitors that there are no rattlesnakes in the vineyards here. They are higher up in the rocky parts of the Rattlesnake Hills, which is also the northern limit of the Yakima Valley. Rattlesnake Hills wine country is situated entirely within the Yakima Valley appellation, and therefore also within the Columbia Valley AVA. It is located in the north-central part of the Yakima Valley on the southern slopes of a portion of the east-west running Rattlesnake Hills, which extend beyond the boundaries of the appellation in both directions.

The southern border of the appellation runs along the Sunnyside Canal, which contributes irrigation water to the vineyards, from Gangl Road in the north to just above the town of Outlook in the south. The town of Zillah is just about in the middle of the southern border of the appellation. The appellation's boundaries begin at the 850-ft. (259-m) elevation and include the southern slopes of the Rattlesnake Hills up to the 3000-ft. (914.4-m) peak, well beyond the point of viticultural viability.

Elevation is a key element distinguishing the appellation from surrounding areas. Farther south, the valley flattens out at lower elevations, making grape growing more problematic because of frost danger. On the west and east sides of the appellation, the viticultural distinctions are less clear, which has fueled controversy over the establishment of this AVA. The soil profiles are similar to those seen elsewhere in the surrounding Yakima Valley: generally silty and loamy, with perhaps less of a sandy quality.

The topography of the Rattlesnake Hills is mixed and local climate variations make generalization risky. Weather data supplied by two Washington State University–run measurement stations, located within the appellation but not at vineyards, show growing degree day averages between 2683 (1472) and 2870 (1576). But the data gathered by Gregory V. Jones indicate a cooler overall growing season

RATTLESNAKE HILLS WINE COUNTRY AT A GLANCE

Year established: 2006
Number of wineries: 16
Total acreage: 74,400 acres (30,100 ha)
Vineyard acreage: 1500 acres (607 ha)
Predominant soil type: silty loam
Vineyard growing degree days:
    2025-2614 (1107-1434)

Most important grape varieties
cabernet sauvignon, merlot, malbec, syrah, chardonnay, riesling

where vineyards are located, with growing degree days from 2412–2614 (1322–1434), and some places lower. These lower GDD ranges have prompted some Rattlesnake Hills boosters to call their appellation cool-climate, which it is definitely not. This wine country is cool only in relation to its warm-climate environment, and claims about the Rattlesnake Hills being "cool climate" should be avoided.

In winter, the Rattlesnake Hills experience slightly warmer average temperatures than neighboring areas, perhaps because the northern ridges prevent direct polar air from hitting the southern slopes during extreme winter events. Indeed, during the killing winters of 1996 and 2004, the vineyards here seemed to survive better than those elsewhere in the Yakima Valley.

Today the approximately 16 wineries in this wine country proudly promote the Rattlesnake Hills Wine Trail with the language of superlatives: "the prettiest wine region in Washington State," and "the friendliest tasting room staffs in the world." It is certainly true that there are many interesting wines and eclectic tasting room experiences to be had in the Rattlesnake Hills.

The Rattlesnake Hills wine country runs along the southern slopes of a portion of Washington's Rattlesnake Hills, which form the northern border of the Yakima Valley.

WINERIES AND WINES TO SAMPLE

HYATT VINEYARDS

2020 Gilbert Road, Zillah, WA
509-829-6333; www.hyattvineyards.com
Open all year.

Year founded:	1983
Annual production:	25,000 cases
Signature wine:	Merlot ($)
Premium wine:	Roza Ridge Cabernet Sauvignon ($$$)
Value wine:	Nonvintage Cabernet-Merlot ($)
Estate vineyards:	Cherry Hill, Three Rocks, Roza Ridge, Hyatt

Hyatt Vineyards was founded by Leland and Lynda Hyatt in 1983 with a small vineyard. Today they farm 180 acres (72.8 ha) and are producing well-crafted, modestly priced wines from merlot, cabernet sauvignon, syrah, chardonnay, riesling, zinfandel, and, most unusually, black muscat grapes.

Winemaker Andy Gamache produces the main line of wines under the Hyatt name, as well as a second, premium tier called Roza Ridge. The latter wines are made from select lots and feature smaller production and modestly higher prices; they include a cabernet sauvignon, merlot, syrah, and viognier. Hyatt's wines are clean, straightforward examples of the region's fruit.

Hyatt Vineyards winery, Washington.

86

SILVER LAKE WINERY

Rattlesnake Hills tasting room:
1500 Vintage Road, Zillah, WA
Woodinville tasting room:
15029 Woodinville-Redmond Road, Woodinville, WA
509-829-6235; www.silverlakewinery.com
Tasting rooms open all year.

Year founded:	1987
Annual production:	61,000 cases
Signature wine:	Cask Roza Riesling ($)
Premium wine:	Grand Reserve Merlot ($$$)
Value wine:	Chenin Blanc ($)
Estate vineyards:	Roza Hills

Silver Lake Winery was founded in 1987 by a small group of University of Washington professors and friends, and it released its first wines in 1989. From a production of 2000 cases, the winery has grown to over 60,000 cases, and through an unusual arrangement is jointly owned by over 1200 individuals. The parent company, Washington Wine & Beverage Company, also owns the Glen Fiona and Hoodsport wine brands.

Winemaker William Ammons works with fruit from the Roza Hills Estate Vineyard to craft three levels of wine: a Cask Series of immediately quaffable wines, a Reserve Series of premium wines, and a Grand Reserve Series of limited-production wines. Silver Lake's wines are fruity expressions of clear varietal fruit.

Red Mountain Wine Country

Red Mountain isn't really red (it may have gotten its name from the auburn hue of the native grasses in spring), it's not much of a mountain, and its parched, wind-blown landscape isn't likely to be any wine lover's vision of vinous heaven. But in the world of Northwest wine, it would be difficult to find a hotter—literally and figuratively—source for great wine grapes than Washington's smallest AVA, Red Mountain.

Before the 1970s, no one had any thought that this desert land would someday become wine country. In 1972, two intrepid investors and budding wine aficionados, Jim Holmes and John Williams, purchased 86 acres (34.8 ha) of what was essentially scrub land on the southwest side of Red Mountain. A few years later, they planted wine grapes, and in 1980 they bottled the first commercial wines from Red Mountain wine country.

Red Mountain rises from the surrounding landscape like a beached upside-down boat hull northeast of Benton City. Along the gentle southwestern slopes above the Yakima River, at elevations between 600 and 1000 ft. (182.8–304.8 m), a green patchwork of vineyards spreads amidst an otherwise unbroken expanse of sagebrush and beige dirt. That dirt offers the first and perhaps most significant quality that defines Red Mountain's grape-growing desirability. Typical of the region, the soils here were formed by both glacial flood deposits and windblown erosion. Variable in composition and thickness—there are at least eight different types of soil in the vineyard areas of the AVA—the multiform soils of Red Mountain share the important qualities of being remarkably dry and alkaline.

Kick up the ground in many spots on Red Mountain and you'll likely find water-worn, white-encrusted rocks in the fine, sandy, silty loam. The white material is calcium carbonate, a coveted soil component shared with some of the greatest vineyards of Europe. The alkaline nature of these soils, plus their permeability to water, make it difficult for grapevines

RED MOUNTAIN WINE COUNTRY AT A GLANCE

Year established: 2001
Number of wineries: 14
Approximate total acreage:
    4040 acres (1635 ha)
Approximate vineyard acreage:
700 acres (280 ha)
Predominant soil type: silty, sandy, or stony
    loam, with pockets of calcareous rock
Vineyard growing degree days:
    2687–2803 (1475–1539)

Most important grape varieties
cabernet sauvignon, merlot

to extract the nutrients they need, causing a natural stress that helps create intense fruit.

With summer daytime temperatures averaging around 90°F (32°C) and growing degree days at some sites reportedly reaching 3000 (1649), Red Mountain wine country has enough heat and sunlight energy to ripen just about any warmth-loving grape, and in fact the area is often the first in Washington to harvest. Yet nighttime temperatures can fall to 50°F (10°C) toward the end of the growing season, an unusually wide diurnal variance.

Winter can be more challenging. Temperatures regularly fall below 20°F (−6.6°C) in December and January, and the area is subject to some of the same periodic killing freezes as much of the region. Spring and fall frosts can also pose threats, but the constant gentle to gusty wind down the slopes of Red Mountain generally preclude the need for fans or other frost mitigation techniques.

Topography mediates temperature extremes to the grapes' benefit. The Yakima River Valley runs along the western edge of the appellation, forming a sink for cooler air coming from the higher elevation north in the summer. As this air passes through the

gap between the northwest tip of Red Mountain and the southeast tip of the Rattlesnake Hills, it is channeled through the vineyards, cooling the vines and keeping them dry, thereby reducing disease and mold dangers. Likewise in winter, the warmer air coming off the Yakima River helps reduce the severity of frost threats.

Red Mountain's vineyards receive no more than 6 or 7 in. (15–17 cm) of rain annually. While this means irrigation is vital, it also means that the area sees very little cloud cover. Red Mountain accumulates some of the most intense sunlight hours anywhere in the Northwest, an enviable asset for balanced fruit ripening.

All of these factors give Red Mountain fruit a distinctive character. While some attribute the color richness in Red Mountain wines to the alkaline soil, or the fruit brightness to diurnal temperature swings, or the force of tannin and structure to the nearly constant air movement, the reality of *terroir* is that it is more easily described than explained. Whatever its causes, the fruit and wines that come from Red Mountain have a unique character, one desirable enough for Red Mountain grapes to be among the most expensive in Washington state.

Red Mountain wine country is most famous for its red grapes. Most of the major red grape varieties are easily grown in this AVA. The wines made from these grapes display great concentration of berry aromas and flavors, deep coloration and extraction, and a minerality that runs through the tasting experience from entry to finish. Red Mountain wines are usually highly structured, with plenty of taut tannins and crisp acidity—qualities that make for wines that are tightly wound and assertive when young but with profound, layered complexity when properly and patiently aged.

The Bordeaux varieties are prized here, with cabernet sauvignon and merlot being the two most widely planted, though cabernet franc, malbec, and petit verdot are present as well. Red Rhône grapes are becoming increasingly important, with significant

Col Solare winery sits at the base of Red Mountain, Washington, with vineyards gently sloping to the southwest.

Cabernet sauvignon grapes relish the warmth of Red Mountain wine country, Washington.

plantings of syrah and small amounts of high-quality mourvèdre and counoise. Italian varieties, including sangiovese and nebbiolo also have a toehold in the AVA. Chardonnay, sauvignon blanc, and sémillon are the white grapes most widely grown, but riesling, chenin blanc, roussanne, viognier, gewürztraminer, and even pinot gris are also present. Like the reds, Red Mountain white wines show distinct power, with lots of succulent, ripe, almost tropical fruit flavors.

Red Mountain wine country is more important as a source of grapes for some of Washington's best wines than it is as a destination for wine touring, though Hedges Family Estate, Fidélitas, Kiona, and Terra Blanca wineries have notable tasting rooms. Some of the most famous names in Red Mountain are vineyards not wineries. While you can view some vines from the road, vineyards like Ciel du Cheval and Klipsun have no facilities for visitors. And though many wineries proudly proclaim Red Mountain as the source of fruit for some of their wines, that does not mean they have tasting rooms actually in the Red Mountain wine country.

WINERIES AND WINES TO SAMPLE

CADENCE

9320 15th Avenue South, Unit CF, Seattle, WA
206-381-9507; www.cadencewinery.com
Open by appointment only.

Year founded:	1998
Annual production:	2500 cases
Signature wine:	Bel Canto ($$$$)
Premium wine:	Bel Canto ($$$$)
Value wine:	Coda ($$$)
Estate vineyards:	Cara Mia

Owners Gaye McNutt and Benjamin Smith have built for their Seattle-based winery an enviable reputation as one of Washington's most respected artisan producers. Particularly adept at making finely tuned blends (the winery's name is a reference to the qualities of harmony, balance, and precision), they are also skilled in sourcing from quality vineyards, with a firm emphasis on fruit from their estate vineyard on Red Mountain.

Cadence wines are primarily Bordeaux-style blends that display powerful, lively, clear fruit flavors, with expansive aromas, strong structure and satisfying balance. In 2006, the winery released its first wines from its 10.5-acre (4.2-ha) Cara Mia Estate Vineyard on Red Mountain, including the Bel Canto cabernet franc–driven blend, and Camerata, which is cabernet sauvignon–driven, with a small amount of cabernet franc. It also secures fruit from Ciel du Cheval, Klipsun, and Tapteil Vineyards.

COL SOLARE WINERY

50207 Antinori Road, Benton City, WA
509-588-6806; www.colsolare.com
Open by appointment only.

Year founded:	1992
Annual production:	8000 cases
Signature wine:	Col Solare ($$$$)
Premium wine:	Col Solare ($$$$)
Value wine:	Shining Hill ($$$)
Estate vineyards:	Col Solare

Since its first vintage in 1995, Col Solare (Italian for shining hill) has become one of the preeminent wine brands of the Northwest. The winery historically made only one wine, Col Solare, but has recently added a second label, Shining Hill. A collaboration between Washington's Chateau Ste. Michelle and Italy's Marchese Piero Antinori wineries, the cabernet sauvignon–driven Col Solare blend consistently achieves some of the highest critical ratings of any Northwest wine. In 2007, the Tuscan-inspired, contemporary estate winery opened. Resident winemaker Marcus Notaro works with Renzo Cotarella, head enologist for Marchesi Antinori, to make wines from the state-of-the-viticultural-art 30-acre (12.1-ha) estate vineyard.

The Col Solare blend is known for both power and concentration. Aromas are rich and complex, tannins are surprisingly soft and supple for Red Mountain fruit, and the finish lingers long. While Col Solare wines have the trademark bright and fresh Washington fruit character, they also possesses Old-Worldlike structure and power: Col Solare can be drunk pleasurably when young, but should also age gracefully for decades. The Shining Hill label uses premium fruit from prime vineyards that didn't make it into the Col Solare blend each vintage, producing a wine that requires less time in barrel and bottle to show its character.

FIDÉLITAS

51810 N. Sunset Road, Benton City, WA
509-588-3469; www.fidelitaswines.com
Open all year; limited hours.

Year founded:	2000
Annual production:	3500 cases
Signature wine:	Optu Red Wine ($$$)
Premium wine:	Champour Vineyard Cabernet Sauvignon ($$$)
Value wine:	Sémillon Columbia Valley ($$)
Estate vineyards:	uses purchased fruit

Owner-winemaker Charlie Hoppes is a respected figure in Washington's wine world, having gained a thorough knowledge of the region's varying vineyards while spending many years making wine for Ste. Michelle Wine Estates. At Fidélitas, he crafts wines for himself and his loyal following of friends and customers.

Hoppes's Red Mountain winery gives him an impressive base for working with fruit from the best vineyards in the state across many appellations. Fruit is treated with careful attention to bring out its best qualities in the finished wine. The Optu blend is a personal statement about balance, complexity, and craft, employing Bordeaux varieties from key vineyards. The Boushey Red is blended from grapes grown at Boushey Vineyards and is a concentrated, vibrant wine. If anything, the Champour Vineyard Cabernet Sauvignon is even more dense and luscious, with supple tannins and deep complexity. Also popular are the fresh, mouth-coating Sémillon Columbia Valley and the white Optu blend. Fidélitas exemplifies the personal, craft-oriented side of Washington's wine industry at its best.

HEDGES FAMILY ESTATE

53511 N Sunset Road, Benton City, WA
509-588-3155; www.hedgesfamilyestate.com
Open during the season; limited hours

Year founded:	1987
Annual production:	90,000 cases
Signature wine:	Hedges Three Vineyards ($$)
Premium wine:	Single Vineyard Limited Wines ($$$)
Value wine:	CMS by Hedges White ($)
Estate vineyards:	Hedges, Bel'Villa, Les Gosses, Magdalena

Tom Hedges was an early visionary of Red Mountain, and it was largely through the work of Hedges Family Estate that Red Mountain became an AVA. The chateau winery and tasting room is an appropriate crown to his efforts. A shrewd businessman who combines a personal passion for wine with practical commercial savvy, Hedges has built his winery into Washington's largest family-owned winery, known for delivering top-quality wines at reasonable prices.

The 37-acre (14.9-ha) Hedges Estate Vineyard was planted in 1991 with cabernet sauvignon, merlot, and cabernet franc. In 1997, a second, 40-acre (16.1-ha) estate vineyard, Bel'Villa, was planted, the highest elevation vineyard in Red Mountain wine country. The Hedges Three Vineyards, Two Vineyards, and Single Vineyard labels come from estate fruit. The winery also makes a value-focused tier of blended wines using purchased Columbia Valley fruit, which they have branded CMS by Hedges. When red, CMS stands for a marriage of cabernet, merlot, and syrah; when white, it's chardonnay marsanne and sauvignon blanc. At all levels, the wines are superb, as is the chateau tasting experience at Red Mountain.

The Hedges Family Estate Chateau is surrounded by vineyards.

HIGHTOWER CELLARS

19418 E 583 PR NE, Benton City, WA
509-588-2867; www.hightowercellars.com
Open during the season; limited hours.

Year founded:	1997
Annual production:	2500 cases
Signature wine:	Cabernet Sauvignon ($$$)
Premium wine:	Red Mountain Red Wine ($$$$)
Value wine:	Murray Cuvée ($$)
Estate vineyards:	Out of Line

Kelly and Tim Hightower form the spousal winemaking team at this craft-oriented boutique winery. Since its first vintage in 1997, the winery has purchased fruit from Red Mountain. So when the opportunity arose to purchase 15 acres (6 ha) of Red Mountain land complete with water rights, the Hightowers jumped at it. In 2004, they planted 10 acres (4 ha) of cabernet sauvignon, merlot, cabernet franc, petit verdot, and malbec. While still sourcing grapes from Horse Heaven Hills and Walla Walla Valley, the estate vineyard gives the winery extra *terroir* diversity.

Hightower's Red Mountain Red Wine is a classic example of the power of Red Mountain fruit, with rich, almost jammy dark flavors. The cabernet releases are focused and mouth-filling, with flavors of cassis and plums complemented by a veil of dusty earth.

KIONA VINEYARDS AND WINERY

44612 North Sunset Road, Benton City, WA
509-588-6716; www.kionawine.com
Open all year.

Year founded:	1975
Annual production:	35,000 cases
Signature wine:	Estate Cabernet Sauvignon ($$$)
Premium wine:	Chenin Blanc Ice Wine ($$$ 375 ml)
Value wine:	Riesling ($)
Estate vineyards:	Kiona, Ranch at the End of the Road, Heart of the Hill, Nine Canyon, Terril

John Williams and then-partner Jim Holmes purchased the first Red Mountain land to be used as a vineyard in 1975 for about $400 an acre (the partnership was dissolved many years ago). Kiona Vineyards is now also run by son Scott Williams, who with his father farms 300 acres (121.4 ha) of vineyards, including the original 12 acres (4.8 ha). Known best for its cabernet sauvignon, Kiona was the first winery in America to make lemberger, which remains a highly popular wine for them.

With the oldest vines in this wine country, Kiona makes big, burly red wines that are true to the *terroir*. Its wide wine selection also includes merlot, syrah, sangiovese, and zinfandel, plus (unusual for the appellation) a dry riesling, chardonnay, and even a chenin blanc ice wine—all from estate vines.

TERRA BLANCA WINERY

34715 N DeMoss Road, Benton City, WA
509-588-6082, www.terrablanca.com
Open all year.

Year founded:	1997
Annual production:	30,000 cases
Signature wine:	Onyx Red Mountain ($$$)
Premium wine:	Reserve Riesling Ice Wine ($$$ 375 ml)
Value wine:	Viognier ($)
Estate vineyards:	Terra Blanca

Owner-winemaker Keith Pilgrim grew up in Napa Valley and studied enology, geology, and viticulture at the University of California, Davis. He purchased 300 acres (121.4 ha) on treeless Red Mountain in 1997, and began planting grapes for his aptly named Terra Blanca (white earth) winery.

An impressive winery, tasting room, and visitor facility now crown the estate. Terra Blanca's signature wine is a classic Bordeaux-style blend using estate-grown cabernet sauvignon, cabernet franc, merlot, malbec, and petit verdot.

Snipes Mountain Wine Country

One of Washington's newest appellations encompasses some of its oldest vineyards. On Snipes Mountain in eastern Washington, in 1917 William B. Bridgman planted one of the earliest vinifera vineyards in the Northwest with varieties including sauvignon blanc, sémillon, muscat, and zinfandel. A few of these original vines are still producing grapes today, used by the modern incarnation of the Upland Winery in a special, limited production wine.

In 1963, a group of amateur Washington winemakers, who had just formed Associated Vintners, purchased land from Bridgman on Harrison Hill just to the east of Snipes Mountain. Here Bridgman had planted his first table grape vineyard in 1914, and 46 years later Associated Vintners put into the same ground some of the earliest modern plantings of gewürztraminer, grenache, chardonnay, sémillon, and cabernet sauvignon. Some of these vines are still producing grapes and are made into wine. It is an interesting historical curiosity that vines planted in the early years of the twentieth century are still producing grapes, and some of the earliest modern plantings of vinifera remain productive as well.

Snipes Mountain itself is an uplifted section of earth just north of the Yakima River, west of the town of Sunnyside and south of the hamlet of Outlook. Measured from the valley floor elevation that ranges between 680 ft. and 780 ft. (207.2–237.7 m), Snipes Mountain peaks at just above 1300 ft. (396.2 m) elevation. The south-to-southwest edge of the rise—to call it a mountain gives it more substance than it may merit—can be very steep, and exposes glacial gravel-strewn ground that includes ancient sediments, basalts, and riverbed deposits. The northern slopes of Snipes Mountain are gentler and covered more evenly with loess.

For winegrowing, the two distinguishing features of this area are the steep slope on the southern exposure, which is warmer than the northern slope, and the very rocky ground, which is uncommon in the Yakima Valley.

SNIPES MOUNTAIN WINE COUNTRY AT A GLANCE

Year established: 2009
Number of wineries: 1
Total acreage: 4145 acres (1677 ha)
Vineyard acreage: 665 acres (269 ha)
Predominant soil types: rocky, coarse
    sediment, and loess
Vineyard growing degree days:
    2850–3950 (1565–2176)

Most important grape varieties
cabernet sauvignon, gewürztraminer, merlot

WINERIES AND WINES TO SAMPLE

UPLAND ESTATES

6141 Gap Road, Outlook, WA
509-839-2606; www.uplandwinery.com
Open by appointment only.

Year founded:	2006
Annual production:	650 cases
Signature wine:	Old Vine Cabernet ($$)
Premium wine:	Muscat Ice ($$$)
Value wine:	Gewürztraminer ($)
Estate vineyards:	Upland

The Newhouse family purchased what used to be William Bridgman's Upland Vineyards in 1972. A part of a larger farming operation, the vineyard lands were expanded to about 700 acres (283.2 ha) and the fruit was sold to various wineries. In 2006, Todd and Amber Newhouse crushed the first grapes for their new Upland Estates, resurrecting a venerable name in Washington wine history. In 2007, they released a well-received gewürztraminer, followed in 2009 by a cabernet sauvignon, malbec, sauvignon blanc, another gewürztraminer, and a muscat.

The Old Vine Cabernet comes from vines planted in 1973, and the Vintage Muscat Ice, remarkably, was made from the original vines planted by Bridgman in 1917. Only 90 cases of the muscat ice wine were made in 2009, and represent an unusual opportunity to taste a piece of Washington's history.

Walla Walla Valley Wine Country

Stand at the windy edge of Spring Valley Vineyard's estate vine rows 12 mi (19.3 km) northeast of the town of Walla Walla, and you will see a view unlike that obtainable in any other wine country in the world. To the north, a seemingly infinite ocean of lonely, wheat-swathed swells undulate out to the horizon, nary another vineyard in sight. Except for the virid vines next to you, the only colors you see are the pale blue of the sky and flaxen-hued hummocks that comprise the wheat fields of eastern Washington's Palouse region. Move down into the lower lands, especially south of town, and the scene changes, becoming more familiar. Here carpets of vine rows settle evenly across gently rolling inclines and smooth bottomland, a more expected wine terrain. Here, each year more vines are planted.

Part of Walla Walla Valley's wine allure comes from the dramatic beauty of its varying topography. Part also comes from the complexity of its soils and the compatibility of its climate to grape growing. And undeniably, part of Walla Walla's appeal is the almost cultish celebrity that has attached to certain small-production local wine brands.

There has been an explosion of new Walla Walla Valley wineries in recent years. It almost seems as if wineries are being started here not because of the availability of great fruit—a significant amount of the wine produced by Walla Walla wineries still comes from fruit grown outside of the appellation—but because of a desire to cash in on the cachet of simply being based in the Walla Walla Valley.

With an eastern border along the western foothills of the Blue Mountains, fertile wheat land of the Palouse to its north, and just east of the confluence of the Columbia and Walla Walla Rivers, Walla Walla Valley wine country encompasses a trapezoid-like area that ranges from fertile river bottomland to wind-buffeted bluffs nearly 2000 ft. (609.6 m) high. Approximately two-thirds of the appellation is in Washington, but an important third extends south over the border into Oregon.

The modern history of Walla Walla Valley winegrowing began in 1974, when now legendary Northwest winemaker Gary Figgins planted a single acre of cabernet sauvignon and "a bit" of riesling. In 1977, Figgins bonded the region's first contemporary winery, Leonetti Cellar, and in 1978 he released the first modern vintage of Walla Walla Valley wine. He was then the lone winegrower in a land of wheat, onion, and fruit growers.

Early wine growth in the region was slow. Two years after Figgins planted his first vines, friend and neighbor Rick Small planted Walla Walla's second

> ## WALLA WALLA VALLEY WINE COUNTRY AT A GLANCE
>
> Year established: 1984
> Number of wineries: 100*
> Total acreage: 322,800 acres (130,632 ha)*
> Approximate vineyard acreage:
>   1600 acres* (648 ha)
> Predominant soil types: loess (consisting of windblown silts, sands, and loam), cobblestone, and some volcanic ash.
> Vineyard growing degree days:
>   2653–2911 (1456–1599)†
>
> **Most important grape varieties**
> merlot, cabernet sauvignon, syrah
>
> *Figures apply to the entire appellation including Oregon.
> † Figures apply only to Washington portion of the appellation.

From Spring Valley Vineyard in the northern portion of Washington's Walla Walla Valley wine country, you can take in expansive views.

Gary Figgins and son Chris in the barrel room at Leonetti Cellar, the first winery in Washington's Walla Walla Valley wine country.

(*opposite*) The southern part of Washington's Walla Walla Valley wine country is a patchwork of vineyards.

vinifera vineyard on family land previously used for wheat farming. In 1981, Small and his wife Darcey Fugman-Small bonded the area's second winery, Woodward Canyon. Two years after that, Walla Walla's third winery, L'Ecole No. 41, was founded by Baker and Jean Ferguson. And in 1984, Waterbrook Winery became the region's fourth winery.

From the start, the early Walla Walla Valley wines garnered rave reviews from national wine critics. While Leonetti Cellar achieved an elite status, with customers sometimes waiting years to get on its list to buy, the others became known for making superb-quality and somewhat more easily obtainable wines. With these wineries' recognition came growing respect for the Walla Walla Valley as a place to grow grapes, not just make wine, and new vineyard developments began adding important resources to the region.

By 1984, Walla Walla's esteem and potential were acknowledged through the approval of an AVA application. Even so, growth did not take off. By 1990, the wine country still had only 6 wineries on approximately 100 acres (40.4 ha) of vineyards. It really wasn't until the turn of the twenty-first century that the pace of wine development accelerated. Today, things in Walla Walla are dramatically different. In 2008, Figgins and his now-acclaimed winery celebrated their thirtieth vintage. Today, over 100 wineries now call Walla Walla Valley home, and the wine country is among the fastest growing, most attention getting anywhere in North America.

The town of Walla Walla offers quaint tasting rooms and plenty of wine country charm.

(*opposite*) The distinctive cobblestone soils of Walla Walla Valley wine country are highly desirable.

Walla Walla Valley's success is partly because it is perhaps the most amenable wine country to visit in eastern Washington. Walla Walla hospitably attracts and accommodates volumes of visitors with a choice of fine restaurants and cozy lodging options, natural complements to wine touring. These amenities, in turn, have helped encourage and support new winery development.

From a purely winegrowing perspective, the Walla Walla Valley offers the same foundational set of favorable growing conditions found elsewhere in the Columbia Valley: low rainfall, high growing heat, long growing season, and cold winters. But specific vineyard sites can vary significantly in any number of features, and as the area matures certain subregions are becoming defined.

The western portions of Walla Walla Valley are warmer, more arid, and lower lying than the eastern side. During the growing season, daytime temperature averages rise from the high 40s°F (7°C–9°C) during March, as the vines come out of dormancy, to the upper 80s°F (26°C–31°C) in July and August when the vines are in full flush. Though the area is consistently warm, it is generally not too hot. Maxi-

mum daytime summer temperatures occasionally reach into the high 90s°F (35°C–37°C). This consistent heat is potent for grape growing: while growing degree days average around 2800 (1537), some vineyards have reported in excess of 3000 (1648) GDD. The frost-free growing season is long, ranging from 190 to 220 days depending on the site.

Summers are also dry; soils get parched, so irrigation is a prerequisite almost everywhere. Precipitation for July, August, and September averages less than 2 in. (5 cm). Average annual rainfall at lower elevation vineyards is around 13 in. (33 cm), mostly in winter, but some high sites in the eastern part of the appellation can receive up to 20 in. (50 cm), mostly in winter. At least one vineyard here is dry-farmed, a most unusual approach in eastern Washington.

Spring Valley Vineyards showcase the beauty of Walla Walla Valley's higher elevation northern terrain.

(*opposite*) Pepper Bridge Vineyard portrays the lower elevation, gently rolling terrain of the southern part of Walla Walla Valley in Washington.

100

Walla Walla winters can be cold, and pose the most significant grape growing risk in the region. Average daytime temperatures drop quickly into the low 40s°F (4°C–7°C) in the fall, and stay in the 30s°F (−1°C to 3°C) for most of the winter. Average winter lows reach into the 20s°F (−6 to −4°C). For low-lying vineyards and those with poor air drainage, growers usually employ wind machines or other frost-mitigation techniques to prevent damage, and some go to the expensive effort of burying dormant canes for the winter as protection against killer freezes. Periodically, the Walla Walla Valley is hit by arctic blasts from the north delivering sustained temperatures well below 0°F (−17.7°C). Such extreme cold can kill some vines almost no matter what the grower does. Own-rooted vineyards (vines that are not grafted onto a rootstock) and older vines are better able to survive these exceptional conditions, but once or twice a decade, acute conditions can imperil a vintage.

In addition to the variability of climate, the unique geologic history of the Walla Walla Valley has resulted in a virtual laboratory for vintners to explore the concept of *terroir*. Today only a little of the basalt bedrock is exposed, mostly in the southern portion of the appellation. These outcroppings have been decaying for eons, adding eroded basalt to the composition of local soils. In some places, ambitious vineyardists are ripping through this decomposed basalt, some of which sits under thin layers of silt, and planting vines in the resulting basalt-infused ground. It is still too early to tell what kind of wines this distinctive soil will produce, but another kind of similarly rocky Walla Walla soil offers some hints.

Along the floodplain of the Walla Walla Valley in the southern part of the appellation is another group of exceptionally stony soils where the ground appears to be little more than water-worn cobblestones. Poor in nutrients and nearly unable to hold water, this rock-rich ground has gained considerable prestige as the source of distinctive wines, especially those of the Rhône persuasion. When vigneron Christophe Baron, of Cayuse Vineyards, saw this unusual land, he noticed a resemblance to the Châteauneuf-du-Pape region of France. And indeed, the area has become known for producing unusually mineral- and herb-laden, meaty syrah wines reminiscent of the Old World region. Because of the extremely sparse nature of the soils, grapes struggle mightily and deliver a naturally small yet highly concentrated crop. Also, the rocks are very good at retaining heat, which helps the plants ripen their fruit. Though the cobblestone ground is different from the basalt-based vineyards in the appellation, the two soils share a stone-heavy composition, very low organic matter, and excessively dry dirt. The *terroir* character of the cobblestone-grown fruit is becoming better known all the time, and we await what the basalt soils will yield.

Most of the other Walla Walla Valley vineyards are on silty loam and loess soils that range in depth from just a few feet to as much as 70 ft. (21.3 m). They are fast draining, tend to have a neutral pH, and often have low amounts of organic matter. The soil texture is fine grained, and high amounts of mixed quartz, mica, and other minerals from regional volcanic activity often interlace the loess. The mineral content in particular seems to result in wines that have an almost edgy quality of sharp fruitiness, perhaps an emerging characteristic of *terroir*.

Because the Walla Walla Valley wine country is still so young, it may be too early to be talking *terroir* here. A European winegrower would likely laugh at the idea that a wine country less than 40 years old could possess reliably distinguishable regional *terroirs*. Yet the Walla Walla Valley's rapid development is revealing noticeable differences in wine character, partly depending on soil variances. Red wines grown in the warmer, deep loess of flatter, lower elevation sites display rich, darker flavored fruit. Wines grown on higher elevation slopes often have more red fruit characteristics, while cobblestone-sited vineyards result in meaty, somewhat more herbaceous wine qualities. More time in the ground will reveal whether these characteristics prove to be regional *terroirs* of Walla Walla Valley wine country.

Ironically, Walla Walla's early fame with merlot and cabernet sauvignon had more to do with wine-making skill than the character of Walla Walla fruit. Much of the grapes that went into the early vintages actually were grown outside of the appellation. Still largely true today, the appellation's wineries use purchased fruit because until recently there was only a relatively small amount of local fruit available, and because wineries have diversified their fruit sources outside of Walla Walla Valley as insurance against local fruit loss from periodic killer freezes. But extensive vineyard development means that there is more Walla Walla Valley–grown fruit becoming available, and so more will be known in coming years about locally grown flavors of each grape variety.

Merlot grown in Walla Walla Valley displays dark saturated color and powerful fruit concentration, with overtones of black cherry and plum flavors. Frequently there are tones of tobacco, leather, and spice, adding complexity and interest. Cabernet sauvignon typically expresses classic cassis aromas and flavors, ringed with notes of cedar, pine, and floral aspects, also often displaying notes of cocoa. When grown at sites with a longer season, the fruit has an excellent combination of power and elegance, with fine-grained tannins and a broad, lush palate.

Syrah is certainly the grape of the moment in Walla Walla Valley. Unlike the Bordeaux varietals, syrah is almost always made as a 100-percent varietal wine. Widely considered to grow well in almost all the subregions of Walla Walla, syrah has the potential to become the appellation's signature wine. Walla Walla's syrah wines show good minerality wherever they are grown, and they are usually supple, sometimes fat-feeling, with bright plum and blackberry flavors. At higher elevations, additional acidity and elegance can be detected, with a slightly more spicy aspect, while down in the cobblestones, syrah takes on a meaty aspect.

There are many other red grapes grown in Walla Walla Valley, though only a few others are made into any significant quantity of wine. These red wines in-

clude a small amount of sangiovese, some barbera, dolcetto, cabernet franc, malbec, petit verdot, nebbiolo, grenache, and other varieties. Though chardonnay, riesling, and even some pinot gris are grown in Walla Walla Valley, little of it has shown profound character. Except for the sémillon, which often has a rich buttery quality that has gleaned a cultish reputation among wine drinkers seeking a more exotic white wine. Viognier also shows potential.

Part of the excitement of the Walla Walla Valley wine country's future is in the exploration of growing new grapes in the region's varied soils that might produce distinctive wines. After all, in the 1980s, when Walla Walla was building it's reputation for Bordeaux varieties, no one really expected that 20 years later a Rhône grape would help make Walla Walla famous.

Grapes fresh from the vineyard are poured into fermentation tanks at L'Ecole No. 41 Winery, Washington.

WINERIES AND WINES TO SAMPLE

ABEJA

2014 Mill Creek Road, Walla Walla, WA
509-526-7400; www.abeja.net
Open only to wine club members and inn guests.

Year founded:	2000
Annual production:	4000 cases
Signature wine:	Cabernet Sauvignon ($$$)
Premium wine:	Cabernet Sauvignon Reserve ($$$$)
Value wine:	House Red ($$)
Estate vineyards:	Heather Hill, Mill Creek

Abeja has developed a loyal following for its rich cabernet sauvignon wines, though it also produces well-made merlot, syrah, chardonnay, and viognier. Located on a century-old, beautiful farmstead in the foothills of the Blue Mountains, the winery and luxury inn provide an idyllic setting for making great wine.

Abeja's winemaking approach is to combine modern technology with classic techniques and a focus on quality. Believing that cabernet sauvignon may become the signature variety for Washington state, Abeja's winemaker, John Abbot, sources premium grapes from around the Columbia Valley and applies his previous experience working in Napa Valley and eastern Washington to crafting the best wines possible. The finely tuned Walla Walla Valley syrah and viognier bottlings are popular as well. Combine the wines, the winery, and the charming inn accommodations, and Abeja offers the perfect place for wine.

CAYUSE VINEYARDS

17 E. Main Street, Walla Walla, WA
509-526-0686; www.cayusevineyards.com
Not open.

Year founded:	1997
Annual production:	3500 cases
Signature wine:	Cailloux Vineyard Syrah ($$$$)
Premium wine:	Bionic Frog Syrah ($$$$$)
Value wine:	All other wines ($$$$)
Estate vineyards:	Cailloux, En Chamberlin, En Cerise, Coccinelle, Armada

Christophe Baron is an uncompromising fellow who makes uncompromising wines that are incredibly good and disconcertingly difficult to come by. Like a handful of other cult Northwest producers, he maintains a tightly controlled list of those he sells his wines to.

Baron is a persuasive advocate of biodynamic farming methods, and tasting his wines may well convert the skeptic of this unconventional approach to farming. Famous for his spicy syrah wines with complicated notes of game and dried herbs, Baron has virtually defined the lean and savory style of Walla Walla Valley syrah. He has also planted Rhône and Spanish varieties, such as granache, tempranillo, and mourvèdre. Baron famously found the cobblestone-filled fields in the Oregon portion of this AVA that so reminded him of Châteauneuf-du-Pape, and now others are scrambling to emulate his approach by planting in the rocks. His wines are distinctive, with characters very different from the more luxurious house style of plump Walla Walla Valley wines. If you can beg, borrow, or buy a bottle, don't hesitate!

GRAMERCY CELLARS

1825 J B George Road, Walla Walla, WA
206-553-9177; www.gramercycellars.com
Open by appointment only.

Year founded:	2005
Annual production:	2000 cases
Signature wine:	Walla Walla Valley Syrah ($$$)
Premium wine:	John Lewis Reserve Syrah ($$$$)
Value wine:	Inigo Montoya Tempranillo ($$$)
Estate vineyards:	JB George, Octave

Greg Harrington is a kind of wine prodigy. Not only was he the youngest American to pass the Master Sommelier Exam at the age of 26 (not to mention having worked with chefs such as Emeril Lagasse and Wolfgang Puck), he has also been an unqualified rave success with his first winery venture, Gramercy Cellars.

Gramercy Cellars is a highly respected, in-demand boutique winery crafting incredibly layered, succulent, sophisticated syrah wines. These wines have an enviable combination of power and definition, resulting in part from a philosophy of minimal intervention. Harrington is developing two estate vineyards in the Walla Walla Valley wine country, which are planted to syrah, tempranillo, and Bordeaux varieties. This winery is a small producer with a big future.

K VINTNERS/CHARLES SMITH WINES: THE MODERNIST PROJECT

820 Mill Creek Road, Walla Walla, WA
509-526-5230; www.kvintners.com
Open by appointment only.

Year founded:	2001
Annual production:	5000 cases
Signature wine:	K Syrah
Premium wine:	Royal City Syrah ($$$$+)
Value wine:	Viognier ($$)
Estate vineyards:	Phil Lane

Charles Smith has a bigger than life personality and makes bigger than life wines, especially syrah. His K Syrah line of wines features (besides his penchant for puns) different vineyard sources reflecting different stylistic expressions. His latest incarnation, called Charles Smith Wines: The Modernist Project, includes highly touted wines of great intensity and popularity designed to be consumed immediately.

Smith's wines are bold, rambunctious bottles with eccentric names that are highly memorable, displaying his marketing acumen as much as his winemaking skills. Some of his syrahs come from the vineyards of Christophe Baron of Cayuse (El Jefe, for example), while others are sourced from premium spots known for syrah. He also makes a few blends: The Boy is 88 percent grenache and The Creator has 60 percent cabernet sauvignon. Whatever the composition or moniker, the wines are 100 percent delicious.

L'ECOLE NO. 41

41 Lowden School Road, Lowden, WA
509-525-0940; www.lecole.com
Open all year.

Year founded:	1983
Annual production:	35,000 cases
Signature wine:	Estate Perigee ($$$)
Premium wine:	Pepper Bridge Vineyard Apogee ($$$)
Value wine:	Columbia Valley Sémillon ($$)
Estate vineyards:	Seven Hills

L'Ecole No. 41, named after the 1915 schoolhouse that is the winery's headquarters and tasting room, is a signature Walla Walla Valley winery, the third to be established in the appellation. Now owned by Martin and Megan Clubb, L'Ecole is known for crafting extremely well-made wines full of clear fruit character and poise. Its Seven Hills Estate Vineyard is also a key source of fruit for other top area wineries, but Marty does the best job of making wine from his own grapes.

The Apogee (made from Pepper Bridge Vineyard) and Perigee (Seven Hills Vineyard) Bordeaux-style red blends are excellent examples of Walla Walla Valley fruit. The flavors are rich and round, with a stout sense of structure that is mouthwatering. Perhaps most famous for merlot, L'Ecole makes different versions—Columbia Valley, Seven Hills Vineyard, and Walla Walla Valley—each one showing distinct character. Sémillon is another specialty, made here probably better than anywhere else in the Northwest.

L'Ecole No. 41's tasting room in Lowden, Washington.

LEONETTI CELLAR

1875 Foothills Lane, Walla Walla, WA
509-525-1428; www.leonetticellar.com
Not open.

Year founded:	1978
Annual production:	6000–7000 cases
Signature wine:	Cabernet Sauvignon ($$$$)
Premium wine:	Reserve ($$$$+)
Value wine:	Sangiovese ($$$$)
Estate vineyards:	Loess, Mill Creek Upland, Seven Hills

Leonetti Cellar kicked it all off in Walla Walla. Gary Figgins was the first to make wine in the appellation, and he has gone farther in vinous sophistication than anyone else in the region. His brand is the ultimate in prestige. It is rare to find Leonetti wines: they are essentially allocated to private list customers. But do look for them on wine lists at the best restaurants. The Reserve, in particular, is highly prized. A small-production, traditional Bordeaux-style blend composed of estate-grown grapes, it is built for aging, with a succulent, intense, and beautiful style.

Leonetti wines are made with uncompromising care and commitment. Using fruit from estate vineyards that are lovingly tended and specially sourced grapes from other prestige vineyards, the wines represent the essence of each variety—cabernet sauvignon, merlot, and sangiovese—plus the personality of each vineyard. Gary's son Chris now joins in managing the winemaking and viticulture, taking this foundational Washington winery solidly into the next generation.

LONG SHADOWS VINTNERS

1604 Frenchtown Road, Walla Walla, WA
509-526-0905; www.longshadows.com
Open by appointment only.

Year founded:	2002
Annual production:	12,000--15,000 cases
Signature wine:	Chester-Kidder ($$$)
Premium wine:	Pedestal ($$$$)
Value wine:	Poet's Leap ($$)
Estate vineyards:	27 Benches

Allen Shoup is the legendary genius behind the unique confederation of individual wineries known as Long Shadows Vintners. As CEO of Stimson Lane (the corporate entity today known as Ste. Michelle Wine Estates) for 20 years, Shoup was instrumental in helping raise the quality of Washington winemaking and in putting the state on the map of the world's most respected wine regions. When he retired from Ste. Michelle, Shoup drew upon his connections to entice an international band of high-profile winemakers to each make a single wine from Washington fruit as part of his Long Shadows venture. The intent was not only to create the best possible wines, but also to showcase the power of Washington's vineyards.

Under the Long Shadows umbrella, California's Randy Dunn makes Feather, a pure Washington cabernet sauvignon, French winemaking icon Michel Rolland produces the Bordeaux-style red blend called Pedestal, and acclaimed German winemaker Armin Diel crafts the Poet's Leap riesling. Also, Agustin Huneeus, Sr., and Philippe Melka bring their Napa Valley experience to the making of the Pirouette red blend, Australian John Duval makes a syrah called Sequel, and the Tuscan father-son team of Ambrogio and Giovanni Folonari make the Saggi blended red wine. Gilles Nicault is the resident winemaker for Long Shadows, and produces the Chester-Kidder red blend. All Long Shadows wines are made from Washington fruit, including some biodynamically grown, and all are of extremely high quality. There is perhaps no other winemaking venture anywhere that

Woodward Canyon wines are crafted to go with food, rather than to be consumed as a cocktail. Consequently, they are fresh and vibrant in style, with sustaining acidity and noticeable structure containing the ripe fruit. Their Old Vines Cabernet Sauvignon typifies the power and poise of their wines. Using fruit from vines planted in the 1970s, this wine has tremendous depth and intricacy of flavors, wrapped in a haze of campfire smoke and earth tones. The rare Charbonneau red blend is not made every year, but always packs plenty of power and concentration thanks to the quality of fruit from the eponymous vineyard source. The Estate Red Wine uses the low yields that naturally result from the spare conditions at the certified organic vineyard to produce concentrated flavors, yet has a generous, supple texture. A second label, Nelms Road, offers more affordable, larger production Woodward Canyon-made merlot and cabernet sauvignon from Walla Walla Valley and other Washington vineyards.

Horse Heaven Hills Wine Country

Standing on a knoll in the Horse Heaven Hills wine country, you can easily visualize wild horses cantering unimpeded across the rolling, windswept slopes. This image was supposedly the origin of the name when in 1857 cowboy James Kinney discovered his herd of horses contentedly grazing the native grasses—heaven for a horse, indeed! Today, this lonely upland plain is more a heaven for wine grapes.

Located south of the eastern half of Yakima Valley and straddling the ridge that rises up from the Columbia River, Horse Heaven Hills wine country is home to nearly a third of Washington's wine grape production, as well as the source of grapes for Washington's vaunted perfect Parker score wines. Consistent heat, constant wind, and trademark Washington acidity create a showcase example of the state's wine marketing mantra: the perfect climate for wine.

The Horse Heaven Hills appellation consists of a large swath of land, approximately 50 mi (80.4 km) long by 20 mi (32.1 km) wide bordering the Co-

HORSE HEAVEN HILLS WINE COUNTRY AT A GLANCE

Year established: 2005
Number of wineries: 6
Total acreage: 573,800 acres (232,200 ha)
Average vineyard acreage:
    9063 acres (3667 ha)
Predominant soil types: silty loam
Vineyard growing degree days:
    2468–2979 (1353–1637)

Most important grape varieties
merlot, cabernet sauvignon, syrah, chardonnay

lumbia River in the south and lying almost 30 mi (48.2 km) west of Walla Walla Valley wine country. Much of the northern border of the appellation is the southern border of the Yakima Valley AVA, and the wine country is entirely subsumed by the Columbia Valley appellation.

The land's topography is generally south sloping, with a northerly crest at about 1800 ft. (548 m), angling down to about 200 ft. (60.9 m) at the shore of the Columbia River. Across this open desertlike incline, north-south drainage fissures periodically cut through the land surface as small streams and creeks wend their way down to the Columbia.

The soils here are a combination of windblown silts and sand with glacial sediments, alluvium, and volcanic ash. There is a higher amount of eroded basalt rubble in some places, partly because of the Columbia River's eons of cutting through the bedrock, but generally the Horse Heaven Hills soils are not substantially different from most of south-central Washington's other wine countries.

Similarly, key aspects of the region's mesoclimate resemble those of other nearby appellations. The Horse Heaven Hills are dry, with an annual average of 2 to 9 in. (5–22.8 cm) precipitation, which is a little more than the Yakima Valley and about

The gentle slopes, wide expanse, and constant wind of Washington's Horse Heaven Hills are ideal for growing wine grapes.

Windy and dry conditions help protect vines in Washington's Horse Heaven Hills from disease.

WINERIES AND WINES TO SAMPLE

COLUMBIA CREST

Highway 221, Columbia Crest Drive, Paterson, WA
509-875-4227; www.columbiacrest.com
Open to the public all year.

Year founded:	1984
Annual production:	2,100,000 cases
Signature wine:	Grand Estates Merlot ($)
Premium wine:	Walter Clore Private Reserve Red ($$$)
Value wine:	Two Vines Riesling ($)
Estate vineyards:	Columbia Crest

Columbia Crest is Washington's largest winery by volume, and perhaps the most impressive producer in terms of wine value. Relying on the winery's large estate vineyard, winemaker Ray Einberger has loads of fruit to work with and makes the most of them. Einberger pioneered the development of the winery's Reserve wines, including setting aside places within the winery where handcrafted attention can be given to individual lots. The Walter Clore Private Reserve Red table wine (named after one of Washington's most important wine pioneers) is an extraordinary value in a sophisticated Bordeaux-style blend.

The H3 brand of wines showcase cabernet sauvignon, merlot, and chardonnay that typify this wine country's character. The Grand Estates line of wines focuses on pure varietal flavor, and includes merlot, cabernet sauvignon, shiraz, chardonnay, riesling, pinot grigio, and sauvignon blanc. For sheer wine-drinking value, the Two Vines series delivers an unbeatable combination of easy-drinking quality and low price.

Wahluke Slope Wine Country

Undoubtedly the largest gravel bar you've ever seen, Wahluke Slope wine country is 15 mi long (24.1 km) and hundreds of feet high, desolate, and remote. The appellation is one of Washington's most important winegrowing regions, accounting for approximately 20 percent of the state's vinifera production. But this wine country has only a few wineries.

Situated almost in the middle of the Columbia Valley AVA, Wahluke Slope is bounded in the north by the Saddle Mountains, a basalt ridge 2700 ft. (822.9 m) high, and in the west and south by the spectacular steep cliffs of the Columbia River, which turns an almost 90-degree angle toward the east, cradling the Wahluke Slope in its crook. Mattawa, on the western edge of the slope, is the only significant town in the appellation. The slope is one huge south-facing alluvial fan (the AVA petition calls it a mega-alluvial plain) formed of gravels and sand left behind by the Missoula Floods. The ancient gravels are topped by thick layers of windblown sand and loess. The homogeneous nature of the Wahluke Slope is unique in Washington, and helps make grape growing relatively easy, since the uniform terrain means growing conditions are consistent no matter where on the Slope grapes are planted.

The appellation encompasses over 82,000 acres (33,184 ha) between the 425 ft. (129.5 m) elevation along the Columbia River to 1480 ft. (451.1 m) along the south slope of the Saddle Mountains. The Wahluke Slope is very warm to hot, with heat accumulation exceeding 3000 GDD (1648), and dry, with a scant 5.9 in. (14.9 cm) of precipitation. The heat means Wahluke Slope fruit ripens reliably, and the dryness and abundant wind means growers can control vine vigor through irrigation.

Despite its dearth of wineries, the Walhluke Slope is home to over 20 vineyards, some of substantial size, and is the source for many of Washington's better known wine brands. Château Ste. Michelle's Indian Wells wines, Snoqualmie Rosebud Vineyard Cabernet Sauvignon, Fidelitas, and Barnard Griffin

all use Wahluke Slope grapes for their wines, and labels such as Saint Laurent, Desert Wind, Fielding Hills, Millbrandt Vineyards, and Arbor Crest have estate vineyards on the Wahluke Slope.

It seems that most any grape can be grown well in this wine country. In addition to the powerhouse trio of cabernet sauvignon, merlot, and syrah, the appellation grows tempranillo, petit verdot, cinsault, barbera, malbec, sangiovese, tinto cão, sousão. And though one wouldn't expect a cool-climate grape do well here, I have tasted an award-winning pinot noir from the Wahluke Slope. The appellation started out as a white wine region, and still grows riesling, char-

The consistent soils and topography of Washington's Wahluke Slope wine country make for large vineyards.

WAHLUKE SLOPE WINE COUNTRY AT A GLANCE

Year established: 2006
Number of wineries: 2
Total acreage: 82,600 (33,400 ha)
Approximate vineyard acreage:
    5200 acres (2104 ha)
Predominant soil type:
    ancient alluvial deposits
Vineyard growing degree days:
    2674–3164 (1466–1740)

Most important grape varieties
merlot, cabernet sauvignon, riesling

The vineyards of Washington's Lake Chelan wine country are located on both the north and south shores of the lake, along glacial benches at high elevations.

It's too soon to speak of a characteristic Lake Chelan *terroir*, but a few early generalizations can be made. Crisp white wines, for instance, seem to be made well in the area, especially on the cooler southern side of the lake. Fresh riesling, gewürztraminer, and pinot gris wines have been early standouts, with the ever-present chardonnay also showing well. Among the red varieties, pinot noir is being experimented with, and small plantings of other red varieties, including barbera and merlot, are gaining a foothold.

As Lake Chelan viticultural experience grows, the region will begin to focus more clearly on the grapes that best match the appellation's climate. In the meantime, most Lake Chelan–based wineries will continue to bring in grapes from elsewhere in the Columbia Valley to supplement what they can grow in their home ground. Wine tourists are increasingly drawn to the area as much for its beautiful scenery, outdoor activities, and pleasing accommodations, as for its growing wine culture.

WINERIES AND WINES TO SAMPLE

C. R. SANDIDGE WINES

145 East Wapato Way, Manson, WA
509-682-3704; www.crsandidgewines.com
Open all year; limited hours.

Year founded:	1998
Annual production:	1500 cases
Signature wine:	Whistle Punk ($$)
Premium wine:	Tri*Umph ($$$)
Value wine:	Glam Gams Rosé ($)
Estate vineyards:	uses purchased fruit

Winemaker Ray Sandidge brings both international wine experience and a long history of making wine in Washington to the new Lake Chelan appellation. Through the winemaking skills of Ray and the sales and marketing acumen of brother Robert, C. R. Sandidge Wines has contributed significantly to developing both vineyard resources and winemaking capabilities in this young wine country. Ray Sand-

idge is a constant presence in the appellation and consults with numerous vineyards and wineries.

For its own wines, Sandidge sources grapes from select growers throughout the Columbia Valley who agree to meet specific conditions, including reduced yields and imposing water stress at appropriate times. Sandidge's Tri*Umph red blend is an award-winning creation that delivers juicy, forward fruitiness backed with firm but fine-grained tannins. The popular Whistle Punk is a tasty, freshly forward red blend with great blackberry flavors. The Sandidge dry viognier is packed with summer fruit flavors.

Enjoying a taste of wine from Lake Chelan wine country.

Columbia Gorge Wine Country

The Washington side of the Columbia Gorge wine country is about half the size of the Oregon side, and mostly encompasses the valleys running north and south between the towns of White Salmon and Lyle. The appellation is long and narrow, primarily following the White Salmon River's valley to Trout Lake in the north. Though slightly cooler than the Oregon side by about 200 (93) GDD, the difference is not dramatic, and doesn't affect the kinds of grapes that can be grown here. For more information on this wine country, see the Columbia Gorge entry in the Oregon section, page 207.

COLUMBIA GORGE WINE COUNTRY AT A GLANCE

Year established: 2004
Number of wineries: 33*
Total acreage: 186,890 acres (75,700 ha)*
Washington portion acreage:
    64,200 acres (26,000 ha)
Vineyard acreage: 800 acres (323 ha)*
Predominant soil types: mixed volcanic, loess, and loam
Vineyard growing degree days:
    1483–2441 (806–1338)†

Most important grape varieties
pinot noir, gewürztraminer, pinot gris, chardonnay

*Figures apply to the entire appellation.
† Figures apply to Washington portion of the appellation only.

Underwood Vineyards on the Washington side of the Columbia River Gorge underscores the natural beauty of this wine country. Oregon's Mount Hood rises majestically to the south.

WINERIES AND WINES TO SAMPLE

MARYHILL WINERY

9774 Highway 14, Goldendale, WA
877-627-9445; www.maryhillwinery.com
Open all year.

Year founded:	1999
Annual production:	80,000 cases
Signature wine:	Proprietor's Reserve Syrah ($$)
Premium wine:	Proprietor's Reserve Cabernet Sauvignon ($$$)
Value wine:	White Riesling ($)
Estate vineyards:	uses purchased fruit

Owners Craig and Vicki Leuthold chose the right spot to open their winery in 2001. The site has a commanding view of the Columbia River and enough ground space to be an important outdoor entertainment venue. Add to that a wide range of well-made wines, and you have a memorable experience when visiting Maryhill.

It is difficult to say which wines bring Maryhill more accolades, but its Proprietor's Reserve Syrah consistently scores highly for its meaty aromas and rich blueberry core. Also impressive are a Reserve Cabernet Franc that delivers spice-tinged plum flavors, a distinctive and dense Reserve Malbec full of juicy black fruitiness, and a succulent Bordeaux-style red blend called Reserve Serendipity. With a style that favors strong oak treatment and richly ripe fruit, Maryhill's red wines, which also include sangiovese, cabernet sauvignon, merlot, zinfandel, and grenache, have gained a large and loyal following. Not to be outdone in whites, Maryhill offers both a stainless steel- and barrel-fermented chardonnay, crisply styled pinot gris and sauvignon blanc, a flavorful viognier, and a white blend. For the sweeter palate, look for the muscat canelli, white riesling, gewürztraminer, and a vintage port-style offering.

SYNCLINE WINE CELLARS

111 Balch Road, Lyle, WA
509-365-4361; www.synclinewine.com
Open during the season; limited hours.

Year founded:	1999
Annual production:	5000 cases
Signature wine:	Syrah ($$)
Premium wine:	Cuvée Elena ($$$)
Value wine:	Rosé ($$)
Estate vineyards:	Steep Creek Ranch

James and Poppie Mantone make impressive wines in an out-of-the-way place. They met while working in Oregon's Willamette Valley wine world, but relocated to the Washington side of the Columbia Gorge in 2001. Their first vintage consisted of 76 cases of pinot noir planted at Celilo Vineyard in 1972 (yes, that would be Washington pinot noir). The name for their young winery is taken from a local geological formation called the Bingen Syncline, dramatic nearby 300-ft. (91.4-m) cliffs at the eastern end of Columbia Gorge wine country.

Syncline's focus is Rhône varieties, including mourvèdre, roussanne, syrah, and viognier—plus a little non-Rhônish pinot noir from Celilo Vineyard. Its Cuvée Elena is a sophisticated mélange of grenache, mourvèdre, syrah, and cinsault that has a wonderful brambly fruit and wild aspect. Syncline's wines generally are well structured, have good acidity, and refined fruitiness; they are stylish, not flamboyant, and decidedly delicious.

OREGON

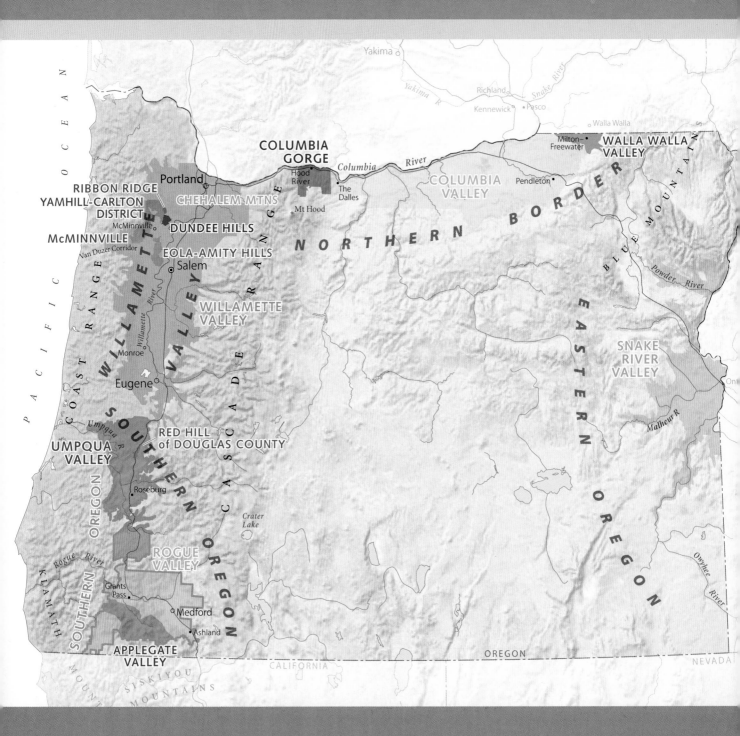

Yakima

Yakima R

Richland

Snake River

Kennewick • Pasco

• Walla Walla

WALLA WALLA VALLEY

Milton-Freewater

PACIFIC OCEAN

COLUMBIA GORGE

Columbia River

Hood River

COLUMBIA VALLEY

Pendleton •

Portland

RIBBON RIDGE
YAMHILL-CARLTON DISTRICT

CHEHALEM MTNS

The Dalles

NORTHERN BORDER

McMinnville

DUNDEE HILLS

• Mt Hood

McMINNVILLE

EOLA-AMITY HILLS

Van Duzer Corridor

• Salem

BLUE MOUNTAINS

Powder River

COAST RANGE

WILLAMETTE VALLEY

WILLAMETTE VALLEY

Willamette River

CASCADE RANGE

Monroe

SNAKE RIVER VALLEY

Eugene •

SOUTHERN OREGON

EASTERN OREGON

Malheur R

Umpqua R

RED HILL of DOUGLAS COUNTY

UMPQUA VALLEY

Roseburg •

Crater Lake

ROGUE VALLEY

Rogue River

Owyhee River

Grants Pass •

KLAMATH

Medford •

• Ashland

OREGON

APPLEGATE VALLEY

CALIFORNIA

NEVADA

SISKIYOU MOUNTAINS

OREGON'S WINE COUNTRIES AT A GLANCE

Vineyard acreage:	19,400 acres (7851 ha)
Number of wineries:	400+
Annual cases produced:	2,331,900 (in 2009)
Economic impact of wine:	$1.5 billion

Most important grape varieties
pinot noir, pinot gris, riesling, chardonnay, cabernet sauvignon, syrah, merlot, gewürztraminer, pinot blanc, viognier

Wine countries (AVAs)
Willamette Valley
    Chehalem Mountains
    Dundee Hills
    Eola–Amity Hills
    McMinnville
    Ribbon Ridge
    Yamhill–Carlton District
Southern Oregon
    Umpqua Valley
        Red Hill of Douglas County
    Rogue Valley
    Applegate Valley
Columbia Gorge*
Columbia Valley*
    Walla Walla Valley*
Snake River Valley†

*Shared with Washington. †Shared with Idaho.

These vines at Tualatin Valley Vineyards are hand-tended throughout the year, like at most Oregon vineyards.

LIFE IN OREGON'S wine countries is slower paced, more personal, and less pretentious than in many other wine regions. Winemakers here wear jeans, not chinos; boots, not boat shoes. They speak more of sustainable farming than creative branding, of biodynamics instead of market dynamics. In its lack of affectation, it has been said that Oregon today is like Napa Valley 30 years ago. Indeed, Oregon's wine countries still have the small-scale feel of rural authenticity and individuality that once characterized Napa Valley. You can drive up to any number of Oregon wineries and, without appointment, be personally treated to an unhurried

tasting and tour by the winemaker or the spouse, son, daughter, niece, or nephew. In the tasting rooms, you can still stumble on that singular Oregon wine find—just 300 cases made, available only at the winery—that you'll not see reviewed in the national wine press or sitting on the shelves at your local wine store. And it is still common to find tasting rooms without fees, parking lots without buses, and winery buildings that really are old barns.

Oregon is appealingly small scale; there are no really large wineries. Average annual production for the state's over 400 wineries is around 3500 cases, and none of the biggest wineries make over 200,000 cases a year. Compare this output to California or Washington, where there are multiple wineries that individually make more wine in a year than all Oregon's wineries put together.

Most of Oregon's wines are hand grown and hand made. There are perhaps two or three mechanically harvested vineyards in the state; everywhere else, vines are pruned, shoot-thinned, and leaf-pulled by hand. On average, each vine gets touched by a worker between four and eight times during the growing season. At harvest, grape clusters are individually inspected, manually cut, and hand-hauled from the vine rows in 40-lb. (18.1-kg) bins. And in nearly all Oregon wineries, when grape clusters arrive from the field they are manually inspected and hand-sorted to eliminate material other than grapes from getting into the fermenters. Individual vineyard blocks are typically fermented separately in small, ½-ton or 1-ton bins. Ferments are monitored around the clock, and adjustments and punchdowns are often done by hand. Technology is certainly employed, but usually in the service of quality, not speed or mass production.

Overleaf: Grape varieites listed in order of tons produced, 2009 Oregon Vineyard and Winery Report, U.S. Department of Agriculture, National Agricultural Statistics Service.

Oregon also has almost no corporately owned wineries. The overwhelming majority of the state's wineries and vineyards, including some of the largest and most prestigious producers, are individually or family-owned businesses, many in the second generation of ownership. Most were (and still are) started on a shoestring, limping through years of building customer loyalty and advancing their winemaking skills before finding financial success. Consistent with the private ownership of Oregon's wineries is the unusually independent spirit of the state's winemakers, winegrowers, and winery owners. "Oregon is a state of individualists," wrote the New York Times wine writer Frank Prial in 1991, when there were only about 80 wineries in the state. Today, with over five times that number, Prial's observation is still valid.

From the beginning, Oregon's wine community was built by free thinkers pursuing distinctly personal wine ambitions. This maverick ethos resulted in the planting of grape varieties in places where conventional wisdom said they would not thrive (Willamette Valley pinot noir and pinot gris in the 1960s and 1970s, for example) and in the production of wine varieties that had never been seen in the Northwest before (southern Oregon tempranillo in the 1990s and grüner veltliner in the early 2000s, to name two). This attitude has also meant that Oregon is home to a wide variety of distinctive wine styles as winemakers strive to express their own idiosyncratic sensibilities.

This independence, however, is tempered by a shared commitment to communal good. Early on, Oregon's winemakers understood the value of protecting what they were building. They agreed to fund viticultural research and industry marketing by imposing on themselves the largest industry tax in the world. They also fought for and enacted the nation's strictest state wine labeling laws to ensure a high level of wine quality and label integrity for consumers. And they became leaders in land use regulation, helping preserve agricultural land in the face of encroaching development.

Jason Lett is second-generation winemaker at The Eyrie Vineyards. He exemplifies the artisan, craft-oriented nature of Oregon's wine culture.

During harvest, grape clusters are picked by hand and placed in small totes for gentle transportation to the winery, where clusters are sorted to eliminate non-grape material.

In keeping with these values, and through a common desire to pass on to future generations a healthy wine ecosystem, Oregon has also been a pioneer in sustainable, organic, and biodynamic viticulture. Oregon is home to the first winery in the nation (Sokol Blosser Winery) to receive a Leadership in Energy and Environmental Design (LEED) certification from the U.S. Green Building Council, as well as the first Gold LEED Certified winery in the country (Stoller Vineyards).

On its bucolic surface, Oregon's wine countries exude an honest and independent, rural and artisan spirit that makes touring the state's wineries a very different experience from visiting many other wine regions. If you are looking for wineries with Versailles-scale gardens, neo-Renaissance castles, museum gallerylike tasting rooms, or celebrity architect-designed buildings, there's not a lot in Oregon to interest you. But if you seek the embodiment of winemaking passion—whether in the guise of individuals grubstaked by families and friends, young second-generation winemakers working to modernize the family wine business, or successful businesspeople earnestly applying their resources and energies to making the best wine they can, Oregon offers much. If you want to see how craft and character—of the land and place as much as the grower and winemaker—can be tasted in a glass, then Oregon is for you.

But Oregon is changing—growing up, some might say, selling out according to others—and is seemingly at risk of becoming a more ostentatiously and glamorous wine destination every day, or at least less like the Oregon of the past.

Even Oregon's most famous wineries, like Domaine Drouhin Oregon, can offer visitors an intimate tasting experience.

132

King Estate is an example of how modern wineries are changing Oregon's traditional wine country landscape.

HillCrest is Oregon's oldest winery, and still produces excellent wines.

How Oregon's wine countries should be further developed is an active issue of debate within much of the state's wine world. As the posh wine country lifestyle becomes more popular, more people are looking to Oregon as the land of vinous opportunity. Priced out of tonier and more famous wine countries, unprecedented amounts of investment and development monies for both wineries and wine-tourism amenities are moving into the relative bargain that Oregon presents. This influx is changing the character of the state's wine countries.

Oregon today has more faux chateaus, flashy villas, and architectural paeans to a mythical Old World heritage than ever before. Hummer limousines are no longer out of place. One Willamette Valley winery offers advice for customers who want to know where best to land their personal jets when touring local wine country. And it seems that any new winery, no matter how inexperienced, wants to sell you a $50 bottle of Willamette Valley pinot noir because . . . well, because it's Willamette Valley pinot noir.

The comparison to Napa Valley 30 years ago? It irks a lot of Oregon's winemakers. Partly because they can see its truth—success necessarily breeds popularity, imitation, and investment—and partly because they can see a future that is different from their past. Oregon's contemporary wine country can appear a far cry from its bootstrapped roots. In a wine community that was entirely built by the sweat of individuals who were doggedly committed to doing their own thing, it can be difficult to respect newcomer outsiders who pay their dues by check.

Perhaps, though, all the concern over protecting the heritage and integrity of Oregon's wine personality from the threat of monied greenhorns is

Biodynamic Wine

Oregon is a global leader in biodynamic wine. A controversial farming practice, biodynamics is sometimes thought of as taking organic farming to the next level, or over the edge. Some of Oregon's most famous pinot noir wineries—Beaux Frères and Bergström are just two examples—employ biodynamic techniques, though they rarely make a public point of it. Biodynamic winegrowing is only beginning elsewhere in the Northwest.

Formulated by the Austrian polymath Rudolph Steiner in the 1920s, the principles of biodynamic agriculture seek to connect the microecology of a farm to the überecology of the cosmos. Bio-dynamics views the farm, or vineyard, as a self-sustaining living organism, and employs methods designed to uphold and improve the health of the whole farm, not just a field or a crop. Crops are carefully rotated to restore soils and to increase biodiversity on the land. As a self-contained organism, no inputs, including fertilizers no matter how organic, from outside the farm are allowed, and all the agents of fertility or feed come from recycling organic materials that the farm itself generates.

Though the basic tenets of biodynamics seem idealistic and worthy, what riles many people are the esoteric, some say looney, methods that bio-dynamics employ. One practice involves the appli-

Paul de Lancellotti, of de Lancellotti Family Vineyards, is one of Oregon's leading biodynamic practitioners. Here, he prepares cow horns for burying as part of that practice.

Vigneron Christophe Baron works his biodynamic vineyards in Oregon's Walla Walla Valley with a draft horse instead of a tractor.

cation of a compost tea obtained by stuffing cow horns with manure and herbal teas, burying them over the winter, digging them up in the spring, mixing the contents with water, and spraying the liquid over the ground. Other preparations are designed to contribute some element of beneficial energy to the farm. And all farm practices are strictly scheduled according to lunar, solar, and planetary alignments.

But does this framing practice improve wine? Biodynamic practitioner Michael Etzel, partner and winemaker at Oregon's Beaux Frères, is ambivalent. In a 2006 interview, he said: "I do believe there is an improvement in the wines . . . but I am also maturing as a winemaker, and I can't say with certainty that the wines are better because of the biodynamics." Still, Etzel believes biodynamic practices are beneficial. "I can say that biodynamics makes me a better farmer. It demands that I be more attentive and involved with the vineyard on a daily basis . . . it is more holistic farming, you're working with everything your *terroir* has to offer. By using these preparations and improving the life in the soil, I'm able to get a healthier plant that hopefully transforms the flavors of the soil into the grapes and into the wine."

Oregon winemaker Tony Soter strolls the edges of his Mineral Springs Vineyard at the end of a summer day.

overblown. Perhaps the strength of character within Oregon's wine community will mitigate the potential ravages of development. And perhaps—just perhaps—much of that new money flowing into the state is arriving because the newcomers respect what Oregon is, and want to join, sustain, extend, and even advance the quality, temperament, and virtuosity of Oregon's wine countries.

OREGON'S WINE GEOGRAPHY

Because of its geographic diversity, one cannot generalize about Oregon wine. The state's four broad growing regions, which include the Willamette Valley, southern Oregon, eastern Oregon, and what I call the northern border region, are more varied in climate and topography than those of Washington. Though often thought of only as pinot noir country, Oregon's mix of viticulture climates makes for the most successfully varied winegrowing areas in the Northwest.

On the surface, it would seem that Oregon's geography mimics that of Washington. Like its neighbor to the north, Oregon is dramatically divided west to east by the two-mile high backbone of the Cascade Range, and two-thirds of the state lies east of these mountains as vast, sparsely populated high-elevation desert. But unlike Washington, the great bulk of Oregon's vineyards and wine production occur in the western third of the state. And unlike Washington, Oregon is best known for its cool-climate wine countries.

Spreading south from Portland like an oak leaf, the Willamette Valley is Oregon's largest wine country and is home to over 80 percent of the state's vineyards and wineries. Only about 40 to 50 mi (64.3–80.4 km) from the Pacific Ocean, the Willamette Valley experiences a marine-influenced temperate climate that makes it the most successful cool-climate wine country in the Northwest.

Bergström Vineyard exemplifies the beautifully manicured vineyards of Oregon's Willamette Valley wine country.

OREGON PINOT NOIR
GAINS INTERNATIONAL ATTENTION

The 1975 South Block Reserve Pinot Noir from The Eyrie Vineyards helped bring worldwide attention to Oregon wine.

The potential of Oregon's cool-climate Willamette Valley was dramatically demonstrated at two wine tastings held in France in 1979 and 1980. The story has been proudly recounted many times in Oregon because it brought international credibility to the young wine region.

In 1979, the French magazine *GaultMillau* held a Paris tasting they called the Olympiades du Vin. Included among the Burgundies was a pinot noir from a then obscure Oregon producer, The Eyrie Vineyards, made by a young winemaker named David Lett. It was a surprise, if not an outright shock, that the 1975 South Block Reserve from The Eyrie Vineyards placed second.

Robert Drouhin, the third-generation head of the famed Burgundy *négociant* Maison Joseph Drouhin, perhaps perturbed to find an upstart pinot from such an unlikely place besting some of his own Grand Cru bottlings, recreated the *GaultMillau* tasting a year later on his home turf in Beaune, the heart of Burgundy. The result was the same.

Convinced that Oregon's cool-climate Willamette Valley held true promise as a new region for growing top-quality pinot noir, Robert's daughter Véronique Drouhin-Boss interned in the Willamette Valley for the 1986 vintage, and a year later the Drouhin family purchased vineyard land in the Red Hills of Dundee, opening their Domaine Drouhin Oregon winery in 1989. The Drouhin's investment gave Oregon's cool-climate wine country the stamp of credibility it needed: Burgundy was coming to Oregon to make pinot noir. Quickly, new wineries began springing up along the Willamette Valley's western hillsides to produce pinot noir, a phenomenon that continues unabated.

growing regions. Unlike the Willamette Valley, where available winegrowing land is limited and expensive, Oregon's warm-climate growing regions offer a varied and viticulturally underexplored geography rife with opportunity. Today, the most significant area of warm-climate viticulture is in the Southern Oregon AVA, though winery development in the northern border region is accelerating and someday is likely to press into eastern Oregon.

Driving south from Eugene, the land and its life changes. The rolling prairies and lush agricultural plains of the Willamette Valley give way to sparse range and grazing land as you climb through geologically folded, craggy, mountains. Trees change too: the prominence of Douglas fir and deciduous broadleaf trees gives way to Oregon white oak, Pacific madrone, and ponderosa pine.

The climate for wine grapes becomes warmer and drier, and appropriate vineyard sites are at higher elevations, often over 1000 ft. (304.8 m), and are more difficult to find among the smaller valleys and flood plains of the Klamath and Siskiyou Mountains. Average growing degree days in southern Oregon are 300 to 400 (148–204), higher than in the Willamette Valley, but many individual sites are even warmer, some reported to exceed 3000 (1649) GDD. The warm to very warm growing regions of southern Oregon enable the successful ripening of a wider range of vinifera grapes than is possible in the Willamette Valley. Consequently, the area produces the full panoply of Bordeaux varieties, and is increasingly planting Rhône and Spanish grapes, as well as experimenting with varieties that have previously not

Del Rio Vineyard in the Rogue Valley wine country. The warmer climate of Southern Oregon allows for the ripening of a wider range of grape varieties than in the Willamette Valley.

the wines they produce. Such single-vineyard wines often command a price premium, with the theory that a single vineyard's distinctive *terroir* is more desirable than an anonymous blend of different vineyards. The proposition is debatable.

A vineyard name on a wine label by itself isn't necessarily meaningful. These days, it seems that every new Oregon pinot noir producer, regardless of its winemaking history, proudly puts a previously unknown vineyard name on the bottle and then charges more for it. The value of a single-vineyard name only accrues over the years, as vines grow deeper into the soil and wines from that vineyard consistently deliver distinctive character. Only the most tried and true vineyard names should justify a premium bottle price. It might also be argued that single-vineyard wines are overrated. Which is more important to the character of a pinot noir, the land (the expression of *terroir*) or the hand (the winemaking technique)? The hand of the winemaker can always outplay the nuance of the *terroir*, if the winemaker wants it to.

Blended pinot noir wines are the best example of hand over land. Most well-established pinot producers have at least one release they consider to be their signature blend, a combination of grapes from different vineyards that the winemaker composes to reflect a particular style or expression. Often these wines are labeled reserve or have cuvée somewhere in the name of the wine. These wines represent the best craft the winemaker can employ for expressing the character of a vintage, a growing region, or a personal palate. The wise consumer knows that often the best wines in a winery's range are the reserve-level blends.

Broadly speaking, there are two predominant styles of Oregon pinot noir, which I call the poised and the plush. Whether expressed in a blend or a single-vineyard wine, these two pinot expressions are common. Winemakers who strive for the elegant, more poised style, try to let the *terroir* talk in the wine. They do this, they often say, by getting out of the way of the wine, by minimizing manipulations that alter the inherent characteristics of the fruit they harvest. They intervene in the natural winemaking process as little as possible, even to the point of relying for fermentation on the native yeasts that grow on the grapes and live in the winery. Such winemakers use oak judiciously, only applying it as an accent to the wine rather than as a central theme.

Pinot noir makers of the plush school are usually more involved in managing the winemaking. They may delay picking the grapes until they achieve higher levels of sugar to increase both alcohol and concentration. They may also delay fermentation for many days while the newly harvested grapes are left to cold soak in their own juice to extract and concentrate color, flavor, and tannin structure. To initiate fermentation, they may choose a specific strain of yeast that will achieve a particular sensory aspect they wish to emphasize in the finished wine. They may chaptalize—add sugar—in cooler years to achieve higher alcohol content. And typically, they will use plenty of new oak barrels to help realize the rich, sometimes heavy toastiness often thought desirably compatible with pinot noir.

Between poised and plush, neither is considered better than the other; they are both viable and popular wine styles. There are as many modes of pinot noir as there are winemakers producing it.

Pinot Gris

The most widely planted white grape in Oregon and second-most planted overall is pinot gris, the so-called gray mutation of pinot noir. We're talking pinot gris, the French wine, not pinot grigio, the Italian: they are the same grape but made into very different styles of wine. Oregon's wine industry has deliberately chosen to emulate the French model for making pinot gris. It has only been recently that the term pinot grigio has been allowed on Oregon wine labels.

Pinot gris grapes are lighter in color than pinot noir, yet darker than pinot blanc grapes. Though pinot noir and pinot gris vines look identical, ripening

146

pinot gris clusters display a mixture of berry colors from dusky green, to grayish blue, to rosy pink, often in the same cluster. Like its pinot noir cousin, pinot gris is an early ripening variety best adapted to a cool climate.

The ancestral home of pinot gris is Burgundy, where it is also known as pinot beurot, and is an approved variety in many of the region's appellations. It is also widely grown in eastern Europe, Germany, and in Italy, where it is most often turned into an inexpensive, light, easy-quaffing wine, pinot grigio. The grape's emotional home, however, is Alsace. Alsatian pinot gris can be distinctive wines of power and depth that range from dry to intensely sweet, and are considered to be especially food-friendly. It is this Alsatian pinot gris that Oregon's wine community has historically sought to make.

Pinot gris was brought to the Northwest by David Lett in the late 1960s. His 160 vines were perhaps the first pinot gris planted anywhere in North America. Throughout the first two decades of Oregon's wine history, pinot gris was a pleasant if not particularly popular variety. But beginning in the mid-1990s, the relentless hand-selling done by Willamette Valley winemakers to show the food affinity of pinot gris, plus a greater focus on quality farming and winemaking, began to pay off with new demand that continues growing today.

The typical flavors of Oregon pinot gris include pear, melon, and green apple, plus a honeysucklelike aroma. There are often notes of lemon-lime spice and toasted nuts, which are sometimes considered a signature of the variety. The wine tends to have good body in the mouth, and sometimes has a slight rosy hue, especially if given any skin contact. The aromas can be subtle, but often have a sense of spicy flower blossoms.

Capturing and showcasing these aromas and flavors can be challenging. Timely picking is key to quality Oregon pinot gris. Unlike its pinot noir cousin, pinot gris loses acidity rapidly near peak ripeness, demanding that winemakers pay close attention at harvest

time, because sufficient acidity is vital to maintaining the fruit and spice characters of the grape.

There are two axes of stylistic choice for the pinot gris consumer to consider: degree of dryness and presence of oak. Truly dry pinot gris wines display crisp pear, melon, or citrus flavors, and an edge of spice that can be subtly reminiscent of clove or allspice. Most often these wines are fermented in steel to help retain brightness and fruit clarity, but sometimes an element of wood fermentation or barrel aging is applied for roundness.

Many Oregon pinot gris wines are made with some degree of residual sugar left over from fermentation. When the amount is moderate, the sweetness can add a level of textural richness and easy-drinking appeal, as well as contributing flesh to the fruitiness and heightening the aromas. These lightly off-dry wines also frequently have some measure of oak, contributed either through fermentation or aging in

Pinot gris grapes.

ed in Oregon, achieving greatness with the grape has proven elusive. Even so, a lot of cabernet sauvignon is successfully made in Oregon, and its popularity is undeniable. After many years of tasting the state's cabernet sauvignon wines, however, I find they rarely achieve the depth, complexity, and finesse that can more frequently be found in those from Washington.

Though Oregon's warm-climate wine countries generally have the proper heat units to grow late-ripening cabernet sauvignon, reliable viability is very site specific. Cabernet sauvignon typically matures in mid to late October, but in some regions a shorter growing season means that early fall frosts can endanger full ripening unless the grape is planted only in the warmest sites.

If a site is even a little too cool, cabernet sauvignon will not reliably reach full ripeness, resulting in green or vegetal flavors. Lowering yields can help accelerate ripening and achieve better varietal flavors, but this approach is costly and not as widely practiced as it might be. Conversely, if a site is too warm, cabernet sauvignon can become quickly overripe, adding sugar, losing acidity, and accumulating excess tannins in the skins if not picked at the right time. Wine made from such grapes can be flabby, jammy, or harsh. Adding citric acid during winemaking and extended barrel aging can add structure, but they can also alter flavors and be too easily overdone.

At its best, Oregon cabernet sauvignon displays clean and pure black currant and cherry fruit flavors, with layered complexity added by measured application of French oak aging (which tends to be softer, though more expensive, than American oak). Frequently, however, Oregon cabernets are aged long in wood, often in heavily toasted new American barrels that impart heavy doses of vanilla, spice, and smoke that can overwhelm the fruit. Riper versions of the wine, when less encumbered by oak, offer notes of

jammy cassis and currants, with accents of violets and chocolate.

A pleasing trend of lighter cabernet sauvignon wines has emerged in Oregon the last few years. These wines are made with less aggressive oak treatment and more forward, juicy fruitiness, making them easier to enjoy as single varietal wines when young, and as good components for more accessible blended wines.

Other Important Grapes

Oregon's next most produced grape varieties are, in order, syrah, merlot, gewürztraminer, pinot blanc, and viognier. Of these, syrah is perhaps the most important. Syrah wine in Oregon is a fairly new phenomenon, having been widely made only since around 2000. Most syrah comes from the Rogue Valley, where the grape tends to produce brooding wines with dark fruit flavors, heavy textures, and plenty of plush sweetness. Syrah is also widely grown in the Walla Walla Valley appellation, and the wines made from those grapes tend to have more bright tones, redder fruit flavors, and a more evenly balanced composition.

The top 10 list of Oregon wine grape varieties does not include two grapes that consumers should know about. Both tempranillo and cabernet franc have the potential to become signature grapes for southern Oregon's wine countries in years to come. Tempranillo is a newcomer to the Northwest. This great Spanish grape is the mainstay of Rioja and Ribera del Duero red wines, but until the mid 1990s, it was almost unknown in Oregon and the Northwest. Earl and Hilda Jones, of Abacela winery in Roseburg, produced the first commercial vintage of tempranillo in the Northwest in 1997. The subsequent success of the variety has led to a surge in new tempranillo plantings throughout Oregon's warm climate regions, and increasingly in Washington and Idaho as well. There are even a few successful plantings in the cool-climate Willamette Valley.

Oregon tempranillo displays deep black fruit qualities mediated by a sense of minerality and spice. It

---

Old cabernet sauvignon vines at Valley View Winery in Oregon's Applegate Valley wine country.

REX HILL WINERY

30835 N Highway 99W, Newberg, OR
800-739-4455; www.rexhill.com
Open all year.

Year founded:	1982
Annual production:	20,000 cases
Signature wine:	Dundee Hills Pinot Noir ($$$)
Premium wine:	Shea Vineyard Pinot Noir ($$$$)
Value wine:	Oregon Pinot Gris ($$)
Estate vineyards:	Rex Hill

Rex Hill, founded by Paul Hart and Jan Jacobsen, was one of the earliest wineries to bottle single-vineyard pinot noir in Oregon. Today the winery is owned by A to Z Wineworks, one of the largest wineries in Oregon, and managed by partners Bill and Deb Hatcher, and Cheryl Francis and Sam Tannahill.

Rex Hill's wines are made from old-vine grapes, whether biodynamically grown, estate-owned, or purchased, and have tremendous aging capacity as well as great depth and elegance. Winemakers Sam Tannahill, Cheryl Francis, and Michael Davies produces the wines with a focus on organic and biodynamic farming. While A to Z also makes large volumes of value-priced wines under the A to Z brand, Rex Hill specializes in small-production, craft-style wines.

SCOTT PAUL WINES

128 South Pine Street, Carlton, OR
503-852-7300; www.scottpaul.com
Open all year.

Year founded:	1999
Annual production:	3000 cases
Signature wine:	Le Paulée Pinot Noir ($$)
Premium wine:	Audrey Pinot Noir ($$$$)
Value wine:	Cuvée Martha Pirrie ($$)
Estate vineyards:	Azana

Scott and Martha Wright, with help from winemaker Kelley Fox, craft only pinot noir wines that are proudly "old school." Scott does not hold with the bigger-is-better philosophy of some pinot noir makers, and treats his carefully sourced grapes with kid gloves. His three stylings of pinot noir display beautiful fruit, graceful balance, and excellent length. They are fine polished wines that go wonderfully with food.

Though current wines are sourced from key Willamette Valley vineyards, including Momtazi, Ribbon Ridge, and biodynamically farmed old-vine pinot noir at Maresh Vineyard, Scott has recently planted his first estate vines, Azana Vineyard, in the Chehalem Mountains. A former general manager of Domaine Drouhin Oregon, Wright has leveraged his French connections into also becoming an importer of selected Burgundy producers. At his tasting room in Carlton, you can sample Oregon and France side by side.

Dundee Hills Wine Country

In some ways, the Dundee Hills wine country is the heart of Oregon's red wine soul. It was here that the first pinot noir in the Willamette Valley was planted, and it was from here that the state's flourishing pinot noir industry blossomed across northern Oregon.

In the Dundee Hills, it's all about the soil: it is dry, sparse, and red. The volcanic Jory soil that covers 80 percent of this wine country is the result of decomposed basalts, and is treated like gold by some pinot noir growers. For most of its history (and on USGS topographic maps), the region has been known as the Red Hills of Dundee, and that was the name first proposed for the AVA. But in a move that can be variously interpreted, a slightly prior AVA application was made for the name Red Hill in southern Oregon, forcing the Dundee petitioners to rename their appellation.

By any name, the Dundee Hills are a discrete, roughly circular uplift of land south of part of the Chehalem Mountains appellation and east of much of the Yamhill–Carlton District wine country. The town of Dundee is included in the northeastern AVA boundary, and the southeastern border essentially follows Highway 99W. Like its neighboring wine countries, the appellation's boundary begins at the 200 ft. (60.9 m) contour line, separating it from the

DUNDEE HILLS WINE COUNTRY AT A GLANCE

Year established: 2005
Number of wineries: 25
Total acreage: 12,500 acres (5100 ha)
Vineyard acreage: 1700 acres (687.9 ha)
Predominant soil type: red volcanic Jory
Vineyard growing degree days:
    1839–2077 (1003–1136)

Most important grape varieties
pinot noir, pinot gris

Vines at Ayoub Vineyard in the Oregon's Dundee Hills are beginning to enter senescence, a kind of seasonal old age that precedes dormancy.

Willamette Valley floor, and extends to just beyond 1000 ft. (304.8 m) elevation.

In climate, the Dundee Hills appellation is slightly warmer than neighboring Yamhill–Carlton District, and receives somewhat less rain than the Chehalem Mountains to the north. It is protected from more severe weather by surrounding landforms, and is not subject to the frost dangers of lower elevations.

The pinot noir wines grown in the Dundee Hills are noted for their bright, elegant red fruit flavors, ranging from strawberry to raspberry to cherry. While darker black cherry notes are not uncommon, silky-textured red cherry flavors with earthy, trufflelike aromas are integral to the Dundee Hills pinot noir signature. Additional qualities of light spice, minerality, and cola are also present in wines from this appellation.

Grapes have apparently been grown in the Dundee Hills since the early part of the twentieth century, but the allure of the area for vinifera had to wait for the first generation of modern pinot noir pioneers. David Lett planted this wine country's first pinot noir and pinot gris vines in 1965, and was rapidly joined by others. Since then, the Dundee Hills appellation has become a prestige locale among pinot noir winemakers and an important wine-touring destination.

WINERIES AND WINES TO SAMPLE

ARCHERY SUMMIT

18599 NE Archery Summit Road, Dayton, OR
503-864-4300; www.archerysummit.com
Open all year.

Year founded:	1995
Annual production:	10,000 cases
Signature wine:	Arcus Pinot Noir ($$$$)
Premium wine:	Estate Pinot Noir ($$$$+)
Value wine:	Premier Cuvée ($$$)
Estate vineyards:	Archery Summit, Red Hills, Arcus, Renegade Ridge, Looney

Archery Summit was created by the late Gary Andrus (formerly of Pine Ridge Winery in Napa Valley), who designed an impressive gravity-flow winery (where all grape, juice, and wine movement is accomplished by gravity rather than mechanical pumps) expressly for pinot noir, and brought to Oregon a flair for wine marketing that helped drive national attention. Always a prestige winery, it was the first in Oregon to release a $100 pinot noir in greater than single-barrel quantities. Archery Summit has never spared effort or expense in making its wines, even under different ownership.

Winemaker Anna Matzinger continues the tradition of excellence with her expert way of bringing out the best in both the vintage and the vineyard. With classic Dundee Hills vineyard sites to work with, she has plenty of quality fruit for making her elegantly powerful wines. The Arcus and Red Hills releases are particularly powerful, with great bursts of dense cherry and blackberry flavors balanced by ample acidity and backed by polished tannin grip. Difficult and expensive wines to come by, Anna's pinot noirs are among the most desired in the Willamette Valley, and for good reason.

ARGYLE WINERY

691 Highway 99W, Dundee, OR
503-538-8520; www.argylewinery.com
Open all year.

Year founded:	1987
Annual production:	40,000 cases
Signature wine:	Extended Tirage Brut Sparkling Wine ($$$$)
Premium wine:	Spirithouse Pinot Noir ($$$$)
Value wine:	Willamette Valley Pinot Noir ($$)
Estate vineyards:	Lone Star, Spirit Hill

It is difficult to know just what kind of a winery Argyle is. Winemaker Rollin Soles is so adept at making sparkling wine, pinot noir, chardonnay, and one of the finest rieslings in the Northwest that you just can't put Argyle into a neat category.

The quality of Argyle's sparkling wines alone would be enough for any single winery. The Extended Tirage Brut and the Knudsen Vineyard Brut are among the finest made in America. But Soles also crafts superb pinot noir, including the deep, sometimes brooding Nuthouse and the refined, floral-spicy accented Spirithouse. Soles was one of the first Oregon winemakers to work with Dijon clone chardonnay, producing a delightfully fresh style, and his riesling program is one of the best and longest running in the Northwest. Perhaps Argyle doesn't get quite as much attention as some of Oregon's newer wine names, but there is no winery that can beat Argyle for substance and quality across such a spectrum of wines.

170

DOBBES FAMILY ESTATE

240 SE 5th Street, Dundee, OR
503-538-1141; www.dobbesfamilyestate.com
Open all year.

Year founded:	2003
Annual production:	3500 cases
Signature wine:	Grande Assemblage Pinot Noir ($$)
Premium wine:	Meyer Vineyard Pinot Noir ($$$$)
Value wine:	Willamette Valley Pinot Gris ($$)
Estate vineyards:	uses purchased fruit

Winemaker Joe Dobbes is a dashing figure in Oregon winemaking circles—dashing from vineyard to vineyard during harvest, managing one of the broadest set of winemaking commitments in the state. Dobbes Family Estate is his focus, though his consulting skills are in high demand. His personal wines push pinot noir to the limit, getting from each vineyard what seems to be the pure essence of the vine. The Meyer Vineyard release, for instance, is about as pure an expression of Dundee Hills *terroir* as you are likely to find. Each of Dobbes's single-vineyard pinot noirs has a distinctive personality that well reflects the grape source. In his cuvées, Dobbes imparts his own spin, resulting in concentrated, bold wines.

Dobbes's winemaking experience includes southern Oregon as well. In addition to his Willamette Valley pinot noir, he also makes excellent syrah and viognier from warm-climate Oregon vineyards.

DOMAINE DROUHIN OREGON

6750 NE Breyman Orchards Road, Dayton, OR
503-864-2700; www.domainedrouhin.com
Open all year.

Year founded:	1988
Annual production:	18,000 cases
Signature wine:	Willamette Valley Pinot Noir ($$$)
Premium wine:	Louise Drouhin Pinot Noir ($$$$)
Value wine:	Arthur Chardonnay ($$)
Estate vineyards:	Drouhin Family

Domaine Drouhin Oregon is one of Oregon's most important producers. The credibility of the Drouhin family of Burgundy fame, bestowed on Oregon when

they established their winery here, cannot be overstated. And since that time, in vintage after vintage, Domaine Drouhin consistently has produced some of the state's finest wines. As a Burgundian who has made more Oregon vintages than most Oregon

Domaine Drouhin Oregon.

171

winemakers, Vèronique Drouhin-Boss's unique perspective results in wines that clearly reflect both the vineyard and the vintage.

The Willamette Valley Cuvée is well balanced, accessible, and beautifully reflects each vintage. The Laurène Pinot Noir is from the estate vineyard, fermented with native yeasts, and exposed to no more than 20 percent new French oak, resulting in a profound expression of Dundee Hills *terroir*. The rare Louise Drouhin Pinot Noir is Drouhim-Boss's personal pick of the best few barrels in the cellar. And the Burgundian-style Arthur Chardonnay blends partly oak-fermented wine for roundness with steel-fermented wine for freshness.

Ably managed in Oregon by David Millman, with constant attention from Vèronique and her father Robert in France (and multiple trips to Oregon through the year), Domaine Drouhin is perhaps the quintessential example of a truly international winery.

DOMAINE SERENE

6555 NE Hilltop Lane, Dayton, OR
503-864-4600; www.domaineserene.com
Open all year; limited hours.

Year founded:	1989
Annual production:	28,000 cases
Signature wine:	Evenstad Reserve Pinot Noir ($$$$)
Premium wine:	Monogram Pinot Noir ($$$$+)
Value Wine:	Yamhill Cuvée Pinot Noir ($$$)
Estate vineyards:	Fleur de Lis, Gold Eagle, Côte Sud, Clos du Soliel, Jerusalem Hill, Etoile, Grace, Mark Bradford, Winery Hill

Sitting high atop the Dundee Hills, the Tuscan-style Domaine Serene winery is a Willamette Valley landmark, as are its wines. Ken and Grace Evenstad came to Oregon in 1989 to grow and make pinot noir. Applying their considerable resources, they developed three vineyard estates totaling 462 acres (186.9 ha), making Domaine Serene one of the largest vineyard owners in the state. Vines are dry farmed using sustainable practices and cropped for low yields for intense, balanced fruit.

Domaine Serene pinot noir wines are beautifully balanced with succulent fruit, excellent acidity, and deep layers of complex flavors. Domaine Serene's wines include single-vineyard releases from different estate vines, with the complex Mark Bradford and spicy Grace Vineyard being my favorites. Winemaker Eleni Papadakis also produces a prestige Monogram cuvée, small amounts of stylish chardonnay, and makes viognier and syrah under the Rockblock brand. Domaine Serene's stature is well justified by the highest quality of wine in the bottle.

ERATH WINERY

9409 NE Worden Hill Road, Dundee, OR
503-538-3318; www.erath.com
Open all year.

Year founded:	1972
Annual production:	120,000 cases
Signature wine:	Estate Selection Pinot Noir ($$$)
Premium wine:	La Nuit Magique Pinot Noir ($$$$)
Value wine:	Pinot Blanc ($)
Estate vineyards:	Prince Hill, Niederberger

Dick Erath was one of the earliest founders of the Oregon wine industry. Arriving in 1968, planting

Dick Erath, who planted wine grapes in the Dundee Hills as early as 1969, is one of Oregon's pioneer modern winemakers.

vines a year later, and making his first 216 cases of Willamette Valley pinot noir in 1972, he went on to build Erath into one of the state's largest wineries. Now owned by Washington's Ste. Michelle Wine Estates, Erath's name and wines continue through the able winemaking hands of Gary Horner.

Erath is best known for its pinot noir wines, including a classic Oregon blend from prime vineyard sites around the state. A selection of single-vineyard pinot noirs presents a taste tour of the Willamette Valley, while the sultry blend La Nuit Magique presents a remarkably palate-pleasing wine for the pinot noir perfectionist. Erath also makes a solid selection of pinot gris, gewürztraminer, riesling, and pinot blanc whites, as well as a rare Willamette Valley dolcetto. These are classic wines from a classic Oregon winery.

THE EYRIE VINEYARDS

935 NE 10th Avenue, McMinnville, OR
503-472-6315; www.eyrievineyards.com
Open all year; limited hours.

Year founded:	1966
Annual production:	10,000 cases
Signature wine:	Estate Pinot Noir ($$)
Premium wine:	Reserve Pinot Noir ($$$)
Value wine:	Pinot Gris ($$)
Estate vineyards:	The Eyrie Vineyard, Rolling Green Farm, Daphne and Stonehedge, The Three Sisters

When David Lett, affectionately known as Papa Pinot, founded The Eyrie Vineyards, he also helped create what was to become one of the most respected pinot noir–producing wine countries in the world. The Eyrie Vineyards is the foundational Willamette Valley pinot noir winery. Alas, Lett passed away in 2008, but his talented son Jason continues the legacy.

Famed for graceful expressions of pure pinot fruit, Lett intrudes on the winemaking process as little as possible and revels in the character of his old-vine estate, with its own-rooted, dry-farmed vines. The Estate and Reserve pinot noir wines are stylishly elegant, as are the chardonnay and pinot gris offerings. Lett also makes the rare muscat ottonel and pinot meunier, plus a pinot blanc. There is no better way to experience the true essence of Dundee Hills pinot personality than sampling The Eyrie Vineyards' wines.

LANGE ESTATE WINERY & VINEYARDS

18380 NE Buena Vista Drive, Dundee, OR
503-538-6476; www.langewinery.com
Open all year.

Year founded:	1987
Annual production:	14,000 cases
Signature wine:	Three Hills Cuvée Pinot Noir ($$$)
Premium wine:	Lange Estate Vineyard Pinot Noir ($$$$)
Value wine:	Willamette Valley Pinot Noir ($$)
Estate vineyards:	Lange, Red Side

Purely a family endeavor, winery founders Don and Wendy Lange are joined by son Jesse in producing sumptuous pinot noir wines that gracefully embody the Dundee Hills character. Their estate vineyard is perfectly sited for pinot noir and carefully farmed for low yields to obtain the best possible fruit ripening and flavor. Fruit is processed in small lots and gently handled, from vine to barrel, to maintain optimum character. The Estate pinot noir wines have lots of minerality underlying the juicy red cherry fruit, and have sufficient structure to age well.

Besides its estate vines, Lange has been making pinot noir from the Freedom Hill Vineyard in the Coast Range foothills longer than any producer. These earthy, substantial wines often show their best character after a few years in the cellar. Lange is also a pioneer with pinot gris: it was the fourth producer in the United States to work with the grape and the first to produce a barrel-fermented version.

PANTHER CREEK CELLARS

455 NE Irvine Street, McMinnville, OR
503-472-8080; www.panthercreekcellars.com
Open all year.

Year founded:	1986
Annual production:	7500 cases
Signature wine:	Winemaker's Cuvée Pinot Noir ($$)
Premium wine:	Shea Vineyard Pinot Noir ($$$)
Value wine:	Elton Vineyard Chardonnay ($$)
Estate vineyards:	uses purchased fruit

Panther Creek Cellars was founded by winemaker Ken Wright, but he sold it when a partnership dissolved. The winery grew in prominence over the years because of the efforts of subsequent owners Ron and Linda Kaplan and winemaker Michael Stevenson. Now owned by Liz Chambers, Panther Creek produces wines that are still ably made by Stevenson in a bold, forward style. He works closely with famous-name growers, which include Shea, Freedom Hill, Temperance Hill, and Vista Hills, using only prime pinot noir fruit.

Working diligently and gently, Stevenson coaxes succulent character out of his fruit. Good tannin backbone gives his wines a firm structure—they age well—but forward fruit makes them easily accessible. A stylish chardonnay from Elton Vineyard and a good pinot gris from Melrose Vineyard in the Umpqua Valley round out the selections.

SOKOL BLOSSER WINERY

500 NE Sokol Blosser Lane, Dayton, OR
503-864-2282; www.sokolblosser.com
Open all year.

Year founded:	1971
Annual production:	80,000 cases
Signature wine:	Dundee Hills Pinot Noir ($$$)
Premium wine:	Estate Cuvée Pinot Noir ($$$$)
Value wine:	Evolution ($)
Estate vineyards:	Sokol Blosser

Susan Sokol Blosser and Bill Blosser began planting their pinot noir vineyard in 1971, and they released their first wines in 1977. The success of Sokol Blosser Winery is testament to the energy and wisdom of the early winemakers, who took land others saw little use for and transformed it into one of the world's great wine regions. Today, Sokol Blosser is run by the second-generation sibling team Alex and Alison Sokol Blosser, who are adding new energy to the venerable label.

Focusing on organic and sustainable practices throughout the property—the underground barrel cellar was the first LEED-certified winery building in the country—winemaker Russ Rosner crafts impeccable pinot noirs from different blocks of the estate vineyard. Rife with Dundee Hills fruit, these wines are classic expressions of Oregon pinot noir. Despite its pinot fame, more people probably know the winery for its wildly successful, inexpensively priced Evolution white blend and Meditrina red blend.

STOLLER VINEYARDS

16161 NE McDougall Road, Dayton, OR
503-864-3404; www.stollervineyards.com
Open all year.

Year founded:	1995
Annual production:	9000 cases
Signature wine:	Stoller SV Estate Pinot Noir ($$$)
Premium wine:	Cathy's Reserve Pinot Noir ($$$$)
Value wine:	Stoller JV Pinot Noir Rosé ($$)
Estate vineyards:	Stoller

Bill and Cathy Stoller began their vineyard in 1996 by planting 10 acres (4 ha) each of chardonnay and pinot noir. Today they farm 176 acres (71.2 ha) of land that has been in the Stoller family since the 1920s; at one time it was the largest turkey farm in the state. The winery was added in 2005. Designed to state-of-the-art environmental standards, it was the first Gold-Certified LEED winery in the United States.

Winemaker Melissa Burr focuses exclusively on pinot noir and chardonnay from the estate vines. The SV range includes selected lots and barrels of wines made from senior vines, while the JV line is a broader blend of fruit from younger, junior vines from across the estate. All Stoller wines are crafted with skill and precision, delivering an extremely high level of quality. Stoller Vineyards also supplies fruit to a number of premium Willamette Valley wineries, including Chehalem, in which the Stollers are partners.

Eola–Amity Hills Wine Country

Farther south in the Willamette Valley, the Eola–Amity Hills wine country rises up approximately 1000 ft. (304.8 m) from the valley floor, with a profile that, with some imagination, looks a bit like a left-facing seahorse. At its northwesterly head, the 16-mile (25.7-km) chain of north-south hills begins just northeast of the town of Amity, with the northern reaches of the AVA composed of the Amity Hills. The appellation continues southward into the Eola Hills portion, crossing the Yamhill–Polk County line before the tail curves eastward, ending at the Salem Highway, just west of the Willamette River and the city of Salem.

Along these hills, the wine country encompasses slopes starting at 200 ft. (60.9 m) and extending to the ridgetops at around 1160 ft. (353.5 m). Vineyards are scattered throughout the wine country, with exposures that include the expected south and southwestern orientation, but also some east- and west-facing sites.

Soils here are predominantly volcanic in origin and include some Jory, though the majority is of a variant type called Nekia. Like Jory, these are red-colored soils, but they are shallower, at 1 to 3 ft. (30.4–91.4 cm), and contain less clay so they drain water readily. Some sedimentary soils can be found, particularly on the western ridges, and at lower elevations alluvium soils also appear. It is not uncommon for multiple soil types to be found in a single Eola–Amity Hills vineyard.

The Eola–Amity Hills share the general Willamette Valley climate pattern of warm, dry summers and mild, wet winters. There are important mesoclimate differences created by the AVA's location opposite the mouth of the Van Duzer corridor. This gap

EOLA-AMITY HILLS WINE COUNTRY AT A GLANCE

Year established: 2006
Number of wineries: 25
Total acreage: 39,200 acres (15,900 ha)
Vineyard acreage: 1500 acres (607 ha)
Predominant soil type: volcanic Nekia and
    Gelderman, with some sedimentary soils
Vineyard growing degree days:
    1818-2048 (992-1120)

Most important grape varieties
pinot noir, pinot gris, chardonnay, pinot blanc

in the Coast Range funnels marine air straight onto the Eola–Amity Hills, and so it is difficult to generalize about heat accumulation here. At mid elevations, especially on the eastern slopes of the appellation during the growing season, extra heat can linger because of the effects of a frequent inversion layer. At night, cooler air flowing from the Van Duzer corridor to the west climbs over the tops of the Eola–Amity hills and spills down the eastern slopes to the Willamette Valley floor. This cooler air crowds out the valley floor's warmer air, which rises to the vineyards' elevations and helps keep the vines warmer longer. At some elevations on the eastern side, temperatures can actually be higher than on the valley floor, resulting in more rapid ripening at some sites. This effect also means that vineyards on the western side of the wine country are much cooler, since they receive the brunt of the marine flow. Strong diurnal swings in the appellation, most noticeably on the western slopes, help slow overall ripening and help the grapes retain acids.

These environmental distinctions create the character of Eola–Amity Hills wines. The pinot noirs tend to have deeper color as well as darker fruit tones, with flavors of black cherry, black raspberry, plum, and even cassis. Higher acidity gives the wines

The Eola Hills rise up from the floor of the Willamette Valley, providing excellent slopes for vineyards.

a slightly bolder mouth feel, and notes of earthiness provide textural heft. Eola–Amity Hills wines are also noted for nuances of dried herbs and spice.

While pinot noir is the predominant grape of this wine country, the varied mesoclimates sustain more diversity of grapes than is found in the neighboring appellations. Plantings of viognier, tempranillo, gamay noir, grüner veltliner, and even syrah provide interesting accents to the otherwise overwhelming pinot noir, pinot gris, chardonnay complexion of the appellation.

The first vinifera vines in the area were planted in 1971 at what is now Amity Vineyards. Additional vineyards were planted slowly, and by 1983, just 273 acres of wine grapes were producing in the area and only two wineries were making commercial wines. So for years, the Eola–Amity Hills wine country retained a sense of being at the rural edge of things, and was visited less often than wine countries closer to Portland. Today, the appellation has taken on new status as a prime pinot noir wine country. Over 95 vineyards are strewn across the hills, and the region is home to some of the most respected wine labels in Oregon, making Eola–Amity Hills a visible and visited Oregon wine country.

WINERIES AND WINES TO SAMPLE

AMITY VINEYARDS

18150 SE Amity Vineyards Road, Amity, OR
503-835-2362; www.amityvineyards.com
Open all year; limited hours.

Year founded:	1974
Annual production:	13,000 cases
Signature wine:	ECO•WINE Willamette Valley Pinot Noir ($$)
Premium wine:	Winemaker's Reserve Pinot Noir ($$$)
Value wine:	Pinot Blanc ($$)
Estate vineyards:	Amity

Myron Redford is a Willamette Valley wine legend. He arrived in Oregon in 1974, with the purpose of making dry-farmed, cool-climate wines. When famed wine critic Robert M. Parker Jr. wrote in 1985 that an Amity Vineyards wine was "one of the best pinot noirs I have ever tasted," the world began paying more attention to the Willamette Valley, and to Amity Vineyards.

Something of an iconoclast, Myron was an early practitioner of organic and sustainable farming, nonirrigated vines, and using only neutral oak in the making of his wines. Sometimes this approach put him at odds with market fashion, but Myron was content to make famously authentic wines that were true to his sites as well as his soul. Amity pinot noir wines are full of varietal flavors, often with meaty overtones, and restrained in their expression. Besides pinot noir, Myron has led a resurgence in pinot blanc quality, and produces an outstanding set of riesling and gewürztraminer wines, from bone dry to late-harvest sweet. Myron and his wines are true Oregon originals.

BETHEL HEIGHTS VINEYARD

6060 Bethel Heights Road NW, Salem, OR
503-581-2262; www.bethelheights.com
Open during the season; limited hours.

Year founded:	1977
Annual production:	13,000 cases
Signature wine:	Bethel Heights Estate Pinot Noir ($$)
Premium wine:	Casteel Reserve Pinot Noir ($$$$)
Value wine:	Pinot Blanc ($$)
Estate vineyards:	Bethel Heights, Justice

Twin brothers Ted and Terry Casteel (Ted manages the vines, Terry makes the wines) are iconic figures in Oregon, both for their expertise and their generosity in sharing it. Many are the vintners who gained early experience under their tutelage. The winery was founded when the brothers and their spouses (Pat Dudley and Marilyn Webb, respectively) purchased what is today one of the premier pinot noir vineyards in the Northwest. Now joined by the second generation, Ben and Mimi Casteel, Bethel Heights is poised to sustain its legacy well into the future.

The 70 acres (28.3 ha) of producing vines grow fruit that differs among the vineyard blocks, expressed in the Southeast Block and West Block pinot noir releases. The Casteel Reserve is a big, polished estate blend that typifies Eola–Amity Hills character. And don't miss the whites. All Bethel Heights' wines are superbly crafted.

Ted and Ben Casteel of Bethel Heights Vineyard, Oregon.

CRISTOM VINEYARDS

6905 Spring Valley Road NW, Salem, OR
503-375-3068; www.cristomwines.com
Open during the season; limited hours.

Year founded:	1992
Annual production:	10,000 cases
Signature wine:	Sommers Reserve ($$$)
Premium wine:	Jessie Vineyard Pinot Noir ($$$)
Value wine:	Estate Pinot Gris ($$)
Estate vineyards:	Marjorie, Louise, Jessie, Eileen, Emilia, Germaine, Viognier, Syrah

After a 1991 visit to the International Pinot Noir Celebration, Paul Gerrie decided to move his family to Oregon and pursue a passion for pinot noir. Concentrating on the fruit grown at Cristom's 65 acres (26.3 ha) of vineyards, winemaker Steve Doerner takes a noninterventionist stance and lets the land speak in the glass more than his hand.

Each of Cristom's multiple single-estate vineyard pinot noir wines is a crystalline expression of a part of the estate. Eileen Pinot Noir is planted on Jory soil and shows a balanced red cherry focus; Louise Pinot Noir comes from the oldest vines and displays a rich fruitiness with light spice; Marjorie wines are floral and supple with great length; Jessie wines are darker and spicier. While these pinot noirs show the differences of *terroir* among vineyards, Doerner is also a master of blending. His Mt. Jefferson Cuvée and Sommers Reserve are artful expressions of Willamette Valley and vintage character. Cristom has also pioneered syrah and viognier in the Willamette Valley, varieties usually found in warm-climate Oregon.

EVENING LAND VINEYARDS

572 Patterson Street NW, Suite 101, Salem, OR
503-395-2520; www.eveninglandvineyards.com
Open by appointment only.

Year founded:	2007
Annual production:	4000 cases
Signature wine:	Seven Springs Vineyard Estate Pinot Noir ($$$)
Premium wine:	Seven Springs Summum Pinot Noir ($$$$+)
Value wine:	Seven Springs Gamay Noir ($$)
Estate vineyards:	Seven Springs

While the Evening Land name is new to Oregon, the vineyard the winery leases is not. Seven Springs Vineyard has long been a premier source for some of the Willamette Valley's best fruit. Now under long-term lease to the owners of Evening Land Vineyards (which also owns ground in California), the 65-acre (26.3-ha) site is the primary source for the wines bearing the Evening Land name.

Resident winemaker Isabelle Meunier is Burgundy-trained, and works closely with legendary Burgundy-based consulting winemaker Dominique Lafon of Domaine des Comtes Lafon. Together this international team has upgraded the vineyard with the goal of wringing all the *terroir* they can out of this ideal site without imposing any preconceived winemaking style or formula. Early wines—pinot noir and chardonnay—have been exceptionally clean, lean in style, with great fruit depth, an earthy foundation, and plenty of good acidity. The Evening Land Vineyard name is just beginning, but it is clearly a winery intent on making an impact.

ST. INNOCENT WINERY

5657 Zena Road NW, Salem, OR
503-378-1526; www.stinnocentwine.com
Open during the season; limited hours.

Year founded:	1988
Annual production:	6700 cases
Signature wine:	Winemaker's Cuvée Pinot Noir ($$$)
Premium wine:	Shea Vineyard Pinot Noir ($$$)
Value wine:	Freedom Hill Vineyard Pinot Blanc ($$)
Estate vineyards:	Zenith

Owner-winemaker Mark Vlossak was exposed to wine early by his father, a wine importer. Learning from Oregon wine pioneer Fred Arterberry Jr. in the 1980s, Vlossak founded St. Innocent in 1988. He opened a new winery building and tasting room in 2007, which helped him meet the increasing demand for his wines.

Vlossak makes his wines to accompany food, so they tend toward higher acidity, controlled oak, and vibrant flavors. St. Innocent pinot noir wines are made primarily from fruit from eight well-known Willamette Valley vineyards, including Shea, Temperance Hill, Justice, White Rose, and Momtazi. Vlossak has an ownership interest in Zenith Vineyard, which is producing increasing amounts of pinot noir for his classically made wines. St. Innocent also produces vineyard-designated pinot gris and pinot blanc, an unusual practice, and chardonnay.

McMinnville Wine Country

The McMinnville wine country is the Willamette Valley's westernmost subappellation, located just south of the Yamhill–Carlton District and northwest of Eola–Amity Hills. Named after the town of McMinnville, the appellation spans the eastern slopes of a section of Coast Range foothills southwest of the town. The southern boundary of the McMinnville wine country runs along the northeastern edge of the Van Duzer corridor, and vineyards in this part of the appellation experience plenty of daily cooling air that helps extend ripening. The slopes in the north tend to be warmer and drier because of their proximity to the higher Coast Range foothills, and can be ready for harvest earlier.

Soils in the appellation are shallow, well drained, very mixed in type, and among the oldest (38 to 55 million years old) of any in Oregon's wine countries. Both marine sedimentary (Willakenzie) and basalt-based volcanic (Nekia) soils are found. Underlying the soils is an unusual bedrock type not found in other appellations, the Nestucca Formation, which consists of mixed marine sandstone and mudstone with intrusions of marine basalts that originally formed underwater, and is sometimes exposed in vineyard areas. In some vineyards, a mixture of these and other soils can be found.

From such a small appellation, it is difficult to define a distinctive wine style. Nevertheless, pinot noir wines from the McMinnville wine country seem to have greater intensity of dark fruit character than wines from other regions, with somewhat more tannin structure and assertive earth and spice notes. Generally, wines grown on these Coast Range foothill vineyards age well in the cellar and can be a little less approachable when young.

MCMINNVILLE WINE COUNTRY AT A GLANCE

Year established: 2005

Number of wineries: 6

Total acreage: 36,900 acres (14,900 ha)

Vineyard acreage: 600 acres (242.8 ha)

Predominant soil types: marine sediments, volcanic, and mixed sandstone and basalt outcroppings

Vineyard growing degree days: 1858–2059 (1014–1126)

Most important grape varieties

pinot noir, pinot gris, pinot blanc, riesling

Momtazi Vineyard is a biodynamically farmed vineyard in McMinnville wine country, Oregon.

WINERIES AND WINES TO SAMPLE

COEUR DE TERRE VINEYARD

21000 SW Eagle Point Road, McMinnville, OR
503-472-3976; www.cdtvineyard.com
Not open.

Year founded:	1998
Annual production:	1000 cases
Signature wine:	Estate Pinot Noir ($$$)
Premium wine:	Renelle's Block Reserve Pinot Noir ($$$)
Value wine:	Pinot Gris ($$)
Estate vineyards:	Coeur de Terre

Lisa and Scott Neal are diehard pinot noir growers and makers who are proud of managing the entire winegrowing process themselves. In a greenhouse on the estate, they graft their vines from their original 3-acre (1.2-ha) vineyard, Renelle's Block, and work to establish balanced vines that individually produce only a small amount of intense fruit. Vines are treated carefully throughout the year, including shoot placement in the spring by hand, and they use only organic practices.

The resulting wines are intensely personal expressions of the vineyard. The Renelle's Block Pinot Noir displays appealing, focused dried fruit notes accented by oak, while the Estate pinot noir emphasizes more red, bramble fruit character. The winery's pinot gris is crisp and refreshing. Coeur de Terre Vineyard owes its name to a huge heart-shaped rock uncovered during the vineyard planting, a fitting emblem for a family labor of love.

COLEMAN VINEYARD

22734 SW Latham Road, McMinnville, OR
503-843-2707; www.colemanwine.com
Open only by appointment.

Year founded:	1991
Annual production:	5000 cases
Signature wine:	Coleman Estate Pinot Noir ($$)
Premium wine:	Coleman Estate Reserve Pinot Noir ($$$)
Value wine:	Coleman Racy Red Pinot Gris ($)
Estate vineyards:	Coleman

Kim and Randy Coleman are archetypical Oregon vineyard and winery artisans. In 1991, they began planting their vineyard, and today they hand-farm 13.5 acres (5.4 ha) of pinot noir and 9 acres (3.6 ha) of pinot gris. Randy Coleman handles the vineyard side, Kim Coleman focuses on winemaking, and they both perform sales and marketing. Yields are kept to around 2 tons per acre or less, the vines are dry-farmed, and sustainable practices are employed throughout.

Coleman Vineyard pinot noir wines can be dark and rich in concentration, partly reflecting the appellation, but they also have great length and complex aromatics. The Reserve is a blend of Pommard and Dijon clones that combines forward fruitiness with plenty of earth, tannin, and smoky qualities, for a wine that is complex but not overpowering. The pinot gris is a tasty, solid example of the variety, and

the Glacial Rock Late Harvest Pinot Gris is a delightful dessert wine. Coleman Vineyard wines are excellent examples of the *terroir* of the Coast Range foothills.

MAYSARA WINERY

15765 SW Muddy Valley Road, McMinnville, OR
503-843-1234; www.maysara.com
Open all year; limited hours.

Year founded:	1997
Annual production:	13,000 cases
Signature wine:	Jamsheed Pinot Noir ($$)
Premium wine:	Mitra Pinot Noir ($$$$)
Value wine:	Pinot Gris ($$)
Estate vineyards:	Momtazi

Moe and Flora Momtazi took a 532-acre (215.2-ha) abandoned wheat farm in 1997 and transformed it into a biodynamically farmed 200-acre (80.9-ha) vineyard growing prime pinot noir, pinot blanc, pinot gris, and riesling. Adding a winery in 2001 was a natural extension, and today winemaker Tahmiene Momtazi is producing a range of wines that well reflect the characteristics of both the vineyard and the appellation.

The Jamsheed Pinot Noir blends Pommard and Dijon clones from across the Momtazi Vineyard into a harmonious whole. The Asha Pinot Noir shows more intensity of red fruit with some spice, while the Delara Pinot Noir delivers more power, concentration, and darker fruit flavors. Mitra, the winery's top pinot noir, is a richly saturated wine that delivers powerful aromas and flavors of plum and chocolate. All vineyard and winemaking practices at Maysara are Demeter-certified biodynamic.

Ribbon Ridge Wine Country

Ribbon Ridge is a distinctive landform 3.5 mi (5.6 km) long by 1.75 mi (2.8 km) wide and 683 ft. (208.1 m) high of uplifted marine sediments located wholly within the Chehalem Mountains AVA, which itself is within the Willamette Valley AVA. Though sandwiched among other appellations, Ribbon Ridge is a distinctive, independent wine country.

To the northeast, Ribbon Ridge is separated from its sibling appellation of Chehalem Mountains by creek valleys, while the Yamhill–Carlton District AVA is just over Chehalem Creek to the west. The Dundee Hills are close by just to the south. This tucked-in location gives Ribbon Ridge a different climate from its neighbors.

The higher ranges of the surrounding hills protect Ribbon Ridge from storms, so this wine country gets less rainfall than its neighbors. It is also blocked by the Dundee Hills from receiving the cooling marine breezes of the Van Duzer corridor, and so the vineyards along Ribbon Ridge's 200-ft. (60.9-m) and higher hillsides can be slightly warmer. This helps lessen spring frost risk and encourages early season growth, as well as promotes long, consistent ripening toward the end of the growing season.

Though neighboring wine countries contain plenty of volcanic soils, there are none on Ribbon Ridge. The entire landform, described by one local winemaker as a giant meatloaf, consists of weathered marine sedimentary soils. The silty soils are relatively deep, remarkably uniform, and finely textured, with some clay loam. Such soils, in combination with the appellation's warmth and dryness, no doubt contribute to the overall sense of power in the appellation's pinot noir wines. More in the masculine style than those of nearby Dundee Hills, they tend to have dark, saturated colors, thick textures, and plenty of dark fruit concentration. Notes of spice—black pepper, clove, cocoa—seem to also be hallmarks of Ribbon Ridge pinot noir. Chardonnay, pinot gris, and some riesling is also grown here, but pinot noir is the predominant grape of Ribbon Ridge.

RIBBON RIDGE WINE COUNTRY AT A GLANCE

Year established: 2005
Number of wineries: 8
Total acreage: 3500 acres (1400 ha)
Vineyard acreage: 800 acres (323.7 ha)
Predominant soil types: marine sediments
Vineyard growing degree days:
 1892–2016 (1033–1102)

Most important grape varieties
pinot noir, chardonnay

Winemaker Harry Peterson-Nedry was the first to recognize the special potential of this place, when he planted a 37-acre (15-ha) parcel in 1980 he called Ridgecrest Vineyard. Others followed suit, valuing the distinctive character of the area's *terroir*. Though it is Oregon's smallest wine country by size, it punches well above its weight in terms of wine quality.

WINERIES AND WINES TO SAMPLE

BEAUX FRÈRES

15155 NE North Valley Road, Newberg, OR
503-537-1137; www.beauxfreres.com
Not open except for two annual open houses.

Year founded:	1987
Annual production:	4000-6000 cases
Signature wine:	Beaux Frères Vineyard Pinot Noir ($$$$)
Premium wine:	The Upper Terrace Pinot Noir ($$$$)
Value wine:	Willamette Valley Pinot Noir ($$$)
Estate vineyards:	Beaux Frères, Upper Terrace

Beaux Frères is one of Oregon's most prestigious wineries, and not just because famed wine critic Robert M. Parker Jr. is a partner. Michael Etzel manages the vineyards with biodynamic care and makes the wine with a perfectionist's hand. The result is a series of blockbuster pinot noirs that show great power and ageability yet have a delightful fruit density that makes them approachable when young.

Three pinot noir releases typify the focused approach at Beaux Frères. The Beaux Frères Vineyard wine comes from the winery's first vineyard planted in 1988, and is a rich, layered wine with silky texture. The Upper Terrace Vineyard's younger, Dijon clone grapes offer dense wines with more structure. And the Willamette Valley is a blend of grapes from select neighboring vineyards. These wines are great but hard to find. Visit Beaux Frères for tastings and tours during the open houses on Memorial Day weekend in the spring and Thanksgiving weekend in the fall.

BRICK HOUSE VINEYARD

18200 Lewis Rogers Lane, Newberg, OR
503-538-5136; www.brickhousewines.com
Open by appointment only.

Year founded:	1990
Annual production:	3500 cases
Signature wine:	Les Dijonnais Pinot Noir ($$$)
Premium wine:	Evelyn's Pinot Noir ($$$$)
Value wine:	Gamay Noir ($$)
Estate vineyards:	Brick House

Former CBS foreign correspondent Doug Tunnell moved back to his native Oregon, and since 1990 has been making stunning, certified organic and biodynamic pinot noir wines. A pioneer in organic winegrowing, Tunnell's beautiful 40 acres (16.1 ha) of rolling vineyards produce balanced pinot noir and chardonnay fruit that he hand crafts into seamless wines. The pinot noir wines possess earthy elegance, from the red cherry–dominated Les Dijonnais to the darker, lightly spicy Cuvée du Tonnelier. Brick House is also one of the few to make a wine from the Beaujolais grape gamay noir; the winery's version is rich, lively, and usually in short supply because of demand. Brick House's chardonnay wines are consistently among the best in Oregon, displaying wonderful balance of clean, clear fruit with light hazelnut and cream notes.

Doug Tunnell is a quiet force in the Willamette Valley. His personal commitment to sustainable farming has influenced the entire industry. His converted barn winery (two open houses take place in the spring and fall) and individualistic wines are virtually the archetype of Oregon's craft winery ethos.

PATRICIA GREEN CELLARS

15225 NE North Valley Road, Newberg, OR
503-554-0821; www.patriciagreencellars.com
Open by appointment only.

Year founded:	2000
Annual production:	10,000 cases
Signature wine:	Estate Vineyard Old Vine Pinot Noir ($$$)
Premium wine:	Notorious Pinot Noir ($$$$)
Value wine:	Sauvignon Blanc ($$)
Estate vineyards:	The Estate

Patty Green and associate Jim Anderson are famed for the quality and range of pinot noir wines they produce. They work with key vineyards around Willamette Valley to make wines that show the diversity of the region's *terroirs*. In fact, you can take a virtual tasting tour of Oregon's pinot noir country just by sampling a lineup of Green's pinots.

While the 52-acre (21-ha) estate vineyard is an excellent source for old-vine pinot noir fruit (and sauvignon blanc), Green sources widely. The wines they make have a jaunty personality that reflects the winemakers' characters almost as much as their vineyards. The Eason has always been a particular favorite of mine, with rich red fruits and subtle earth tones. But the Notorious blend takes the cake as an intense, layered, succulent pinot noir that is worth cellaring.

Yamhill–Carlton District Wine Country

The Yamhill–Carlton District wine country, about 35 mi (56.3 km) southwest of Portland, forms an irregularly shaped upside-down horseshoe-shaped landform surrounding the small towns of Yamhill and Carlton. The appellation begins at the 200 ft. (60.9 m) elevation along the eroded slopes of the Coast Range foothills due north of McMinnville, and goes up to 1000 ft. (304.8 m). The southeast corner of the appellation abuts the Dundee Hills, and Ribbon Ridge is directly to the northeast. To the west are the mountains of the Coast Range.

The vineyards of the Yamhill–Carlton District are located along the low-lying hills to the east of Yamhill and Carlton and on the eastern edges of the foothills west of the towns. The soils here are derived mostly from ancient marine sediments, much older than the sedimentary soils of Ribbon Ridge or the volcanic soils of other nearby wine countries. Of the Willakenzie soil type, Yamhill–Carlton District vineyards are composed of different specific soils, sharing in common high silica content, low water-holding capacity, and shallow depth—rarely deeper than 3 ft. (91.4 cm).

Climatically, this wine country is well protected from extreme weather. The 3000-ft. (914.4-m) Coast Range peaks prevent significant storms from reaching the area, which is especially beneficial toward the end of the growing season. And the Van Duzer corridor is far enough south to not significantly affect the region's vineyards. The Chehalem Mountains to the northeast also help block continental influences from the Columbia Gorge. With a moderately warm growing season, within the broader area's cool climate, grapes here tend to ripen early, which can be advantageous in a cool year. Yamhill–Carlton District vineyards are often among the first picked in the Willamette Valley.

In keeping with the general traits of pinot noir grown on sedimentary soils, the *terroir* characteristics of Yamhill–Carlton wines lean toward black fruit flavors, higher tannins, and lower acidity. Often succulent in texture, with accents of minerality and dried herbs, wines from this wine country are typically deep and expressive without being heavy or coarse.

Note: In early 2010 the TTB accepted a petition to remove the term "District" from the official name of this AVA. If and when it is approved, this wine country will be called simply Yamhill-Carlton.

YAMHILL–CARLTON DISTRICT WINE COUNTRY AT A GLANCE

Year established: 2005
Number of wineries: 26
Total acreage: 58,100 acres (23,500 ha)
Vineyard acreage: 1300 acres (485.5 ha)
Predominant soil types: marine sediments, sandstone, siltstone
Vineyard growing degree days: 1852–2124 (1011–1162)

Most important grape varieties
pinot noir, pinot gris, chardonnay

Elk Cove's Mount Richmond Vineyard is typical of Yamhill-Carlton District terroir.

WINERIES AND WINES TO SAMPLE

ANNE AMIE VINEYARDS

6580 NE Mineral Springs Road, Carlton, OR
503-864-2991; www.anneamie.com
Open all year.

Year founded:	1999
Annual production:	13,000 cases
Signature wine:	Winemaker's Selection Pinot Noir ($$$)
Premium wine:	L'iris Pinot Noir ($$$$)
Value wine:	Cuvée A Müller Thurgau ($)
Estate vineyards:	Anne Amie, Boisseau, Louise, Marilyn, Justin-Grant, Robert

Originally Chateau Benoit, an important early Willamette Valley winery, Anne Amie Vineyards was purchased and renamed by Portland businessman, physician, and philanthropist Robert Pamplin in 1999. Focusing on pinot noir, pinot blanc, and pinot gris, winemaker Thomas Houseman and vineyard manager Jason Tosch apply attentive practices at all points in the winegrowing process. The result is wines that show craft and elegance as well as *terroir*.

Anne Amie pinot noir wines tend to be big in scale, with expansive fruit and character, as well as grip and structure. The pinot gris and pinot blanc are both fresh and crisp with punchy flavors. The Anne Amie riesling is also excellent, made from old estate vines, and shows great intensity and acid zing.

BELLE PENTE VINEYARD & WINERY

12470 NE Rowland Road, Carlton, OR
503-852-9500; www.bellepente.com
Not open.

Year founded:	1994
Annual production:	5000
Signature wine:	Belle Pente Vineyard Pinot Noir ($$$)
Premium wine:	Estate Reserve Pinot Noir ($$$)
Value wine:	Willamette Valley Pinot Gris ($$)
Estate vineyards:	Belle Pente

Brian and Jill O'Donnell farm their 16 acres (6.4 ha) of pinot noir, pinot gris, and chardonnay, all planted, using organic and biodynamic techniques in order to raise the healthiest and most intense fruit they can. Extensive hand sorting and gentle processing at their gravity-flow winery produces wines that possess both poise and potency. Recent Belle Pente–grown pinot noir wines have ripe black cherry flavors with a unique combination of spice and floral notes that provides satisfying complexity.

Belle Pente has also been something of a riesling revolutionary in the Willamette Valley, and along with a few other wineries has helped drive renewed interest in the variety. They also make very good gewürztraminer, pinot gris, and an unusual early muscat–muscat ottonel blend.

ELK COVE VINEYARDS

27751 NW Olson Road, Gaston, OR
503-985-7760; www.elkcove.com
Open all year.

Year founded:	1974
Annual production:	40,000 cases
Signature wine:	Willamette Valley Pinot Noir ($$)
Premium wine:	Roosevelt Pinot Noir ($$$$)
Value wine:	Willamette Valley Pinot Gris ($$)
Estate vineyards:	Mount Richmond, Five Mountain, La Bohème, Windhill, Roosevelt

Pat and Joe Campbell founded Elk Cove Vineyards in 1974 and brought it to prominence as a leading Oregon winery. Today son Adam Godlee Campbell manages the winery and makes the wines, expanding the early reputation for stylish wines. Focusing on pinot noir from estate vineyards, Campbell uses just 20 acres (8 ha) out of 180 available acres (72.8 ha) for his single-vineyard pinot noirs. The Roosevelt Pinot Noir is one of the most complex pinot noir wines produced in the Willamette Valley, while the La Bohème shows greater acidity and verve.

Besides pinot noir, Campbell is a white wine specialist, and makes a range of excellent rieslings, a bracing pinot gris, and a fruity pinot blanc. Though Elk Cove's premier pinot noirs can be difficult to obtain, both the Willamette Valley Pinot Noir and

Willamette Valley Pinot Gris are widely available and offer excellent value.

LEMELSON VINEYARDS

12020 NE Stag Hollow Road, Carlton, OR
503-852-6619; www.lemelsonvineyards.com
Open all year; limited hours.

Year founded:	1999
Annual production:	12,000 cases
Signature wine:	Thea's Selection Pinot Noir ($$$)
Premium wine:	Jerome Reserve Pinot Noir ($$$$)
Value wine:	Tikka's Run Pinot Gris ($$)
Estate vineyards:	Stermer, Meyer, Chestnut Hill, Briscoe, Johnson, Wascher, Rocky Noel

After a diverse background in law and environmental policy, in 1995 Eric Lemelson planted 2 acres (0.8 ha) of pinot noir and pinot gris on a southeast slope at his Carlton-area farm. That was it: he was hooked. Today Lemelson Vineyards organically farms approximately 158 acres (63.9 ha) of pinot noir, pinot gris, chardonnay, and riesling. In concert with winemaker Anthony King, Lemelson makes elegant wines in a beautiful, state-of-the-art winery designed to capture the specific essence of the grape.

While each of Lemelson's individual bottlings shows a different aspect of its vineyards, including blends from fruit grown at different sites, they have a consistency of sweet fruit, silky textures, fine-grained tannins, and dried herb accents. Lemelson's pinot noir wines admirably combine finesse and depth. Not to be missed as well is Lemelson's superb dry riesling and the usually exuberant pinot gris.

PENNER-ASH WINE CELLARS

15771 NE Ribbon Ridge Road, Newberg, OR
503-554-5545; www.pennerash.com
Open all year; limited hours.

Year founded:	1998
Annual production:	8000 cases
Signature wine:	Willamette Valley Pinot Noir ($$$)
Premium wine:	Pas de Nom ($$$$)
Value wine:	Rubeo ($$)
Estate vineyards:	Dussin

Lynn Penner-Ash is one of the most experienced winemakers in the Willamette Valley. She started at Stag's Leap Wine Cellars in Napa Valley and then moved to Oregon to shepherd Rex Hill's success from 1988 through 2002. She left Rex Hill to start, with husband Ron Penner-Ash, the gorgeous winery that today sits atop a Yamhill–Carlton District hill surrounded by vines.

Using her knowledge and skills, Penner-Ash sources fruit from the best vineyards in the state. Her single-vineyard pinot noir wines are exceptional, especially the Carabella and Shea Vineyard releases. Few know better how the grape grows in the Willamette Valley, and Penner-Ash is always able to get the best out of the fruit. Hers are signature Oregon pinot noir wines. And the more adventurous should seek out the small-production viognier that Penner-Ash makes.

SHEA WINE CELLARS

12321 NE Highway 240, Newberg, OR
503-241-6527; www.sheawinecellars.com
Not open.

Year founded:	1996
Annual production:	5500 cases
Signature wine:	Estate Pinot noir ($$$)
Premium wine:	Homer Pinot noir ($$$$)
Value wine:	Chardonnay ($$$)
Estate vineyards:	Shea

Winegrowers Dick and Deirdre Shea have built their Shea Vineyards into one of the most prominent pinot noir names in the world. Starting in 1996, they took over a previously planted sedimentary-soil vineyard and transformed it into a cherished source of pinot noir fruit for some of Oregon's most prominent producers.

Approximately 25 percent of the vineyard's yield is used in the making of Shea Wine Cellars wine. Winemaker Drew Voit and vineyard manager Javier Marin together with Dick and Deirdre Shea produce perhaps the ultimate expression of Shea Vineyard *terroir*. Different bottlings from different blocks of the vineyard reflect different characters. The Homer release blends multiple blocks for a silky, layered, complex, weighty wine that shows why Shea Vineyard fruit is so prized.

SOTER VINEYARDS

10880 NE Mineral Springs Road, Carlton, OR
503-662-5600; www.sotervineyards.com
Open by appointment only.

Year founded:	1997
Annual production:	3000 cases
Signature wine:	Beacon Hill Brut Rosé ($$$$)
Premium wine:	Mineral Springs Vineyard Pinot Noir ($$$$)
Value wine:	North Valley Pinot Noir ($$)
Estate vineyards:	Mineral Springs

Tony Soter spent much of his career building a stellar reputation in California by making wine for such cult brands as Araujo, Spottswoode, Viader, and Dalle Valle, as well as for his own Etude brand. In the late 1990s, he moved his family and business to the Willamette Valley, making the kind of pinot noir wines he felt could only be accomplished in Oregon.

At his Mineral Springs Estate Vineyard, Soter planted 32 acres (12.8 ha) of pinot noir, and released his first vintage from the site in 2005. The initial release displays a mélange of fruit flavors coupled with spice notes that create an exotic character. Soter also makes exceptional sparkling wines, including a Brut Rosé that bursts with flavor and a stylish Blanc de Blancs that is the equal of any Champagne. He harvests his grapes with more ripeness than is traditional for sparkling wine, and minimizes the amount of sug-

ar used in the bottle-fermentation, resulting in rich, bright wines that deliver superb flavor. Few wineries make wine as finely as Soter.

WILLAKENZIE ESTATE

19143 NE Laughlin Road, Yamhill, OR
503-662-3280; www.willakenzie.com
Open all year.

Year founded:	1991
Annual production:	18,000–20,000 cases
Signature wine:	Pierre Leon Estate Pinot Noir ($$$)
Premium wine:	Triple Black Slopes Pinot Noir ($$$$$)
Value wine:	Estate Pinot Blanc ($$)
Estate vineyards:	WillaKenzie

WillaKenzie Estate is named for the sedimentary soil series that underlie the winery's 102 acres (41.2 ha) of predominantly pinot noir vines. Founded by Bernard and Ronni Lacroute in 1991, with the winery and tasting room built in 1995, WillaKenzie Estate is a virtual exploration of pinot noir from a single site. A variety of cuvées offer different expressions depending on the section of the vineyard the fruit came from and the clonal composition of the wine. Limited releases of single-clone pinot noir (Dijon 113, 114, 115, and 777) make for a fascinating comparison.

Winemaker Thibaud Mandet uses strictly sustainable methods for the equally sustainably farmed grapes. WillaKenzie was the first winery to receive the Oregon Certified Sustainable Wine designation. In addition to pinot noir, the winery also makes very fine pinot gris, pinot blanc, pinot meunier, and gamay noir.

Southern Oregon Wine Country

The establishment of the Southern Oregon appellation gave official status and public awareness to what wine industry people knew all along: there was a significant other half to Oregon's wine world. Unlike the tendency to create micro-AVAs in the cool-climate northern part of the state, the winemakers of southern Oregon knew that establishing an overarching appellation that defined the entirety of their warm-climate growing regions would bring needed attention the region's wines. Though all the wineries within the appellation of Southern Oregon are actually located within one of its subappellations (and listed as such here), the definition of Southern Oregon wine country is important to understanding the state's wine character as a whole.

Southern Oregon wine country is roughly 125 mi (201.1 km) long and 60 mi (96.5 km) across at its widest point. It begins in the north about 25 mi (40.2 km) below Eugene, where it touches the southernmost border of the Willamette Valley wine country, and extends south to the Oregon-California border. It takes in the preexisting Rogue Valley, Umpqua Valley, and Applegate Valley AVAs, and the Red Hill of Douglas County, Oregon, appellation. By adding a viticulturally similar, significant area of land between the Rogue and Umpqua appellations, the Southern Oregon AVA became the überappellation that delimits the majority of Oregon's warm-climate vineyards.

Like the Willamette Valley, southern Oregon wine country is protected from ocean air intrusion by the Coast Range in the northern portion and by the Klamath Mountains in the south. Unlike the Willamette Valley, southern Oregon vineyards are at higher elevations—from 900 to 2000 ft. (274.3–609.6 m)—and receive more growing heat. Nearly all of southern Oregon's vineyard areas are classified as warm to very warm. Optimum growing degree days for the appellation range between 2279 and 2716 (1248–1491), compared to 2014–2437 (1101–1336) GDD in the Willamette Valley. This extra heat leads to harvests up to 10 days earlier in southern Oregon

SOUTHERN OREGON WINE COUNTRY AT A GLANCE

Year established: 2005

Subappellations: 4 (Applegate Valley, Red Hill of Douglas County, Oregon, Rogue Valley, Umpqua Valley)

Number of wineries: 60 (located within subappellations)

Total acreage: 2,283,600 acres (924,500 ha)

Vineyard acreage: 2500 acres (1011 ha)

Vineyard growing degree days: 1921-2716 (1049-1491)

Most important grape varieties
cabernet sauvignon, syrah, merlot, chardonnay, tempranillo, viognier

for the same grape variety grown in the Willamette Valley.

Soils and topography of the wine country are also different. Southern Oregon is more mountainous and less homogenous, with good vineyard sites not as obviously abundant as in the north. Successful vineyards can be found on varied geologic features, from steep mountainside slopes to isolated gentle hillsides and even flat bench land. Soils are tremendously varied, but generally developed from decomposed mountainous sediments that are over 200 million years old and have been subject to a variety of geologic forces. Each individual valley and slope has its own composition, which often includes granite rock face erosion, alluvial deposits, and gravel banks; soil types throughout the region vary widely.

Southern Oregon is also considerably drier, especially in the critical growing months between April and September. An average of southern Oregon weather stations shows precipitation of a little more than 34 in. (86.3 cm) annually, compared to an average of just over 43 in. (109.2 cm) in the Willamette Valley.

The terrain of Southern Oregon wine country is more rocky and mountainous than in the Willamette Valley.

Frost-free days, an important measure of loss risk caused by late spring or early fall cold snaps, are fewer in southern Oregon, at an average of 175 days, than in the cooler climate Willamette Valley, which averages 184 days. This number is partly because most of southern Oregon's vineyards are enough inland that they don't gain the benefits of moderating marine weather and partly because of their high elevation. Though the difference in frost-free days may seem paltry, those nine days can be enough to define the difference between a successful vintage and one with measurable crop damage. Indeed, southern Oregon vineyards can face the twin threats of frost damage at the fringes of the growing season and heat damage in the heart of the summer. Careful vineyard manage-

ment is essential, and most vineyards find irrigation a necessity.

Multiple rivers—Umpqua, Applegate, Illinois, Rogue—course through southern Oregon's wine countries, creating many small valleys with varied hillsides, exposures, and mesoclimates. Southern Oregon's wine territory is not part of the Columbia River drainage, and was not subject to the influence of basalt flows or Missoula Floods.

Southern Oregon's hugely varied and relatively remote geography has long made it a land of loners and mavericks. The area's earliest modern winemakers and growers fit right into the local culture, taking fierce pride in doing things independently. Richard Sommer, a perfect example of this ethic, was the founder of Oregon's modern wine industry, and set a tone of creative independence that still permeates much of Oregon's wine culture. A testament to the region's winegrowing capabilities as much as to the spirit of its early winemakers, most of the foundational names of southern Oregon winemaking—Philippe and Bonnie Girardet, the Scott Henry family, the Wisnovsky family, Ted Gerber, and Bob and Lelo Kerivan—are still actively involved in advancing southern Oregon's wine reputation, and many have wineries now run by a second generation of family members.

Despite individual wineries achieving local success, by 2000 the area still had a fragmented wine identity and was home to only about 20 wineries. Even Oregonian wine lovers viewed the area south of Eugene as a scattering of disparate wineries among the mountains and valleys of a region few people visited. Southern Oregon lacked a major population hub; Medford had not yet seen its growth spurt. You had to drive many hours south from Portland or Eugene, or even more hours north of San Francisco, to visit obscure wineries. Where was the Umpqua Valley, anyway?

Those who made the effort to tour southern Oregon's wineries found a region populated by committed, individualistic winegrowers and winemakers whose vineyards and tasting rooms, while frequently out of the mainstream, offered a distinctive wine experience. Visitors found both enthusiasm and an unexpected diversity of wine styles and varieties. For many, myself included, the first taste of an Oregon wine was not one of the state's vaunted pinot noirs, but a more prosaic bottle, such as an unfamiliar baco noir or perhaps a quirky blend called Druid's Fluid. Orthodox wines were made in southern Oregon, but often the outliers stood out. And for that, the region seemed to get little critical respect.

In the years since 2000, a renewed energy has suffused southern Oregon. A strong economy in the first years of the decade boosted population, investment, and travel in the region. Especially around Medford and the I-5 corridor between Grants Pass and Ashland, new wine-business capital has flowed into the area for both vineyard and winery development.

In the early part of the decade, Laurent Montalieu, then winemaker at WillaKenzie Estate in the

Some southern Oregon vineyards are successfully planted on relatively flat land.

Willamette Valley but with deep roots in southern Oregon winemaking, took a group of seasoned Willamette Valley winemakers to view the newly developed Del Rio Vineyard in southern Oregon. What they saw was a large state-of-the-art vineyard producing consistently high-quality, warm-climate fruit. The Willamette Valley winemakers were hooked. Over the next few years, a variety of new, warm-climate wines made from southern Oregon grapes began appearing from previously pinot-only producers. Ironically, it took a few pinot makers using southern Oregon fruit to spur the interest of wine critics in Oregon's warm-climate strengths.

Also vital were the efforts of a handful of new wineries that capitalized on southern Oregon's history of wine experimentation and upped the ante for the region's wine quality. In the 1990s, winemaker Sarah Powell produced wines of high caliber that attracted new attention to the region. Toward the end of that decade, Earl and Hilda Jones moved to southern Oregon specifically to grow and make tempranillo, a Spanish varietal that had never been planted in the Northwest and was little exploited anywhere in North America. With an approach that echoed Richard Sommer's, the Joneses had studied climate records around the country to find the closest possible match to tempranillo's native Rioja region of Spain. They found their match outside of Roseburg in the Umpqua Valley AVA, ironically not far from Sommer's Hillcrest Vineyard. And like Sommer, they began planting grape varieties at their Abacela Vineyards that were entirely new to the Northwest. By employing a scientific approach to their experimentation and paying careful attention to vineyard management and wine quality, Abacela began attracting both critical and popular attention.

Influenced by such successes, new energy has been augmenting southern Oregon's population of long-established wineries. In 2002, Terry and Sue Brandborg established Brandborg Vineyard and Winery in the northwestern portion of the Umpqua Valley AVA, where a relatively cool, marine-influenced climate gives them top-quality pinot noir. Stephen and Gloria Reustle established Prayer Rock Vineyards in the Umpqua Valley in 2001, producing tempranillo, pinot noir, riesling, and the first grüner veltliner wine made in North America. Pat and Loree Spangler purchased an established Umpqua Valley vineyard and winery in 2004, overhauled the winemaking, and have been producing award-winning cabernet franc, viognier, sauvignon blanc, and merlot wines.

In the Rogue and Applegate Valley AVAs, the same thing was happening. In 2002, Kara Olmo and Greg Paneitz brought their winemaking training to Wooldridge Creek Vineyards, adding a new level of wine quality to a venerable vineyard operation. Chris Martin and family purchased the pioneer Troon Vineyard and crafted impressive zinfandel wines, invested in a new tasting room, and developed new estate plantings of less grown varieties. Anne Root and family created EdenVale winery; RoxyAnn Winery was formed outside of Medford; Trium wines were introduced by three area winegrowers.

The commitment of southern Oregon's winegrowers has brought the region into the Northwest wine mainstream, and helped broaden and diversify the market's understanding of the concept of Oregon wine.

Umpqua Valley Wine Country

Long before it became wine country, this area was known as The Hundred Valleys of the Umpqua because of the diversity of landforms that surround the Umpqua River and its tributaries. Three mountain ranges—Klamath, Coast, and Cascades—converge here, resulting in numerous ancient faults, folds, and outcroppings, as well as soil types that include silt, clay, sediments, and alluvial dirt. The lack of uniformity is both a challenge and an opportunity. The diversity of landforms makes it difficult to summarize the climate and topography of the region, but it offers potential for suitable sites for growing most any of the main wine grape varieties.

The northern part of the wine country around the

town of Elkton, for instance, is influenced by marine air coming up the main stem of the Umpqua River. This factor, plus higher elevations, creates sites that can be cool, approaching the same coolness as parts of the Willamette Valley. A more intermediate climate reigns in the wine country's midsection, northwest of Roseburg, where some of the state's earliest vines were planted. Here individual sites can be much warmer, yet still retain sufficient coolness and diurnal variation to ripen traditional cool-climate varieties. Just south of Roseburg, warmer temperatures prevail, and the winemaking focus is more on warm-climate grapes grown primarily on hillside slopes.

The Umpqua Valley wine country is generally wetter than the rest of southern Oregon, with annual

UMPQUA VALLEY WINE COUNTRY AT A GLANCE

Year established: 1984
Subappellations: 1 (Red Hill Douglas County)
Number of wineries: 21
Total acreage: 693,300 acres (280,600 ha)
Vineyard acreage: 1200 acres (485.6 ha)
Predominant soil types: no predominant type
Vineyard growing degree days
   1895–2468 (1035–1353)

Most important grape varieties
pinot noir, pinot gris, chardonnay, tempranillo, merlot, syrah, cabernet sauvignon

Planting a new vineyard block at Abacela Winery in the Upmqua Valley wine country.

precipitation ranging between 30 and 60 in. (76.2–152.4 cm). The northern part of the appellation tends to receive more rain, though everywhere in the wine country the majority of precipitation falls outside of the growing season. The area has low frost risk, with an average growing season of 200 days, though in some locations it can be as short as 175 days.

Summers are warm, with average July maximum temperatures between 81.5°F and 85.6°F (27.5°C –29.7°C), and dry, with only 15 percent of annual precipitation arriving between April and October. Winters are also generally mild, with average minimum temperatures rarely falling below 32°F (0°C),

and so growers infrequently employ special winter or frost mitigation procedures.

Most vineyards in the Umpqua Valley are sited between 350 and 800 ft. (106.6–243.8 m) elevation, and while some are on flat alluvial fans and gravel benches, most are on hillside slopes and rarely go above 1000 ft. (304.8 m). Over 70 different soils are found in the vineyards of the appellation, derived from metamorphic, sedimentary, and volcanic materials, so there is much diversity for vignerons to explore.

Because of the diversity of growing conditions within the appellation, Umpqua Valley produces many different wines. From the northern portions of the appellation come good examples of early ripening grapes, including pinot noir, gewürztraminer, riesling, and pinot gris made into well-styled wines. Elsewhere in the region, the more expected warm-adapted grapes are grown, including syrah, cabernet sauvignon, and merlot, plus tempranillo. The Umpqua Valley is also home to a number of grapes not widely grown elsewhere in the Northwest, including garnacha, albariño, grüner veltliner, dolcetto, malbec, and petit verdot.

WINERIES AND WINES TO SAMPLE

ABACELA WINERY

12500 Lookingglass Road, Roseburg, OR
541-679-6642; www.abacela.com
Open all year.

Year founded:	1995
Annual production:	10,000 cases
Signature wine:	Tempranillo Estate ($$$)
Premium wine:	Tempranillo Reserve ($$$$)
Value wine:	Vintner's Blend ($$)
Estate vineyards:	Fault Line

Earl and Hilda Jones found their vineyard home in Roseburg after searching the country for the place whose climate best matched the Rioja region of Spain, the home of their favorite wine grape, tempranillo. They released the first commercial tempranillo wine in the Northwest (perhaps America) in 1997. Gratifyingly, Abacela continues to emphasize varieties that are seldom seen in the Northwest.

All of Abacela's wines are superbly crafted. The signature tempranillo red wines have succulent fruit well framed with spice, earth, leather, and big black fruits. The garnacha is delightful, with blackberry and licorice tones. Dolcetto, malbec, and petit verdot are unusual and unusually tasty varieties that complement the more expected syrah, merlot, cabernet franc, and blends. Abacela's white wines are limited to two but they are both standouts: a crisp, memorable albariño, and a viognier well balanced with fruit and acidity. Abacela has earned a position as one of the Northwest's signature producers.

BRANDBORG VINEYARD & WINERY

345 First Street, Elkton, OR
541-584-2870; www.brandborgwine.com
Open all year.

Year founded:	2002
Annual production:	8500 cases
Signature wine:	Benchlands Pinot Noir ($$)
Premium wine:	Ferris Wheel Estate Pinot Noir ($$$)
Value wine:	Rosé of Pinot Noir ($)
Estate vineyards:	Ferris Wheel

Terry and Sue Brandborg shrewdly chose a viticulturally promising, out-of-the-way location for their winery when they moved from California to the northwest reaches of the Umpqua Valley appellation. The land around Elkton has supported pinot noir since 1972, yet it is still underdeveloped and affords great opportunity for vineyards.

The Brandborgs quickly established a reputation for first-class winemaking, sourcing fruit from southern Oregon vineyards while they developed their own distinctly cool-climate—under-2000-GDD (1093)—vineyard. Well respected for stylish pinot noirs that prove there are good sources of pinot noir in the cooler reaches of the appellation, Brandborg Winery has brought new attention to pinot noir wines from southern Oregon. It also produces excellent riesling, pinot gris, pinot blanc, and gewürztraminer, and a very fine Umpqua Valley cabernet franc.

REUSTLE–PRAYER ROCK VINEYARDS

960 Cal Henry Road, Roseburg, OR
541-459-6060; www.reustlevineyards.com
Open all year.

Year founded:	2001
Annual production:	5200 cases
Signature wine:	Grüner Veltliner ($$)
Premium wine:	Tempranillo Reserve ($$$)
Value wine:	Riesling ($$)
Estate vineyards:	Prayer Rock

It's a big leap from New York City to a remote vineyard in the Umpqua Valley, but Stephen and Gloria Reustle have accomplished it with grace. They planted the beautiful vineyard in 2001 and are now growing an unusual mixture of grape varieties: pinot noir, tempranillo, syrah, riesling, viognier, sauvignon blanc, merlot, grenache, pinot gris, and grüner veltliner. The 2005 launch of the Reustle–Prayer Rock Vineyards grüner veltliner was the first commercial release of the varietal in the Northwest, and perhaps in North America.

The wines from Reustle–Prayer Rock display an emphasis on careful winemaking and varietal correctness, making for a strong lineup. The riesling is particularly finely executed, with ripe off-dry concentration and good balancing acidity; the tempranillo is balanced and plush, but with substantial structure; the syrah is succulent and satisfying. The one wine to watch from this winery is definitely their grüner veltliner, which seems to advance in sophistication with every new vintage.

SPANGLER VINEYARDS

491 Winery Lane, Roseburg, OR
541-679-9654; www.spanglervineyards.com
Open all year.

Year founded:	2004
Annual production:	3000 cases
Signature wine:	Cabernet Franc ($$)
Premium wine:	Estate Cabernet Sauvignon ($$$)
Value wine:	Sauvignon Blanc ($$)
Estate vineyards:	Spangler

Resurrecting the old La Garza vineyard and winery in 2004, Pat and Loree Spangler moved into the Umpqua Valley wine world with a bang. Demanding high fruit quality from their vineyard sources and applying an energetic commitment to diligent winemaking, Spangler Vineyards has become a potent force in southern Oregon winemaking.

Spangler may be the best in Oregon at making wine from the underappreciated cabernet franc grape. Ripe, aromatic, and full of chocolate and oak, this is a wonderful wine. Two other consistent favorites are the reasonably priced viognier, and the densely packed estate cabernet sauvignon. Spangler Vineyards accomplishes a rare thing: it manages to make excellent wines across the board, even though you would think that might be hard to do with its 17 individual releases.

Red Hill Douglas County, Oregon, Wine Country

Yes, there is an Oregon wine country with but a single vineyard: it is officially called the Red Hill Douglas County, Oregon, AVA. The single winery connected to the single vineyard isn't quite within the borders of the appellation; its operations are at a lower elevation in the town of Oakland.

Red Hill Douglas County, Oregon, is located within the Umpqua Valley and Southern Oregon appellations. This wine country is located to the east of highway I-5 near the town of Oakland between the 800-ft. (243.8-m) contour line and at about 1200 ft. (365.7 m) elevation. Composed of deep Jory soils,

RED HILL DOUGLAS COUNTY, OREGON, WINE COUNTRY AT A GLANCE

Year established: 2005
Number of wineries: 0
Total acreage: 5600 acres (2200 ha)
Vineyard acreage: 220 acres (89 ha)
Predominant soil types: volcanic Jory
Vineyard growing degree days:
    1802–1910 (983–1043)

Most important grape varieties
gewürztraminer, pinot noir

ROGUE VALLEY WINE COUNTRY AT A GLANCE

Year established: 1991
Subappellations: 1 (Applegate Valley)
Number of wineries: 17
Total acreage: 1,146,200 acres (463,800 ha)
Vineyard acreage: 1900 acres (796.9 ha)
Predominant soil types: granitic alluvial gravels
Vineyard growing degree days:
    1982–2716 (1083–1491)

Most important grape varieties
merlot, cabernet sauvignon, chardonnay, syrah, pinot noir

the hill is part of a broader complex of basalt uplifts in this part of the Umpqua Valley.

As in much of the Umpqua Valley, local landforms create small climate pockets. The Red Hill Douglas County, Oregon, appellation appears to be somewhat cooler than the average for the area, and gets a bit more rain. Though this wine country is composed of but a single vineyard, it meets all the criteria established by the TTB for becoming an official AVA.

Rogue Valley Wine Country

In a region of over a million acres threaded with mountain ranges, river valleys, rock escarpments, and high-elevation plateaus, it takes hardy souls to seek out vineyard land. Talk to veteran grape farmers and winery owners of southern Oregon's expansive Rogue Valley wine country, and you'll soon gain an appreciation for the dedication of these people to crafting wines in a rough, rural landscape that is sometimes difficult to access.

The Rogue Valley's warm climate is as conducive to wine-relaxing as it is to winegrowing.

The Rogue River is the dominant geographical feature of this wine country. It flows south into the AVA at the town of Shady Cove, turns west outside of Eagle Point, and flows through Gold Hill and out of the AVA northeast of Grants Pass. It is misleading to call this wine country the Rogue Valley, since that implies a single valley. In fact, vineyards in the appellation run along three valleys of Rogue tributary rivers: the Illinois, Applegate, and Bear Creek.

The Illinois Valley follows the course of the southernmost part of the Illinois River, a major tributary that branches off from the Rogue far to the northwest, outside of the appellation. It roughly forms the southwestern border of the wine country, generally following Highway 199 southwest of Grants Pass, through the towns of Selma, Kerby, and Cave Junction, until it stops almost at the state border. Because of its relative proximity to the coast, this portion of the Rogue Valley AVA receives some marine influence, resulting in a cooler, wetter climate than in much of the rest of the appellation.

The next valley to the northeast is the Applegate Valley, which is a separate appellation. Farther east, Bear Creek Valley, with the population center of Medford, is home to the largest number of wineries in the AVA, and has easy access via Interstate 5. Bear Creek itself flows southeast from the Rogue River east of Gold Hill down to Ashland. Growing degree days in vineyard locations range from 2387 to 2716 (1308–1491), making Rogue Valley the warmest part of the southern Oregon region. Average July maximum temperature is 89°F (31.6°C).

Vineyard sites are located from 900 ft. (274.3 m) to as high as 2200 ft. (670.5), and soil types are not only quite varied but little researched for viticultural suitability. Vineyards sites are often on alluvial fans at the base of mountains or on benches that rise 100 to 300 ft. (30.4–91.4 m) off a valley floor, and more

rarely along the sloped sides of mountains. Because of the high elevations, the growing season in the Rogue Valley is short, ranging from 137 to 169 days, depending on location. Frost is a risk at both ends of the season.

The Rogue Valley's heat makes it prime growing territory for the big Bordeaux and Rhône varieties. Cabernet sauvignon, merlot, and syrah are popular grapes, as are tempranillo and cabernet franc, plus chardonnay, viognier, and pinot gris. Even a bit of good pinot noir is made in some higher elevation vineyards of the Rogue Valley.

WINERIES AND WINES TO SAMPLE

BRIDGEVIEW VINEYARDS AND WINERY

Main winery & tasting room:
4210 Holland Loop Road, Cave Junction, OR
Applegate Valley tasting room:
16995 North Applegate Road, Grants Pass, OR
541-592-4688; www.bridgeviewwine.com
Cave Junction tasting room open all year. Tasting room in Applegate Valley open in season, limited hours.

Year founded:	1979
Annual production:	80,000 cases
Signature wine:	Blue Moon Riesling ($)
Premium wine:	Black Beauty Red Blend ($$$)
Value wine:	Blue Moon Riesling ($)
Estate vineyards:	Bridgeview, Bear Creek, Applegate

Bob and Lelo Kerivan began with what amounted to a hobby 2-acre (0.8-ha) vineyard and parlayed it into one of Oregon's largest wineries, primarily by offering popular, well-priced wines. Based at the extreme southern end of Oregon, Bridgeview has added a tasting room in the more accessible Applegate Valley, where they also have an estate vineyard.

Winemaker René Eichmann produces a range of wines including value-priced chardonnay, viognier, gewürztraminer, cabernet-merlot blend, merlot, pinot noir, and early muscat. The Black Beauty line offers more substantive versions of merlot, syrah,

Pheasant Hill Vineyard is part of the Trium label, producing Bordeaux-style blends from Rogue Valley grapes.

cabernet sauvignon, and a red blend. Bridgeview may, however, be best known for its Blue Moon line of wines that come in a cobalt blue bottle, and in one case, come in a blue bottle shaped like a smiling half moon.

EDENVALE WINERY

2310 Voorhies Road, Medford, OR
541-512-2955; www.edenvalewines.com
Open all year.

Year founded:	1999
Annual production:	7500 cases
Signature wine:	Syrah ($$)
Premium wine:	Tempranillo ($$$)
Value wine:	Midsummer's Eve ($)
Estate vineyards:	uses purchased fruit

EdenVale Winery is located on some of the oldest agricultural land in the Rogue Valley. Anne Root is the driving force behind EdenVale, whose Rogue Valley tasting room in the restored Voorhies Mansion outside of Medford is a mandatory stop for any southern Oregon wine tourer.

Winemaker Ashley Campanella uses fruit from selected area vineyards to craft lush, well-proportioned wines. The EdenVale syrah and tempranillo have earned strong, well-deserved reputations for style and varietal purity. The cabernet franc is a sleeper worth seeking out: like with most of EdenVale's reds, this wine is complex and velvety, with plenty of richness and length.

FORIS VINEYARDS

654 Kendall Road, Cave Junction, OR
1-800-843-6747; www.foriswine.com
Open all year.

Year founded:	1986
Annual production:	27,500 cases
Signature wine:	Pinot Noir ($$)
Premium wine:	Maple Ranch Pinot Noir ($$)
Value wine:	Barrel Fermented Chardonnay ($)
Estate vineyards:	Gerber, Maple Ranch, Cedar, Holland, Three Creeks

Ted Gerber purchased hillside acreage in 1971 in the extreme southern part of Oregon, an area that had yet to see any vinifera vineyards, and transformed it into one of the region's most important wineries. The 20 acres (8 ha) of vineyard land around the winery is unusual: it is a 50-year accumulation of placer mine rock tailings, essentially the upturned rock of ancient stream beds. Vines on this ground dig deep for nourishment and water drains easily.

Foris is famous for cleanly made wines at good prices. Proud of its pinot noir wines, the winery also produces a range of excellent white wines, an intriguing rich cabernet sauvignon reserve that is built to age, and a line of Fly Over wines—red blends and white blends—that make reference (according to one story) to the habit of wine writers to fly over southern Oregon on their way from San Francisco to the Willamette Valley wine country outside of Portland.

ROXYANN WINERY

285 Hillcrest Road, Medford, OR
541-776-2315; www.roxyann.com
Open all year.

Year founded:	2002
Annual production:	15,000 cases
Signature wine:	Claret ($$)
Premium wine:	Parsons Family Reserve ($$$$)
Value wine:	Pinot Gris ($$)
Estate vineyards:	Hillcrest Vineyard

With organically farmed vineyards amid a 100-year old orchard east of Medford, RoxyAnn Winery embodies the rapid advancement of southern Oregon winemaking. Under the direction of regional wine veteran Michael Donovan, RoxyAnn has become a key Oregon winery by producing outstanding warm-climate wines.

Newly named winemaker John Quinones brings a wealth of experience to the winery, along with the intent to maintain the focus on farming the best possible fruit. He concentrates on texture and balance in his wines. The winery led the effort to allow the term claret on Oregon wine labels, and their version is perennially among the best in the Northwest. Their Parsons Family Reserve is a rare and intense red blend, the viognier is full and delicious, and the two RoxyAnn pinot gris bottlings are standouts.

TRIUM WINES

7112 Rapp Lane, Talent, OR
541-535-6093; www.triumwines.com
Open during the season; limited hours.

Year founded:	2003
Annual production:	1000 cases
Signature wine:	Trium Growers' Cuvée ($$)
Premium wine:	Evans Creek Cabernet Sauvignon ($$$)
Value wine:	Pheasant Hill Pinot Gris ($$)
Estate vineyards:	Evans Creek, Gold, Pheasant Hill

Three premier southern Oregon growers decided that they wanted to bottle wine from their own fruit, in addition to selling fruit to other winemakers. The owners of Pheasant Hill Vineyard (Laura and Kurt Lotspeich), Gold Vineyard (Randy and Rebecca Gold), and Evans Creek Vineyard (Vernon Hixson and Nancy Tappan) hired expert winemaker Peter Rosback to produce wine from their fruit.

Trium wines are finely crafted examples of southern Oregon fruit. The Growers' Cuvée is a rich, dark, Bordeaux-style blend that delivers sumptuous flavors and has become an important example of the power of Rogue Valley red blends. Also made are a substantial cabernet sauvignon from Evans Creek Vineyard, viognier from Gold Vineyard, and pinot gris from Pheasant Hill Vineyard, which are well made, delicious wines.

Applegate Valley Wine Country

With local place names like Humbug Creek, Missouri Flat, and Iron Horse Road, you might think you've entered a time warp as you meander along the rural roads of Applegate Valley wine country. But this AVA is the scenic home of a creative coterie of wineries that range from the humble to the ambitious, the tiny to the substantial.

The 50-mi-long (80.4-km-long) Applegate Valley was formed by the flow of the Applegate and Little Applegate Rivers that wind between peaks of the Siskiyou Mountains in the area between Grants Pass in the northwest and Jacksonville in the southeast. One of three broad valleys that make up the bulk of the Rogue Valley AVA, the Applegate is farther inland than the Illinois Valley to the west, but not so far from the coast as the Bear Valley in the east. Protected to the west from both cooling marine temperatures and rainfall by the Siskiyou Mountains that surround it, Applegate Valley receives moderate heat—more than Illinois Valley but less than Bear Valley—and generally dry conditions during the growing season.

APPLEGATE VALLEY WINE COUNTRY AT A GLANCE

Year established: 2001
Number of wineries: 15
Total acreage: 278,190 acres (112,600 ha)
Vineyard acreage: 400 acres (161.8 ha)
Predominant soil types: granitic alluvial gravels
Vineyard growing degree days:
　1852–2630 (1011–1443)

Most important grape varieties
merlot, cabernet sauvignon, chardonnay, syrah pinot noir

Wooldridge Creek tasting room and winery typifies the Applegate Valley's rural charm.

Though the appellation has a multitude of different mesoclimates, growing degree days generally range from 2340 to 2630 (1282–1443) with an average rainfall of 26 in. (66 cm). Such heat accumulation makes the Applegate Valley an obvious candidate for Bordeaux- and Rhone-style warm-climate varietals. And numerous cabernet sauvignon, merlot, zinfandel, syrah, and blended red wines, plus the seemingly obligatory pinot noir, can be found, as well as viognier and chardonnay.

Despite its overall warmth, the Applegate Valley poses challenges to winemakers. It has the shortest frost-free period in southern Oregon at 137 days, compared to 150–165 in other parts of the Rogue Valley. Because of higher vineyard elevations, most-

ly between 1200 and 1700 ft. (365.7–518.1 m), and because the surrounding mountains restrict sunlight late in the day, frost can come early in the autumn and stay late in the spring. This possibility limits the viability of late-ripening grapes, such as cabernet sauvignon, which must be planted at only the warmest sites, despite the apparent sufficient growing season heat. Availability of water is also a challenge. With little rain and moderately high heat, grapevines can become overly stressed toward the end of the season, especially if dry farmed. Irrigation is desirable here, though sometimes unreliable if based on wells.

The valley's topography, however, offers good vineyard sites. Alluvial benches formed from mountain rock erosion provide deep, well-drained flatlands that sit above the valley floor with good sun exposure. The soils are mixed, reasonably fertile, and well drained. The predominant soils are granitic in origin, which imparts a pleasing minerality to the wines, though there are also some sedimentary soils. The valley floor also offers sites with stream deposits, but the potential of cool-air pooling offers a risk of frost damage early and late in the season.

Variations in site conditions throughout the appellation make the choice difficult for the winegrower of which variety to plant where. Not every vineyard in the appellation that is planted to cabernet sauvignon, for instance, will reliably produce ripe fruit. In the past, a lack of viticultural sophistication has led to some not-so-successful decisions, which has meant varied wine quality for consumers. But the situation is changing. More detailed climate and soil data, plus a greater attention to winegrowing and winemaking rigor are resulting in wines of better quality. Consistency remains an issue, especially for smaller producers who might not have either the capital or the experience to make the best wine in all vintages. But it is precisely these issues that can make touring the Applegate Valley wine country rewarding. Because so many of the producers are small, with intimate tasting rooms often staffed by the winemakers or their families, and because so many owners have such individualistic views about winemaking, discoveries abound.

WINERIES AND WINES TO SAMPLE

TROON VINEYARD

Winery tasting room: 1475 Kubli Road, Grants Pass, OR
Carlton tasting room: 250 Kutch Street, Carlton, OR
541-846-9900; www.troonvineyard.com
Tasting rooms open all year; limited hours.

Year founded:	1972
Annual production:	13,000 cases
Signature wine:	Druid's Fluid ($$)
Premium wine:	Vertical ($$$$)
Value wine:	Jeanie in the Bottle ($)
Estate vineyards:	Troon

Dick Troon founded Troon Vineyard in 1972, and became an early pioneer of southern Oregon winemaking, with an eclectic style and great enthusiasm. The Martin family purchased the winery when Dick retired, and under the direction of Chris Martin the winery's scope has greatly expanded and the viticulture has been revamped.

Not lacking in ambition, Troon Vineyard set new price points, with the first wine in southern Oregon to be priced at $100. Troon also pioneered some wines that are unusual for Oregon: it was a zinfandel, little planted in the state, that first carried the C-note price. Winemaker Herb Quady makes a variety of dense, hearty red wines, and has given Troon a particular reputation for zinfandel. The winery has a penchant for playfully named wines, small lots, mostly under 300 cases, and organic principles. Troon is also pioneering new varieties for southern Oregon, including an impressive vermentino (the first in the Northwest), and plantings of primitivo, roussanne, marsanne, and sangiovese.

VALLEY VIEW WINERY

1000 Upper Applegate Road, Jacksonville, OR
541-899-8468; www.valleyviewwinery.com
Open all year.

Year founded:	1972
Annual production:	7000–11,000 cases
Signature wine:	Anna Maria Viognier ($$)
Premium wine:	Pioneer Label Merlot ($$)
Value wine:	Valley View Merlot ($)
Estate vineyards:	Valley View

In 1972, Frank Wisnovsky resurrected the Valley View name, which had been used by Peter Britt for one of the Northwest's earliest commercial wineries, and began Valley View Winery anew. Today, sons Mike and Mark Wisnovsky manage what is clearly one of the most important wineries in Southern Oregon. Using grapes from Valley View's estate vineyard, originally planted in 1972 and 1976 with graftings since then, as well as fruit from prime vineyards in the region, Valley View's long-time winemaker Joe Guerrero makes well-priced wines of rich character.

The Anna Maria Viognier is an Oregon standout, with vibrant acidity and luscious fruit. The merlots have always been plush and hedonistic, while the tempranillo is firm, dense, and rich with cherry and coffee notes. Always good value and reliable, Valley View is a southern Oregon icon.

WOOLDRIDGE CREEK VINEYARD AND WINERY

818 Slagle Creek Road, Grants Pass, OR
541-846-6364; www.wcwinery.com
Open by appointment only.

Year founded:	1978
Annual production:	3000 cases
Signature wine:	Warrick White ($$)
Premium wine:	Warrick Red ($$$)
Value wine:	Gewürztraminer ($)
Estate vineyards:	Wooldridge Creek

Ted and Mary Warrick planted the beautiful 56-acre (22.6-ha) Wooldridge Creek Vineyard in 1976, and for many years provided fruit to a number of Oregon wineries. In 2002, Greg Paneitz and Kara Olmo brought winemaking training and experience to the vineyard, and became partners in Wooldridge Creek Winery. Today Wooldridge Creek produces superbly crafted varietals and blends from the sustainably farmed vineyard.

The Warrick Red and White blends are full-bodied, emotive examples of the power of Applegate fruit. Single-variety wines include a robust cabernet sauvignon with trademark eucalyptus notes, syrah that shows spice and elegance, and a satisfying zinfandel that avoids opulence. A force in Oregon winemaking overall, Kara Olmo and Greg Paneitz are setting the pace for elegantly balanced winemaking in southern Oregon.

Columbia Gorge Wine Country

There can be few places in North America as spectacular for growing grapes as the Columbia Gorge. From a single vineyard vantage, you can scan east to the sparse steppes of the Columbia Basin, west to the cliff-lined passage of the river through the Columbia River Gorge National Scenic Area, and south to the green valleys lying at the base of snow-capped Mount Hood. Throughout the wine country, which is roughly 40 mi (64.3 km) wide, myriad mesoclimates offer plenty of vineyard potential.

Approximately 60 mi (96.5 km) east of Portland, the Columbia Gorge appellation's boundaries encompass the lands below the 2000 ft. (609.6 m) elevation line. The western border is just east of Hood River, and takes in much of the Hood River Valley to the southwest corner near Parkdale below Mount Hood. In the southeast, the appellation skirts the Hood River National Forest and meets up with the southwestern border of the Columbia Valley AVA just west of The Dalles. The appellation crosses the state line and goes north through the White Salmon River Valley to Trout Lake at the foot of Mount Adams.

Channeling one of the mightiest river systems in the hemisphere, the Columbia Gorge is the only sea-level passage through the Cascade Mountains. Untold volumes of water took millennia to carve out today's gorge, leaving magnificent cliffs, bluffs, terraces, and benches throughout the rocky opening. On both sides of the river, for approximately 40 mi (64.3 km) between Hood River in the west and the Highway 97 bridge in the east, wineries and vineyards dot the bluffs and valleys, creating their own integral wine country identity, regardless of their state of residence, or whether they are in the Columbia Gorge or Columbia Valley appellation.

What makes this region so viticulturally interesting, and challenging, is its location at the convergence of three climate zones: marine, continental, and alpine. The variations among these climate types make it difficult to label the Columbia Gorge as strictly cool-climate or warm-climate. It is both,

COLUMBIA GORGE WINE COUNTRY AT A GLANCE

Year established: 2004
Number of wineries: 33*
Total acreage: 186,900 acres (75,700 ha)*
Oregon portion acreage:
   122,700 acres (49,700 ha)
Vineyard acreage: 800* acres (323.7 ha)
Predominant soil types: mixed volcanic, loess, and loam
Vineyard growing degree days:
   1503-2682[†] (817-1472)

Most important grape varieties
pinot noir, gewürztraminer, pinot gris, chardonnay

*Figures apply to the entire appellation.
[†]Figures apply to Oregon portion of the appellation only.

sometimes at the same time, and is more fairly called a transitional-climate region.

The Gorge acts as a funnel, channeling relatively cool, wet marine air surging against the Cascades through its narrow opening. While the river gushes westward, the winds rush eastward, sucked in by the rising warmer air of the interior. The average wind speed through the Gorge is a fairly constant 10 mph (16 kph), with significant and sustained winds easily up to 20 mph (32.1 kph). As the marine air moves east, it also moves up, spilling much of its moisture as rain on the western side of the Cascades. Consequently, westerly vineyards in this wine country receive 35 to 50 in. (88.9–127 cm) of precipitation, though mostly during the winter.

Vineyards at high elevations and in valleys near the taller peaks, especially in the northern part of this wine country, experience colder temperatures sweeping down from the alpine peaks of the Cascade Range. This air helps mediate daytime heat while also creating large diurnal temperature shifts at night.

More easterly vineyards closer to the Columbia Basin experience warmer temperatures and drier summers, putting them in the warm-climate category. Precipitation at the eastern end of the Gorge averages 10 in. (25.4 cm) annually. Even these generalizations, though, are subject to lots of local variation. On the Oregon side of the river, temperatures can be more extreme, ranging from a high of 2682 (1472) GDD to a low of 1301 (705) GDD. Washington's portion of the appellation is cooler, with a maximum of 2441 (1338) GDD and a minimum of 1235 (668) GDD. How cool or warm any one vineyard site is during the growing season depends on its elevation and exposure to wind and sun.

The complex terrain of the region reduces the number of potential vineyard sites. Most of the land along the river is actual cliffs, not slopes. But there

A panoramic view of the Columbia Gorge wine country from Celilo Vineyard on the Washington side of the Columbia River.

Looking east up the Gorge from Celilo Vineyard.

are benches, usually composed of mixed volcanic soils and loess, lying at various elevations and aspects that offer practical vineyard sites. The Hood River Valley in the south, and to a lesser extent the White Salmon River Valley in the north, provide vineyard sites more protected from wind.

Grape growing in the Gorge goes back to the nineteenth century, with the earliest vinifera vines, which are still growing, dating to the early party of the twentieth century. In more recent years, a handful of small wineries first began establishing vineyards in the late 1970s and 1980s, experimenting with different varieties and learning winemaking pretty much as they went along. For a long time, wineries in the area had a variable reputation for quality and consistency.

Within the past decade, significant new vineyard and winery development, plus the attention of committed and experienced winemakers, has been transforming the Columbia Gorge wine country into one with reliable quality and expansive promise. There remains a tendency for many wineries to produce as many different wines as it seems they can man-

WINERIES AND WINES TO SAMPLE

PHELPS CREEK VINEYARDS

1850 Country Club Road, Hood River, OR
541-386-2607; www.phelpscreekvineyards.com
Open during the season, limited hours.

Year founded:	1991
Annual production:	6000 cases
Signature wine:	Estate Reserve Pinot Noir ($$$)
Premium wine:	Cuvée Alexandrine ($$$)
Value wine:	Celilo Rose Rosé ($)
Estate vineyards:	Phelps Creek

It is refreshing to see a winery in the Columbia Gorge making a concerted effort to focus on only a few varieties. Founder of the winery Robert Morus planted his first pinot noir in 1989, and today has built for Phelps Creek a strong reputation for the finicky variety, including a range of wines that showcase different expressions of pinot noir fruit. Phelps Creek is an undoubted star in the Oregon winemaking firmament.

Director of winemaking Rich Cushman has a long history in the Gorge and gets the most from the winery's 30-acre (12.1-ha) estate vineyard, as well as prime grapes from other regional sources. Consultant Alexandrine Roy adds an international component by crafting her own Phelps Creek pinot noir cuvée. In addition to pinot noir, Phelps Creek also produces excellent chardonnay and gewürztraminer, in addition to other wines.

THE PINES 1852

5450 Mill Creek Road, The Dalles, OR
Tasting Room: 202 State Street, Hood River
541-993-8301; www.thepinesvineyard.com
Open all year; limited hours.

Year founded:	2001
Annual production:	5000 cases
Signature wine:	Old Vine Zinfandel ($$$)
Premium wine:	Old Vine Zinfandel ($$$)
Value wine:	Satin ($$)
Estate vineyards:	The Pines

Vineyardist Lonnie Wright's experience with Columbia Gorge fruit goes back to the early 1980s, when he helped renovate what are surely some of the oldest productive grapevines in the Northwest. The vineyard's 8 acres (3.2 ha) of zinfandel vines may have been put in the ground in the late 1880s, and today go into the cult Old Vine Zinfandel made by winemaker Peter Rosback. Additional acreage of syrah and merlot, plus more zinfandel, have been added.

Wright started his winery in 2002 after deciding that his grapes were too good to sell all of them to other wineries. The Pines 1852 offers a range of wines from the estate vineyard and purchased fruit. The Old Vine Zinfandel is a remarkably dense, flavor-packed wine, while the zinfandel from younger, 20-year-old vines is more jaunty and quaffable.

VIENTO WINES

5450 Mill Creek Road, The Dalles, OR
Tasting room: 202 State Street, Hood River
541-298-1981; www.thepinesvineyard.com
Open all year; limited hours.

Year founded:	2001
Annual production:	5000 cases
Signature wine:	Syrah Cuvée R ($$$)
Premium wine:	Syrah Lonesome Spring Ranch ($$$)
Value wine:	Gewürztraminer ($$)
Estate vineyards:	uses purchased fruit

Winemaker Rich Cushman had been making wine in the Willamette Valley, yet sourcing fruit from the Columbia Gorge and the Columbia Valley, until he admitted that his heart really lay in the Gorge. Now a resident of Hood River, Cushman makes wines that define what can be done with fruit from this region, and that have earned him a reputation as one of the state's premier winemakers.

It is difficult to say which are Viento's best wines: the luxurious syrah Cushman makes as both single-vineyard wines and blends (Cuvée R is a standout); or his whites, a dry gewürztraminer and a balanced riesling; or perhaps his tremendously tasty sangiovese rosé. All these wines are beautifully balanced and offer intense fruit. And for a true taste of what is possible with Gorge-sourced and Columbia Valley fruit, there's no wine better than Viento's Cuvée Provençal, a full-bodied, supple blend of grenache and syrah.

Columbia Valley Wine Country

Though the Columbia Valley wine country has its southern border extending into Oregon from The Dalles in the west to the foot of the Blue Mountains along the Washington-Oregon border in the east, there are no active wineries and a mere handful of small vineyards in the Oregon portion of the Columbia Valley appellation.

COLUMBIA VALLEY WINE COUNTRY AT A GLANCE

Year established: 1984
Number of wineries: none in Oregon
Total acreage: 11,393,100 acres (4,610,600 ha)*
Oregon portion acreage:
    2,369,000 acres (958,700 ha)
Vineyard acreage: no significant vineyards
    in Oregon
Predominant soil types: windblown loess,
    sandy silts and loams
Vineyard growing degree days:
    2221–3154 (1216–1734)[†]

Most important grape varieties
little grown in Oregon

*Figures apply to the entire appellation.
[†] Figures apply to Oregon portion of the appellation only.

Walla Walla Valley Wine Country

Though the Walla Walla Valley wine country is almost exclusively associated in people's minds with Washington, a significant portion of its acreage—though not so much its winery population—lies on the Oregon side of the state line. In fact, some of the appellation's best-known Washington wineries, including L'Ecole No. 41, Buty, and Waters, have estate vineyards on the Oregon side of the border, and it is the location of one of Walla Walla Valley's most famous grape sources, Seven Hills Vineyard. Even Cayuse, one of Washington state's most famous boutique wineries, has its winery and estate vineyards in Oregon.

In general, the land lies lower than much of the northern part of the appellation. Growing degree days and annual precipitation do not vary significantly from the rest of the wine country. Oregon vineyards are mostly located on the gently rolling hills just west of the town of Milton-Freewater, and on the ground comprised of cobblestone and rocks that makes up part of the ancient riverbed of the Walla Walla River.

The Walla Walla wine country is described in detail in the section on Washington's wine countries, starting on page 95.

WALLA WALLA VALLEY WINE COUNTRY AT A GLANCE

Year established: 1984
Number of wineries: 4+
Total acreage: 322,800 acres (130,632 ha)*
Oregon portion acreage:
    100,400 acres (49,600 ha)
Vineyard acreage: 1200 acres (485 ha)*
Predominant soil types: loess (consisting of windblown silts, sands, and loam), cobblestone, and some volcanic ash.
Vineyard growing degree days:
    2545–2911 (1396–1599) †

Most important grape varieties
merlot, cabernet sauvignon, syrah

*Figures apply to the entire appellation.
† Figures apply to Oregon portion of the appellation only.

WINERIES AND WINES TO SAMPLE

ZERBA CELLARS

85530 Highway 11, Milton-Freewater, OR
541-938-9463; www.zerbacellars.com
Open all year.

Year founded:	2002
Annual production:	7500 cases
Signature wine:	Columbia Valley Syrah ($$)
Premium wine:	Reserve Cabernet Sauvignon ($$$)
Value wine:	Wild White ($$)
Estate vineyards:	Dad's, Winesap, Cockburn Hills

Zerba Cellars burst onto the scene a few years ago when its inaugural wines swept up multiple gold medals at the Oregon State Fair Wine Competition. Invariably succulent, with clear, vibrant fruit flavors, Zerba Cellars wines lack the jammy, overly oaked qualities of so many of the Northwest's so-called big red wines. Zerba wines have enviable grace and elegance without sacrificing power and concentration.

Owners Cecil and Marilyn Zerba for many years were Walla Walla nursery owners, then converted to vineyards in 2001, and founded Zerba Cellars a year later. Today, winemaker Doug Nierman brings his Sonoma Valley, Napa Valley, and Columbia Valley experience to crafting Zerba wines from estate vineyards and locally sourced fruit. As of 2009, Zerba Cellars was one of just three Walla Walla Valley wineries located on the Oregon side of the wine country.

Snake River Valley Wine Country

The Snake River Valley wine country is a huge territory that extends from Idaho westward into Oregon. The bulk of the appellation is in Idaho (see page 283 for a detailed discussion), but its boundaries cross Oregon's eastern border along the Snake River and Hells Canyon National Recreation Area in the north, to the Idaho-Oregon border just east of Lake Owyhee State Park in the south. Like fingers reaching westward, the Oregon portion of the appellation encompasses large parts of the Snake River drainage,

SNAKE RIVER WINE COUNTRY AT A GLANCE

Year established: 2007
Number of wineries: 2[†]
Total acreage: 5,350,300 acres (2,165,100 ha)[*]
Oregon portion acreage:
  1,537,600 acres (622,200 ha)
Vineyard acreage: 40 acres (10 ha)[†]
Predominant soil types: Very mixed: sandy loam, sedimentary gravels, volcanic clay, loess
Vineyard growing degree days:
  2104–3020[†] (1151–1660)

Most important grape varieties
no significant population of Oregon vineyards yet

[*]Figures apply to the entire appellation.
[†]Figures apply to Oregon portion of the appellation only.

including the Malheur River, Owyhee River, Powder River, and much of the neighboring creeks, tributary systems, and associated valleys up to the 3412-ft. (1039.9-m) elevation.

This desolate, high-desert country is sparsely populated and viticulturally unexploited. Only one or two small vineyard-winery operations have so far attempted to get a foothold in this Eastern Oregon wine country. The success of Idaho's small wine industry, and the similarity of the region to much of Washington's Columbia Valley wine country, would seem to bode well for a vinous future in Eastern Oregon. But so far, such potential is largely unexplored.

BRITISH COLUMBIA

Shuswap
Lake

Kamloops

Salmon
Arm

Vernon

OKANAGAN *Okanagan*
VALLEY   *Lake*

Westbank   Kelowna
Peachland   Kelowna

Summerland   Naramata
              Naramata Bench

COAST

MOUNTAINS

Whistler

Penticton

Okanagan Falls
Okanagan Falls

Similkameen River

SIMILKAMEEN
VALLEY

Keremeos   Oliver   Black Sage Road
Golden Mile

Osoyoos   Osoyoos

Vancouver

Hope

FRASER
VALLEY

Fraser

Langley

River

Abbotsford

BRITISH COLUMBIA
WASHINGTON

Strait of Georgia

Nanaimo

Bellingham

VANCOUVER ISLAND RANGES

Cowichan Valley

Duncan

Saanich
Peninsula

GULF
ISLANDS

VANCOUVER
ISLAND

Victoria

Strait of Juan de Fuca

PACIFIC OCEAN

OLYMPIC
MTNS

Skagit River

CASCADE RANGE

Okanagan River

Everett

Seattle

BRITISH COLUMBIA'S WINE COUNTRIES AT A GLANCE

Vineyard acreage:	9000 acres (3626 ha)
Number of wineries:	200
Annual cases produced:	1.7 million
Economic impact of wine:	$0.5 billion

Most important grape varieties
merlot, chardonnay, pinot gris, pinot noir, cabernet sauvignon, gewürztraminer, syrah, sauvignon blanc, cabernet franc, pinot blanc

Wine countries (DVAs)
British Columbia
    Okanagan Valley
    Similkameen Valley
    Fraser Valley
    Vancouver Island
    Gulf Islands

Richly appreciated by British Columbian wine lovers, the beauty of the province's wine countries can come as a surprise to some not yet aware of the quality of wine and the wine country experience this Northwest province offers.

BRITISH COLUMBIA is perhaps the most impressive, yet least appreciated, wine country in North America. Its charms and sophistication are among the best kept secrets in the Pacific Northwest—at least to those who don't live in British Columbia. Those who do, know the truth: that British Columbia wines and wine countries are the equal in quality and charm of any on the continent. British Columbians have ardent admiration for the wine jewels in their midst. In fact, almost the entire production of the province's wine industry is snapped up by locals. For others to experience British Columbia's exciting wines and alluring wine country, there is only one solution: they must go there.

Few other New World wine regions have come as far as fast as British Columbia. From what amounts to a standing start in 1988, the province's wine industry has grown to nearly 10,000 acres (4046 ha) of vinifera grapes in 2009 from only about 1000 acres (404.6 ha) in 1988. From a mere 17 wineries in 1990, there are now more than 200; since 2004, the winery population has nearly doubled. From a production volume of about 1.2 million gal. (4.8 million l) of wine in the early 1990s, the province now produces 4 million gal. (15.1 million l) of wine.

International accolades roll in for British Columbia's wines. In 1994, Mission Hill Family Estate Winery won the Avery Trophy for the Best Chardon-

nay Worldwide at the International Wine and Spirit Competition in London. In 2004, Jackson-Triggs's winemaker was named the Winemaker of the Year at the San Francisco International Wine Competition. Back at the International Wine and Spirits Competition, Jackson-Triggs won the best worldwide shiraz-syrah wine award in 2006, the first ever for a North American winery. Two years later, Mission Hill Family Estate Winery was awarded the International Wine Challenge Trophy for the world's best icewine.

For a long time, it wasn't clear whether there would ever be a viable fine wine industry in British Columbia. Throughout its history, most of the province's vineyards were planted to nonvinifera grapes. Before the 1980s, it was widely presumed that delicate vinifera vines could not survive British Columbia's winters. The only wines that were made in any quantity came either from other fruits, or were sugar-strengthened products made from a mixed lot of

Overleaf: Acreage from the B.C. Grape Acreage Report, August 15, 2008, compiled by Lynn and John Bremmer, Mount Kobau Wine Services. Grape varieites listed in order of tonnage harvested, British Columbia Wine Institute, 2009.

ICEWINE, ICE WINE, OR SIMULATED ICEWINE?

Canadian wine regulations use the term "icewine"—one word—to describe wine made from grapes that are naturally frozen on the vine. In the United States, the term ice wine—two words—is used to describe the same thing. In technical use, the terms are synonymous.

But it hasn't always been so. For a long time American wines that were made by artificially freezing, and then pressing, grapes were also called ice wine. Canadians rightly protested that this was an inaccurate use of the term. Today's American regulations prohibit the use of the term

ice wine on anything but wines made from grapes that are naturally frozen on the vine, essentially meeting the same natural conditions as Canadian icewine.

But that doesn't stop American (and other) producers from continuing to make dessert-style wines from artificially frozen grapes; they just can't call them ice wines. Such wines are deliberately made to simulate icewine but are marketed under the more accurate label of late harvest-style wine.

Mission Hill Family Estate Winery is one example of the rapid success of British Columbia's wine industry.

hybrid and cross-bred grapes. The few people who planted vinifera vines were considered eccentric at best and were vigorously encouraged to plant hybrids instead. Many did, finally succumbing to the market reality that there was little demand for dry European-style wines at the time. There was no demand for such wines mostly because protectionist regulations hindered importation of nondomestic products, thereby artificially supporting the high-alcohol, sweet, hybrid, provincial wine infrastructure. The provincial market was willing to buy and drink whatever local wines were produced, no matter the quality.

Things began to change in the 1970s when provincial authorities created the Liquor Distribution Branch to help market alcoholic beverages. Soon more of the world's fine wines began to find a market in British Columbia. The contrast in quality between the international wines and those made locally was stark. At the same time, Vancouver was rapidly developing into an international business and culture center, and residents and visitors were demanding more varied and higher quality culinary experiences. British Columbian wines of the era no longer were adequate.

Change came dramatically in 1988, when the Canada–U.S. Free Trade Agreement removed tariffs and trade restrictions on wine. Recognizing that the province's existing wine grape infrastructure could not compete in the new internationalized market, the government paid growers to rip their nonvinifera vines out of the ground. This action effectively wiped the slate clean for British Columbia wine. The province's wine industry would either have to die or adapt by competing on the world's wine stage. British Columbia wine entrepreneurs decisively chose to compete. It was pretty dramatic stuff. Hybrid vines were pulled up everywhere, leaving a little over 1000 acres (404.6 ha) of vinifera to form the enfeebled foundation of what was to become today's world-class wine industry.

A new species of vine was about to be planted in British Columbia's soil—literally and figurative-

ly—and from 1988 onward, its growth pattern would determine the character of the province's wine soul. Two strong branches sprouted from the initial burst of budding enthusiasm for vinifera winegrowing in British Columbia. Along one branch grew strong-willed individualists who explored a personal, sometimes eccentric, path toward vinous fulfillment. Along the other branch, well-financed, but no less vision-driven, individuals and corporations shrewdly applied capital to the development of their wine dreams. Both continue to characterize British Columbia's wine culture.

The winemaking individualists mostly congregate along the edges of the province's limited wine geography. Especially in the cooler west, but also to the north above the Okanagan Valley, committed winegrowers fight against what amounts to a climatic boundary for most vines. Vintages are highly variable in areas where the degrees of growing day heat are barely sufficient and an annual crop cannot always be assured. Discovering which grapes can succeed in such outer reaches is a challenge, and perhaps the reward, for these driven people.

The most prosperous, and usually also the longest lived, of these wineries succeed by hewing to a singular vision, and through hard-wrought experience, dedication, and a willingness to learn. They have achieved the three vital elements to success in winegrowing: learning which grapes grow best at their site, knowing how to craft the best wine they can out of those grapes, and being able to find the customers who will loyally return for more wine. These passion-driven British Columbia wineries value craft and principle above marketing and public relations. They don't have extra energy to put into issues other than their plants, ferments, and barrels. They form the essential artisan core of British Columbia's wine industry.

There is a dark shadow to this approach, however. Often self-educated in wine, some bootstrapped producers seem to revel in their individualism just for the sake of being iconoclastic. Especially in areas

of the province clearly on the margins of growing viability, there can be incentive to cling to ill-advised visions of vinous success, if only to challenge accepted grape growing conventions. As elsewhere in the Northwest, some of these producers make subpar wine. Stubbornly driven in their attempts to realize their dream, they may ignore, willfully or otherwise, realities that prevent them from achieving a quality product. Why, for instance, some would insist on growing obviously late-ripening grapes in areas that are demonstrably too cool for the variety seems a mystery to the outsider. And though these sorts of wineries may well find a local market, they can also resurrect out-of-date impressions of British Columbia's vinous naiveté. But when artisan producers succeed, and many do, they can make brilliant wines. There are several small, iconoclastic British Columbia wineries whose quality helps set the standard for the province as a whole. Small size and uncompro-

mising passion can lead to spectacular wines.

From the inception of the modern British Columbia wine industry, another type of winegrower has also evolved: the well-financed businessman (and they are almost all men) or corporation, which creates or expands a substantial wine brand through the application of capital to winegrowing, winemaking, and wine marketing. In some cases, these have been individuals who are just as driven in their wine dreams as the outlying artisans, only they chose a more mainstream approach and had the means to work on a grander scale. Harry McWatters, for instance, grabbed on to the vinifera vine even before the uprootings of 1988, and personally helped drive

Venturi-Schulze Vineyards has earned to reputation for making top-quality wines in the cool Vancouver Island climate.

Burrowing Owl Estate Winery exemplifies the investment being made in winery and wine touring resources in British Columbia's wine countries.

the industry toward higher standards of quality and winegrowing rigor. And Anthony von Mandl in 1981 bought a down-in-the-mouth winery west of Kelowna and transformed it into one of the most impressive wine estates in North America, and along the way helped raise the standards of wine quality for the entire province.

Corporate drive has also contributed importantly. The growing market success of some British Columbia wine brands led to consolidation and purchases that created wealthy companies, which in turn plowed investment money into new vineyard and winery development. Vincor, for instance, has been instrumental in building the reputation of British Columbia's wines by enhancing viticulture as much as by broadening marketing and distribution. Its partnership with Groupe Taillan to produce the Osoyoos Larose brand, for instance, brought an unprecedented international organization to British Columbia, and along with it, much critical and market attention.

The investment capital flowing into British Columbia has jump-started growth and quality. Financially successful wineries regularly import internationally trained and widely experienced wine specialists, often from California, South Africa, Australia, and Europe. Others send family members or employees to be trained in the wine schools of Germany and France, to bring their knowledge back to British Columbia, which shortens the time it takes to mature the region's depth of viticultural knowledge and broadens the pool of winegrowing talent available throughout the province.

Because of their ability to purchase larger vineyard blocks and support efficient production facilities, the large wineries also achieve economies of scale that deliver higher quality, better consumer value, and greater availability than smaller enterprises often can. They are able to bring more British Columbia wines to more people. And as consumers become better acquainted with British Columbia's wines, they visit the wine countries where the wines originated. Wine-inspired agritourism and culinary tourism are fast-growing contributors to British Columbia's economy.

British Columbia's wine growth has its drawbacks, though. The pace of development pressures natural resources and threatens the environmental quality of British Columbia's wine countries. The Osoyoos area, for instance, is a delicate desert ecosystem increasingly threatened by human development. Some species are at risk. The competing needs for water to support agriculture and housing cause frictions and controversies. As the limited amount of potential vineyard land gets developed, the cost of remaining real estate escalates dramatically: land prices in the Okanagan Valley are among the highest in Canada. Though vineyard and winery development has slowed since the economic downturn in 2008, there will be a time soon when land is either too costly or too precious to support significant new wine development.

Touring British Columbia's wine countries offers the opportunity to experience both the artisan and the corporate winegrowing cultures. Visit the wineries of Vancouver Island and the nearby Gulf Islands, and you can feel as if you're entering another age. The winery tasting rooms have a rural ethos and the winemakers possess at-ease charm that speaks of a more leisurely time when people strolled instead of jogged, there were no cell phones, and tasting wine was a relaxing personal pursuit. Winegrowing here feels more intimate, as if the vintner is inviting you to his backyard to share a few moments of insight over a glass of his wine. Perhaps it is the charm of

Visitors enjoy a glass of wine at the Salt Spring Vineyards Winery, in the Gulf Islands of British Columbia.

The great bulk of British Columbia's land is either too mountainous or too far north for vinifera to grow. Since 52°N latitude is considered the upper limit for reliable wine grape growing, only a narrow slice of the southern part of the province can support grapes. And even then, climate and landform need to coincide to offer productive vineyard sites. In British Columbia, that only happens in a handful of locales, and that it happens at all surprises many. Just comprehending the concept of winegrowing in British Columbia can be challenging to the uninitiated: it's so far north, it's so cold, it's so . . . snowy . . . and wet. But just as many folks first misunderstood the viticultural potential of Washington, Oregon, and Idaho, so those unfamiliar with British Columbia may miss its latent possibilities for fine wine.

The largest, best known, most important of the province's wine countries is the Okanagan Valley. This long, narrow valley surrounding Okanagan Lake is roughly 300 mi (482 km) east of the ocean and is plenty warm for wine grapes. The glacially formed benches along the valley's sides are well suited for vineyards. The Okanagan Valley, and its smaller sibling, Similkameen Valley, slightly to the west, are British Columbia's only warm-climate wine countries.

Cut off from Pacific storms by the mountainous rain barrier to the west, these two valleys are extremely dry and warm. They form a branch of the Columbia River drainage, and are the extreme northerly continuation of the same landforms and essential growing conditions found in the rest of the drainage.

Far to the west of these appellations, the topography is very different, yet follows the same geographic themes we've seen elsewhere in the Northwest. The gargantuan Vancouver Island and the adjacent petite archipelago of Gulf Islands offer vineyard prospects only because of the blessing of a rain shadow. The massive mountains of Vancouver Island's interior prevent significant precipitation from reaching its eastern shore during the growing season, and result-

ing in the seeming paradox of a need for vineyard irrigation in a temperate rain forest biome.

This cool-climate growing region is the northern extension of the Puget Sound climate and geologic zone. The Gulf Islands in the Strait of Georgia are the Canadian portion of the border-blind San Juan Archipelago that includes what in the United States is called the San Juan Islands. Like the Puget Sound AVA, these Canadian island wine countries experience a genuinely cool climate—cool enough that only the earliest maturing vinifera varieties can ripen with regularity, and even they can be problematic in off vintages. More reliable are the multiple hybrids and crosses specifically designed for early ripening. Winegrowing in this geography is winegrowing at the outer limits of reasonableness.

Similarly, the Fraser Valley extending southeast from Vancouver enjoys weather protection from the Vancouver Island Ranges, creating a generally warm and dry growing season that allows for cool-climate grapes to be grown.

THE GRAPES AND STYLES OF BRITISH COLUMBIA'S WINES

In British Columbia, the grape equation is straightforward: late-ripening grapes can only be reliably grown in the Okanagan and Similkameen Valleys, and early ripening grapes are the only trustworthy varieties for the islands and the Fraser Valley. In the warm climate zones, wide diurnal swings and long hours of sunlight create wines with plenty of ripeness and acidity. A hallmark of British Columbian wines is the freshness of the fruit flavors. Even red wines of great density tend to have a brilliant, fresh quality that makes them especially good for pairing with food. The same streak of freshness is apparent in white wines as well, and is quite evident in the best wines made in the cool-climate areas of the province.

Since the Okanagan Valley produces over 90 percent of British Columbia's vinifera fruit, the prov-

ince's most widely produced wines include classic warm-climate varieties. But because of the high latitude, a number of cool-climate grapes are also successfully grown in quantity.

Merlot

British Columbia's Okanagan Valley is home to outstanding merlot wines. Like their cousins to the south, the British Columbia vintners take advantage of the warm climate to reliably ripen merlot fruit, and the cool nights make for ample acidity. Consequently, British Columbia merlots excel at displaying remarkably fresh fruit flavors, as well as showing the leaner, spicier side of the variety—the latter not frequently seen in merlots grown farther south. Merlot wines from the Okanagan Valley are more elegant than plump, savory than sweet, and show spice and herb qualities that are a satisfying complement to the ripe fruit flavors. Thanks to the long sunlit days and the spare sandy soils, Okanagan Valley merlot wines have greater definition, less flabbiness, and more structure than I find in merlots from elsewhere in the

Northwest. The best British Columbia merlots have plenty of plum and blackberry characters but also additional complexity.

As with merlots made anywhere, barrel treatment dramatically alters the inherent fruitiness of the grape. Many British Columbia wineries use American or Hungarian barrels instead of French, which can add spiciness to the wine. Sometimes this quality is overdone when a merlot already displays plenty of its own spice qualities. But when applied deftly, or by using softer French oak, pleasing vanilla and caramel overtones are achieved that can provide a soft counterpoint to otherwise leanly made merlots.

There is a surprising amount of cool-climate merlot made in British Columbia as well. This can be more problematic, depending on the vintage. Merlot does not require the same heat accumulation as the other Bordeaux varieties, but it is by no means a

Wine grapes on the Gulf Islands beginning to ripen in mid-season sun.

227

cool-climate grape. When grown in the cooler western parts of the province, merlot requires extra vineyard methods to ripen, such as tenting to help trap warm air. Techniques such as these are legitimate to employ, but the results can be mixed. Lean, thinner merlots have their own charm, but they rarely achieve the depth, complexity, and satisfaction of wines made from merlot grapes better matched to warmer growing conditions.

Chardonnay

When the 1992 Mission Hill Grand Reserve Chardonnay won the Avery Trophy for Best Chardonnay Worldwide at the 1994 International Wine and Spirits Competition, it was perhaps the first British Colum-

bia wine to attract worldwide interest. The event announced that not only could British Columbia make great wine, it could make great chardonnay wine, one of the most globally competitive categories.

Since then, chardonnay has been a focus for many British Columbia producers, most of whom make excellent, even outstanding, chardonnay wines. But is there an identifiably British Columbian character to the province's chardonnay wines? As always, chardonnay is highly amenable to the winemaker's manipulation, and in British Columbia, it comes in a spectrum of styles. What may distinguish British Columbia chardonnay wines more than any particular style is the overall respect the variety receives. Rather than emphasize simply made, high-volume chardonnay, which is common in many places, the province's winemakers take the grape seriously.

Just look at some of the high-end chardonnays made in British Columbia and the prices they com-

Pinot noir grape clusters approaching picking time in the Okanagan Valley.

mand. Mission Hill Family Estate Winery has added a chardonnay they call Perpetua to its top-tier Legacy line of wines at around C$33, Quails' Gate considers its Stewart Family Reserve Chardonnay to be one of its crown jewels, and prices it at C$30. CedarCreek includes a chardonnay in its exclusive Platinum Reserve product line, also at C$30, while boutique producer Le Vieux Pin offers two small-batch chardonnays, including one priced at C$50. Perhaps the priciest, and most collectible chardonnay rarity in the province is the Micro-Cuvée bottling from the boutique Naramata producer Meyer Family Vineyards at C$65 a bottle. Clearly, chardonnay has cachet in British Columbia.

These premium wines are usually made with some portion of barrel-fermented, and/or barrel-aged juice, in small lots, and are carefully vinified. Most chardonnay grapes come from the warmer vineyards of the southern Okanagan, so it is common for British Columbia chardonnays to display juicy fruit flavors with lush, velvety textures. But there is also the perpetual freshness of British Columbia fruit to add verve to any style of chardonnay wine. Indeed, if there are any hallmarks to British Columbia's chardonnay character, they may be consistent silky texture and fresh white and yellow fruit flavors.

It is interesting that there is not more chardonnay grown in the Vancouver Island and Gulf Island appellations. It grows well in Oregon's cool-climate Willamette Valley (not to mention Burgundy), alongside the pinot noir, so why not in the warmer spots of the islands? If island growers can ripen pinot noir, they should be able to ripen the proper clones of chardonnay. There are wineries here trying to grow merlot and cabernet franc, but wouldn't chardonnay be a more promising match for the climate? Perhaps the trend toward crisp, steel-fermented, no-malolactic-style, cool-climate chardonnay popular elsewhere in the Northwest simply hasn't gained the same traction in British Columbia. Or perhaps there's just no need, since the province's fuller style chardonnays sells so well.

Pinot Gris

The growing popularity of pinot gris everywhere has not escaped British Columbia's winemakers. An early ripening grape, it is a natural choice for the province's cooler regions. Well made cool-climate British Columbia pinot gris wines can be delightful dry, spicy, aromatic, and refreshing, and deliver lively citrus and pear flavors.

As elsewhere in the Northwest, plenty of pinot gris is grown in the warmer regions as well. Okanagan Valley–sourced pinot gris wines have greater depth and richness. And with proper winemaking attention, they retain the fresh, lively character that makes the wine so appealing; acid retention is critical to this character. The flavors of warm-climate pinot gris wines are of peach, apple, and even tropical fruit, with a long, lush mouth feel.

British Columbia's winemakers treat pinot gris with due respect, mostly making clean wines that are true to the varietal rather than trying to impose a predetermined style on the grape. My personal bias is toward the clean, fresh, what I'll call natural style of tank-fermented pinot gris, but some winemakers and a lot of consumers prefer pinot gris to be barrel-fermented and oak-aged. These procedures add depth and complexity and create more mouth-filling, even unctuous wines. The best pinot gris of this style that I have ever tasted came from Averill Creek on Vancouver Island. So, clearly, British Columbia can make wonderful pinot gris of almost any style.

Pinot Noir

Pinot noir is the second most widely grown red wine grape in British Columbia. If Oregon's Willamette Valley pinot noir producers could regularly taste the better pinot noir wines from British Columbia, they would no doubt be impressed. In coming years, Oregon may no longer hold the pinot noir monopoly in the Northwest.

At a 2007 blind tasting of equal numbers of British Columbia and Willamette Valley pinot noir wines, all priced under C$25, a group of expert tasters, including

SELL-OUT REDS
British Columbia's Prestige Blends

In most any wine region, a few wines and a handful of producers achieve an almost feverish market reputation. In British Columbia, a coterie of high-priced, highly sought Bordeaux-style blended wines have become trophies for collectors. Here are some prominent bottlings:

Oculus, from Mission Hill Family Estate Winery. The blend of this Bordeaux-style wine varies with the vintage, but is invariably one of the most collected of British Columbia's wines.

Le Grand Vin, from Osoyoos Larose. This classic, dense combination of Bordeaux grapes is made by Frenchman-turned-Canadian Pascal Madevon. The wine is drawing international attention to the Okanagan Valley.

Nota Bene, from Black Hills Estate Winery. Made since 1999, this single-vineyard blend of cabernet sauvignon, merlot, and cabernet franc has become a standard-bearer for Black Sage Road character.

Pinnacle, from Sumac Ridge Estate Winery. The first of the so-called icon blends, this bold, concentrated Bordeaux-style (though in some vintages syrah is added) wine has tremendous extraction and extra-long barrel aging.

Quintessential, by Church & State Wines. A new entrant into the prestige label category, this aptly named wine has quickly become a high-profile proprietary Bordeaux-style blend.

Quatrain, by Mission Hill Family Estate Winery. One of Mission Hill's Legacy wines, this new blend of merlot, syrah, cabernet franc, and cabernet sauvignon is distinctively juicy and succulent.

Josephine, by Herder Winery & Vineyards. This merlot-driven mélange from the Similkameen Valley, with its vibrant fruitiness and less-than-the-average barrel aging, is quickly becoming a cult bottling.

one, two, and three, by Sandhill Wines, Small Lots Program. Winemaker Howard Soon produces these succulent, sought-after individual blends from different grapes grown on single vineyards in quantities of around 300 cases. The blends one and two are Bordeaux-style, and three is Bordeaux grapes plus sangiovese and barbera.

sommeliers and wine writers from Vancouver (British Columbia), Portland, and Seattle, could not tell the wines apart. Canadians who were certain they'd know their region's pinots and Oregonians who were positive they'd pick the Willamette Valley wines were all proven wrong: the quality of the two wine countries' pinot noir wines in that price range was equal. The British Columbia pinot noir wines showed all the expected characteristics of cool-climate fruit: light color intensity, spicy red-fruit aromatics, silky textures, and plenty of acid-framed red cherry and raspberry fruit flavors. So did the Oregon wines.

Pinot noir is best grown in a cool climate, and consequently in British Columbia, the grape is mostly planted in the north Okanagan Valley (Westbank, Kelowna, Naramata, Summerland-Peachland) and the islands. When carefully grown in the coolest sites, British Columbia pinot noir wines display delightful red cherry, strawberry, and sometimes cranberry flavors, usually on a light frame, with little to no noticeable tannin. These wines stress the light, elegant side of the grape and are most often made for early drinking.

In the north Okanagan Valley, the temperatures are warmer than on the islands, and so pinot noir here has more textural weight, and riper red to black cherry flavors, along with plum and blackberry notes. These wines are usually more concentrated and extracted and, especially when cropped to low yields, have more tannin structure and earthy tones. Such pinot noir wines are built to age better and to show more complexity than many of the cooler region pinot noirs.

So far, British Columbia's pinot noir producers have been controlled in their use of oak, usually preferring a balance between new and older barrels rather than going full tilt on new oak. This approach helps emphasize the natural freshness of the flavors and lets the varietal character show through more readily. While pinot noir grapes are grown in the southern Okanagan Valley, and that part of the appellation can

Moving just-picked pinot noir clusters into fermentation tanks.

(*opposite*) The warm climate of British Columbia's southern Okanagan Valley ripens merlot grapes well.

produce excellent wine from that variety when carefully farmed, generally the farther south you go in the region, the less of a good match it becomes.

Cabernet Sauvignon

Cabernet sauvignon in the Okanagan Valley grows well, gets fully ripe, and displays excellent varietal character, especially, it seems, in the Black Sage Road and Osoyoos areas. Like merlot, it shows the leaner, more elegant side of the grape, and many versions have the classic cigar box, or cedar, notes that are indicative of a well-made cabernet sauvignon. Full fruit flavors of cassis, cherry, and wild berries are hallmarks of British Columbia cabernet sauvignon wines, along with an earthiness that gives weight and complexity. As with many British Columbia red wines, winemakers here tend to be judicious with their use of oak, resulting in more controlled expressions of fruit rather than overt tones of wood. Though not everyone is successful at this, the most prominent wineries regularly make wines with good balance between ripe fruit, tannins, and pleasing oak and vanilla accents.

Much of the province's cabernet sauvignon production goes into Bordeaux-style blended wines, usually contributing tannin structure and depth to the wine. Even so, well-crafted, single-variety British Columbia cabernet sauvignon wines are an elegant expression of a classic warm-climate grape variety.

Other Grapes

British Columbia is home to a surprising amount of well-made gewürztraminer. It was the first vinifera grape to be widely planted and produced in the province and retains its popularity. The variety tends not to be that popular elsewhere in the Northwest, but in British Columbia it is accorded increased winemaking respect. Resultant wines have excellent varietal character, depth, and freshness.

Pinot blanc is another white wine that is made well in the province, though it is not as widely grown as other whites. Vancouver sommelier Barbara Phil-

ip became Canada's first female (and second overall) Master of Wine, in part because of her thesis arguing that pinot blanc had all the right qualities to become British Columbia's signature grape except one: there wasn't enough enthusiasm for the grape in the province. This situation may change as producers are beginning to focus more on this classic variety.

Syrah is clearly an upcoming variety in the warmer reaches of the Okanagan Valley. With enough heat and proper soils, this popular Rhône grape is still in the early stages of its development in British Columbia and clearly has a strong future. British Columiba syrah wines have received a number of international awards, which means more syrah will no doubt be made in the future.

At number 11 on the list of most planted grapes, riesling must be considered one of the lesser grapes of British Columbia—lesser in quantity, but not in quality. A number of wineries make tiny amounts of very high-quality dry riesling, some of the best coming out of the New World and comparable to the finest from Ontario. Though rare, these wines are gaining a cultish following among aficionados of crisp, dry, fruity whites. Riesling is also a preferred grape for ice-wine production, and is perhaps the best-known use of the variety in the province. Two notable producers of riesling wines are Tantalus Vineyards, whose old-vine riesling has a startling clarity and acidity, and Quails' Gate, whose lush, accessible style is very popular. With the resurgence of riesling in the market, perhaps other British Columbia producers will pay it more viticultural attention.

Sparkling Wine

With so much cool-climate viticulture going on in British Columbia, it is not surprising that exceptional sparkling wine is made here. The high natural acidity that can be achieved in the classic pinot noir and chardonnay grapes makes sparkling wine production a natural outcome of the climate.

Some of the larger British Columbia wineries have made important investments in sparkling wine production and are producing hand-crafted *méthode champenoise* wines, but small producers have also made the commitment. Wineries such as Sumac Ridge and Jackson-Triggs produce large volumes of classically made sparkling wine at costs far below imported Champagne. On a different scale, craft producers like Venturi-Schulze, Blue Mountain, and Summerhill Pyramid Winery make more boutique cuvées whose quality attracts top dollar.

The bulk of British Columbia's sparkling wine production is based on classic French models, but the pushing-the-envelope ethic often at play in the province means some eccentric—and sometimes brilliantly so—sparkling wines are made as well. For instance, Venturi-Schulze makes extremely high-quality sparkling wines from unique blends such as: a brut-style combination of auxerrois, pinot gris, and kerner; a semisparkling red blend of pinot noir and zweigelt; and a brut of siegerrebe and kerner. And the large producer Jackson-Triggs has applied innovation to the creation of its distinctive sparkling riesling icewine.

Icewine

If there is one wine the world identifies with British Columbia it is icewine. Made only from naturally frozen-on-the-vine grapes, icewine is an expensive, unctuous delicacy that has earned global fame. To qualify as icewine, the air temperature at harvest must be 17.6°F (−8°C), the grapes can only be specified vinifera varieties, the crushing must be done in a continuous process while the grapes are frozen with no artificial cooling performed, and the sugar level must reach a specified point at fermentation. These are a lot of specifications: British Columbia takes its icewine seriously.

Canada's first commercial icewine was made in 1973 by Walter Hainle, with the help of son Tilman, near his winery in Peachland, in the Okanagan Valley. Today, icewine is made all over the Okanagan Valley, fetching high prices and made from all manner of grape varieties, red as well as white. It is a

messy and arduous process to make icewine, helping account for its cost.

The beauty of icewine is that the flavors are so intense. When the temperature reaches the regulatory standard, the water inside the grape freezes while the sugar-laden juice does not. When the grapes are pressed while still frozen, the concentrated juice seeps out, leaving behind the frozen water. This dense nectar is then fermented, often for very long periods (sometimes up to a year), and turned into icewine.

In the Okanagan Valley, many producers designate specific blocks of grapes in their vineyards as icewine candidates. Since the creation of icewine depends upon Mother Nature, vintners let these grapes hang on the vine well after normal harvest, awaiting the valued first hard freeze. The specified conditions can come as early as the end of October, or as late as March of the next year (in which case the vintage year is the previous year, since it is considered that the grapes were grown during that year's growing season). British Columbia's icewines are seen by some as a novelty and by others as a distinctive category of wine. Like any wine, some producers regularly do a better job of making icewine than others.

BRITISH COLUMBIA'S WINE COUNTRIES

Okanagan Valley Wine Country

The Okanagan Valley is British Columbia's most important wine region. It is the source of 90 percent of the province's wine output, home to some of Canada's biggest wine brands, and offers spectacular vineyard vistas unequaled anywhere in North America. It is also an exciting appellation that has become an international magnet for wine tourists, new winery development, and for winemakers seeking the challenge of helping to develop a still young wine country.

The vast and grand Okanagan Lake, framed by steeply sloping rock banks and sheer scarps, snakes through much of the valley, providing a dramatic

Okanagan Lake is an omnipresent influence on the success of viticulture in British Columbia's Okanagan Valley wine country.

OKANAGAN VALLEY WINE COUNTRY AT A GLANCE

Year established: 2005
Number of wineries: 95
Approximate vineyard acreage:
    9000 acres (3642 ha)
Predominant soil type: mixed gravels, glacial
    till, sand, and clay-loam
Vineyard growing degree days:
    North Okanagan 2192-2408 (1200-1320),
    South Okanagan 2564-2717 (1407-1492)

Most important grape varieties
merlot, pinot gris, chardonnay, pinot noir,
cabernet sauvignon, gewürztraminer, syrah,
sauvignon blanc, cabernet franc, pinot blanc.

backdrop for vineyards and wineries. Wineries of means do all they can to take advantage of their vistas, and on a warm summer day visitors to places like Mission Hill, Gray Monk, Quails' Gate, and Cedar-Creek are treated to a wine country experience unlike any in the Northwest.

Geographically, the Okanagan Valley is a narrow trough of glacially formed lakes roughly 124 mi (200 km) long that drains into the Okanagan River and then into the Columbia River. The valley begins in the north near the southern shores of Shuswap Lake, where a few stalwart wineries grow grapes near the towns of Tappen and Salmon Arm. Farther south, a handful of wineries are located near Enderby, Armstrong, and Vernon, at the northern tip of Okanagan Lake. The main section of the Okanagan Valley starts here, extends south to Kelowna, which is one of the fastest growing cities in Canada, bends westward to Peachland, and then turns south to Penticton.

The Okanagan Valley DVA continues south through Okanagan Falls, Oliver, and Osoyoos, and encompasses Skaha Lake, Vaseux Lake, and Osoyoos Lake. Geologically, the valley continues past the national border and beyond the Washington town of Oroville, but the name Okanagan Valley only refers to British Columbia.

The valley lies in the rain shadow of the Coast Mountains and the Cascade Range, so much of the appellation is semiarid, requiring access to water for irrigation, which is a growing issue as population and development pressures mount in the region. In the northern part of the valley, annual precipitation averages around 16 in. (406 mm). But south of the town of Oliver, true desert conditions prevail, with annual rainfall less than 8 in. (203 mm). The Osoyoos area at the southern tip of the Okanagan Valley constitutes a tiny desert, Canada's only one.

The Okanagan Valley's steep slopes and rugged terrain were initially formed by massive geologic folding, faulting, and erosion some 60 million years ago. These forces created a complex geology that resulted in mixed bedrock of primeval granites and sedimentary formations that underlie today's vineyards. In more recent geologic times, the Okanagan Valley was rent by repeated glacial advances and retreats, which helped carve the current topography and left behind large quantities of unconsolidated rock, gravel, and soil remnants. The last of the glacial events was capped approximately 15,000 to 12,000 years ago by the formation of Glacial Lake Penticton behind an ice dam at the valley's narrow point near present-day Okanagan Falls. When the dam released, perhaps 10,000 to 8000 years ago, the resulting flood caused massive erosion, redistribution and deposition of rocks, gravels, and sediments, and created the basic landforms upon which vineyards now sit.

These processes resulted in convoluted soils and terrain. Even in vineyards as small as a few acres, three or four different soil types can often be found. Vineyard sites run along both sides of the valley on benches and alluvial fans that rise to 300 ft. (91 m) or more above the valley floor, and along the hillsides that bank the lake. These benches are composed of deep, well-drained glacial lake sediments that range from silty and sandy to gravelly and stony. The distribution of these benches, and therefore the vineyards, varies considerably along the length of the valley, and as the topography changes, so do the mesoclimates. Like for the other large-scale Northwest appellations (Columbia, Snake, and Willamette Valleys), these variations make it difficult to describe the Okanagan Valley in the aggregate. There are no official sub-DVAs in the Okanagan Valley (at least not yet), but there are certain subregions beginning to show glimmers of reliable *terroir* distinctions. The Okanagan Valley is developing differing viticultural personalities, depending on the pockets of land where vineyards prosper, including Kelowna, Naramata Bench, Okanagan Falls, Golden Mile, Black Sage Road, and Osoyoos.

Though different, these subregions share an overall warm, dry climate with a long growing season, among the longest in Canada. Average summer

PACIFIC NORTHWEST WINE COUNTRIES GAZETTEER

temperatures in the northern parts of the valley are 68°F to 73.4°F (20°C–23°C) and can reach highs of 80.6°F to 84.2°F (27°C–29°C), with average growing degree days of approximately 2192 (1200). In the south, it is as much as 5°C warmer overall, with some places being considerably warmer than that. Summer afternoon temperatures in many vineyards south of Oliver reach to 95°F (35°C) and more, sometimes for sustained periods. Growing degree days in the Oliver-Osoyoos area range from 2700 to 2800 (1482–1537), though individual sites can vary significantly.

The northerly latitude of the region, combined with clear skies, means vines receive plenty of sunlight, up to 18 hours of daylight in some places. Frost is generally not a danger in the northern part of the appellation because of well-sloped vineyards and the lake effect. But in the south where vines are closer to the valley floor, frost protection procedures are practiced. Winters are cold throughout the appellation, with temperatures averaging 26.6 to 21.2°F (–3 to –6°C). The valley has been subject to occasional arctic weather events in the past. The last significant one was winter 1983, bringing temperatures down to –7.6°F (–22°C). In 2009, unusually cold temperatures damaged some vines and reduced that year's crop yield by approximately 20 percent. It used to be considered prudent to bury young vines as winter protection, but that is no longer done. Severe winter conditions have been rare in recent years, and winter vine kill is not considered a serious danger here.

Modern viticulture in the Okanagan Valley began in the 1920s and 1930s on the high hills to the south of Kelowna, when J. W. Hughes planted mixed table grapes and vinifera grapes. Some of these original vineyard sites still exist, with much replanting. The vineyards were placed on high, sharp slopes to take advantage of good air drainage and to maximize exposure to sunlight.

Today Kelowna-area vineyards extend south and north of the city on the east side of the valley, with sloped vine rows benefiting also from sunlight reflect-ed off the surface of the lake With a location near the 50th parallel, this growing region is one of the coolest in the Okanagan Valley, with average growing degree days of nearly 2200 (1204). Like in the Willamette Valley, pinot noir ripens very well here, as does pinot gris, and especially riesling. Other grapes that produce locally grown wines include chardonnay, pinot blanc, and gewürztraminer, as well as some remnant hybrid grapes that are still occasionally grown.

On the west side of the lake, opposite Kelowna and centered around the slopes surrounding Mount Boucherie, a 60-million-year old volcanic relic, another clutch of vineyards and wineries grow pinot noir, pinot gris, auxerrois, riesling, and a smattering of hybrids including old-vine maréchal foch. Some of these vineyards were planted as early as the 1960s and 1970s, others more recently, but today many of them are uncomfortably interspersed with affluent housing developments that compete for the fine hillside views.

Continuing south along the west side of the valley, vineyards and wineries can be found on alluvial fans and slopes around the towns of Peachland and Summerland, names that allude to the warm climate and agricultural history of the area. These vineyards are well above the lake, in ground that is typically silty to gravelly with relatively high mineral content. The climate here does not vary significantly from the Kelowna area—growing degree days at weather stations in each spot are similar—though the vines on the west side generally receive less light. Pinot noir and gewürztraminer shine along this stretch of the appellation, and in this area some of the earliest sparkling wines in the Okanagan Valley were grown and made.

On the east side of the valley, south of Kelowna and below Okanagan Mountain Provincial Park, there are no vineyards (and little public access) until the town of Naramata. Between Naramata (opposite Summerland to the west) and Penticton, is one of the strongest candidates for true subappellation status, the area known as the Naramata Bench. This

Vines grown on the benches above Okanagan Lake benefit from reflected sunlight and the moderating effects of the water mass.

Vineyards around Mount Boucherie are surrounded by houses and encroaching development.

swath of land starts at the edges of steep bluffs that rise from the lake. Across the broad top of these plateaus, a patchwork of gently sloping vineyards runs from the very edges of the bluffs, back and upward 3 or 4 mi (4.8–6.4 km) to the edge of the eastern mountains that tower above. The views across the lake from these south- and west-facing vineyards are magnificent. The rolling terrain makes for multiple aspects, and as the area develops, it seems that vines can be seen in all manner of dips, slopes, and hillside rolls from Naramata to the hills east of Penticton.

Naramata Bench soils are generally sandy loam,

medium-textured, with some stratified sands, mostly of glacial- or lake-deposited origin. They are well drained, heavier, and contain more organic matter than the soils found in the southern reaches of the Okanagan Valley. Climatically, the Naramata Bench is heavily influenced by the proximity of the lake. Air movement is healthy across the vineyards, from both the lake and surrounding mountains, keeping temperatures cool. The average temperature in July and August is 68.7°F (20.4°C), with maximum average highs approaching 81°F (27.2°C). Winter temperatures are generally not severe, averaging 24°F to 27°F (−4.4°C to −2.7°C). Annual precipitation is a meager 10 to 12 in. (254–304 mm), but interestingly the majority of it falls during the growing season, helping keep vines from becoming too desiccated.

The slopes of the Okanagan Valley's Naramata Bench create excellent growing conditions for a wide variety of wine grapes.

Because of its eastern exposure, vines on the Naramata Bench receive more sunlight hours than those on the west side of the lake, contributing to prolonged, even grape ripening. The bench is also cooler than wine countries to the south, so grapes can be left on the vine longer to develop additional character. Fall frost is rarely a problem, because of the lake effect and good air drainage. Naramata Bench GDD average around 2535 (1391), though specific sites vary.

A wide range of grapes are grown here. Standouts include pinot noir, pinot gris, gewürztraminer, sauvignon blanc, merlot, and cabernet franc. The first syrah in the Okanagan Valley was grown here, and highly respected cabernet sauvignon and Bordeaux-style blends are also produced from Naramata Bench vines. The wines of this region generally show clear varietal character, with good acidity and balance. They are not as plush and rich as the same grapes grown in the south Okanagan, yet their uplifting character is a pleasing counterbalance to the density of wines from warmer parts of the valley.

The Naramata Bench has developed rapidly in recent years, with plenty of new vineyards planted and the creation of small-production boutique labels. The area is alluring and beautiful, which no doubt contributes to its success. The limited amount of available land provides a natural restraint to too much growth.

Okanagan Lake ends at the town of Penticton, which is also the southern terminus of the Naramata Bench, but the Okanagan Valley appellation contin-

ues southward. Below Penticton is Skaha Lake and, at its southern end, the town of Okanagan Falls. Just below the town (locally referred to as OK Falls), wineries are perched on the hills along the eastern side of the Okanagan River. Here marks the southern tip of Okanagan Valley's cooler climate region; from here south the climate gets considerably warmer.

Wineries in this beautiful area have earned special reputations for quality pinot noir, riesling, chardonnay, and gewürztraminer wines, as well as some very fine sparkling wines. The key to their quality—as always—is to carefully match the grape variety to the site, because even though GDD averages here are a warm 2564 (1407), mesoclimate variations allow some sites to produce excellent pinot noir, while others nearby can ripen merlot and syrah.

The valley south of Okanagan Falls is narrow, and the point where it takes a southwesterly bend at Vaseux Lake is marked by the impressive bulk of McIntyre Bluff, rising more than 900 ft. (264 m) off the valley floor. This rock massif marks the climatic border between the Okanagan Valley's cooler climate north and its warmer climate south. Below this point, the weather becomes warmer and dryer, until it is a true desert environment near Osoyoos and the Canada-U.S. border. Growing degree days north of this point range from 2192 to 2408 (1200–1320), while farther south the range is 2564 to 2717 (1407–1492).

The majority of the Okanagan Valley vineyards are located on the open benches that rise up 164 to 328 ft. (50–100 m) from the valley floor south of the town of Oliver, which calls itself the Wine Capital of Canada. On both sides of the valley between Oliver and Osoyoos in the south, vineyard land is highly desirable, increasingly scarce, and decidedly expensive. The wine country of south Okanagan Valley is in many ways the heart of the appellation, and accounts for approximately 70 percent of the grapes grown in the DVA.

Three other subregions comprise the south Okanagan Valley wine country: Golden Mile, Black Sage Road, and Osoyoos. They share the qualities of deep

Vines of the Naramata Bench are highly influenced by their proximity to Okanagan Lake.

(*opposite*) The looming mass of McIntyre Bluff, seen here from Blue Mountain Vineyard, marks the boundary between the Okanagan Valley's cooler north and warmer south.

These estate vines of Tinhorn Creek Vineyards epitomize the *terroir* of the Golden Mile in the Okanagan Valley wine country.

aridity and heat: summer precipitation can be as little as 3 in. (7.6 cm), and temperatures in some vineyards regularly exceed 95°F (35°C)—but each has its own aspect, soil composition, and mesoclimate. Though many might say it is too early in the history of Okanagan Valley wine country to be firmly defining *terroirs* and subappellations, the fact is that most wine people in the region feel they consistently detect discernible differences in the wines from these subregions.

The Golden Mile area extends south of Oliver on an elevated bench along the west side of the valley. Mountains on the west send cooler air cascading through the vines in the summer, yet their mass near the ground gathers daytime heat and also radiates residual warmth for the grapes at night. Varying soil types are found here, but generally soils are well-drained, gravelly loam with some minor amounts of mixed-in clay and sand. Vineyards tend to be southeast and eastern facing, and so they gather maximum morning sun, thought by many to be more advantageous than the harsher afternoon exposure on the opposite side of the valley. The vines do lose the sunlight earlier than vineyards on the western side, so they receive less total heat accumulation.

The Golden Mile area (probably named for the fruitfulness of its former orchards) is slightly cooler than the eastern side of the valley and produces wines with more acidity and elegance. The soils and moderate heat support many aromatic white varieties, including gewürztraminer, sauvignon blanc, and riesling, though many reds, notably pinot noir, cabernet franc, merlot, and, in the right places, cabernet sauvignon, prosper on the Golden Mile.

Across the valley, the growing conditions are different. Black Sage Road parallels the Golden Mile, running along the eastern side of the valley on a huge bench of beach sand. The northern parts of this area have rocky and sandy soils, with sand becoming almost the sole component of the soil toward the south. This ground holds moisture poorly, the sand is deep, and it lacks organic material. Vine roots drive

Black Hills Estate Winery typifies the Black Sage Road area on the eastern side of the Okanagan Valley south of Oliver, British Columbia.

Harvesting red grapes in the south Okanagan Valley.

far here in search of nourishment, and irrigation is vital. The eastside location of Black Sage Road exposes the vines to more daily sunlight hours than vines on the Golden Mile, but this is a mixed blessing. Vines accumulate more heat units during the growing season, but the heat in the heart of summer can be severe, and can cause the vine to shut down its metabolism.

Vines of all types flourish in the area, if managed carefully, and deliver highly sought-after fruit. The wines here show more color extraction, denser body and texture, and deliver blockbuster fruit flavors. All of the Bordeaux-style red grapes flourish, with merlot and cabernet sauvignon being stand-

The vineyards of the Osoyoos Indian Band are the source for Nk'Mip Cellars and Spirit Ridge Vineyard Resort and Spa.

outs. More recently, syrah plantings along Black Sage Road have shown great promise, including the award-winning 2004 Jackson-Triggs Shiraz. Whites also do well, producing lushly textured wines with supple tropical notes, though they can lack the refinement of the same varieties grown on the western side of the valley.

To the south, just above the Canada–United States border, a third emerging region is the benches surrounding Osoyoos Lake. The area is a desert ecosystem, and one that is in peril because of the pressures of development. Similar in climate to the rest of the south Okanagan in terms of aridity and heat, the area is viticulturally distinctive because the moderating effects of the lake help reduce frost risk and lower seasonal temperature extremes in the surrounding vineyards. Soils are parched, sandy, and gravelly, with more clay and sand at lower elevations. Vineyards are located on south-facing slopes along both the west and east sides of the lake. On the west side, light is lost toward the end of the day as the sun sets behind the Coast Mountains. Light lingers longer on the eastern side, giving the vines more accumulated heat.

Wines from the Osoyoos benches possess power and concentration. The majority of grapes grown here are the classic red Bordeaux varieties, though increasingly, Rhône grapes are planted as well. The heat and soils favor reds, and though there are some white grapes grown, the area's reputation is firmly centered on the deep fruitiness and ample structure of its red wines.

Much of the Osoyoos land is owned by the Osoyoos Indian Band, which helped pioneer viticulture in the area and established the first aboriginal-owned vineyard and winery. Many of the larger land tracts are leased or owned in joint ventures with some of British Columbia's biggest wine brands.

WINERIES AND WINES TO SAMPLE

BLACK HILLS ESTATE WINERY

30880 Black Sage Road, Oliver, BC
250-498-0666; www.blackhillswinery.com
Open only by appointment.

Year founded:	1996
Annual production:	6300 cases
Signature wine:	Nota Bene (C$$$$)
Premium wine:	Nota Bene (C$$$$)
Value wine:	Alibi (C$$)
Estate vineyards:	Black Hills

Black Hills is famous for its Nota Bene (Italian for take note) blend of estate-grown cabernet sauvignon, cabernet franc, and merlot, which was one of the earliest British Columbia cult wines. Originally made by Senka Tennant, one of the partners who began the winery and planted the vineyard in 1996, the wine was known for always being sold out and the quonset hut winery for being closed. Since then, the brand has changed hands and has built an award-winning, architectural gem of a new winery. The appeal of Nota Bene has not diminished, and the wine is still difficult to obtain.

Head winemaker Graham Pierce is rigorous in his vineyard and winemaking practices, resulting in a massive, rich, deep Bordeaux-style blend that comes exclusively from the estate vineyard, which is why 4300 cases of Nota Bene is the maximum production. A small amount of tasty chardonnay is also made, plus a delightful sauvignon blanc–sémillon blend called Alibi. And take note: Black Hills Estate is one of the few Northwest wineries making a single-variety carmenère.

BLASTED CHURCH VINEYARDS

378 Parsons Road, Okanagan Falls, BC
250-497-1125; www.blastedchurch.com
Open during the season.

Year founded:	2002
Annual production:	18,000 cases
Signature wine:	Hatfield's Fuse (C$$)
Premium wine:	Amen (port-style) (C$$$$)
Value wine:	Gewürztraminer (C$$)
Estate vineyards:	Blasted Church

The first question anyone asks about this winery is how it came by its name. In 1929 a group of men exploded a small amount of dynamite inside an old local church in order to loosen the nails and make it easier to disassemble and transport. In keeping with such eccentricity, this winery's award-winning label designs are eye-catchingly clever, and feature caricatures of local food and wine personalities.

Fortunately, the wines are not overshadowed by the marketing panache. Blasted Church's wide array of wines are well made, including an eclectic white blend called Mixed Blessing, an unusual wine made from the aromatic chardonnay musqué clone, and a peppery, floral malbec-syrah blend. The pinot noir is a pleasing example of a medium-bodied wine from estate grapes, and the layered syrah is also particularly tasty.

BLUE MOUNTAIN VINEYARD AND CELLARS

2385 Allendale Road, Okanagan Falls, BC
250-497-8244; www.bluemountainwinery.com
Open only by appointment.

Year founded:	1991
Annual production:	12,000 cases
Signature wine:	Brut Sparkling Wine (C$$)
Premium wine:	Pinot Noir Reserve (C$$$)
Value wine:	Pinot Blanc (C$$)
Estate vineyards:	Blue Mountain

Blue Mountain is one of the most beautifully sited vineyards in the Northwest, with sweeping views of McIntyre Bluff and Vaseaux Lake. It also produces some of the finest wines in the region. Ian and Jane Mavety and their children Matt and Christie intensely farm their vines in the belief that the primacy of the land must show through in the wines. They use low-impact, organic, and biodynamic techniques to maintain the health of their soil and the character of their vines. Their first commercial release was 1991, and in subsequent years their wines have been perennial sellouts.

The winery's sparkling wines (brut, rosé, reserve brut, and blanc de blancs) have tremendous depth and crispness, with richer flavors than are typically found elsewhere. One of the finest sparking wines I ever tasted came from Blue Mountain. It is also deservedly famous for its pinot noir wines, which display great Burgundian elegance and restraint without sacrificing fruit or character. They are wonderful expressions of both their soil and the grape itself.

BURROWING OWL ESTATE WINERY

100 Burrowing Owl Place, Oliver, BC
1-877-498-0620; www.bovwine.ca
Open during the season; limited hours.

Year founded:	1997
Annual production:	26,000 cases
Signature wine:	Syrah (C$$$)
Premium wine:	Meritage (C$$$)
Value wine:	Pinot Gris (C$$)
Estate vineyards:	Burrowing Owl

You simply cannot miss noticing Burrowing Owl winery from just about anywhere in the south Okanagan. The building looms over the vines in the Black Sage Road area of the valley as a beacon for wine-seeking travelers. Jim Wyse bought his first piece of vineyard land on the Black Sage Road in 1993, and opened Burrowing Owl winery in 1998. Since then, the original winery has been significantly expanded, with the addition of a 60-seat fine dining restaurant, luxurious 11-room guest house, a 25-m swimming pool, and all the wine country amenities that 100,000 visitors a year might want.

And it makes superb wine, too. The pinot gris and pinot noir are invariably excellent wines, which is interesting considering the pinot noir is grown at the winery's estate vineyard in the very warm Black Sage Road area. Burrowing Owl also makes a complex, intense syrah, an extremely dense but also deliciously age-worthy Meritage blend, and a spicy cabernet franc, among other very good wines.

Visitors are asked to donate C$2 for each wine tasting, and the proceeds are given to the Burrowing Owl Conservation Society of British Columbia to help preserve the endangered species.

CEDARCREEK ESTATE WINERY

5445 Lakeshore Road, Kelowna, BC
250-764-8866; www.cedarcreek.bc.ca
Open all year.

Year founded:	1986
Annual production:	40,000 cases
Signature wine:	Platinum Reserve Pinot Noir (C$$$)
Premium wine:	M (C$$$$)
Value wine:	Proprietor's White (C$)
Estate vineyards:	CedarCreek, Greata Ranch, Desert Ridge, Haynes Creek

CedarCreek is one of Canada's premier wineries, having been named the country's Winery of the Year on two occasions. It regularly produces beautiful wines, especially in its top-tier Platinum Reserve program. Drawing upon estate vineyards in the Kelowna, Summerland, and Osoyoos areas for up to 80 percent of the winery's grapes, CedarCreek employs a range of winemaking tools from gravity feed to micro-oxygenation to produce intense, fruity wines with excellent balance and structure.

CedarCreek offers a small-batch, super-premium line of Platinum Reserve wines made from low-yielding vines and given extra exposure to French oak. Platinum wines include a pinot noir, chardonnay, merlot, a delicious Bordeaux-style blend, and the only Madeira-style wine made in the Okanagan

Visitors to Burrowing Owl Estate Winery enjoy a variety of amenities, including fine dining and lodging.

247

Valley. The Estate Select line delivers prime quality estate-grown fruit, and the more simply labeled CedarCreek line offers delicious varietal wines at value prices. Despite the top reputation of its Platinum wines, the majority of CedarCreek's wines are in the C$20 range, and include select-tier wines that used to go into a now-discontinued higher priced product line. The result is plenty of CedarCreek wines that overdeliver on quality.

DESERT HILLS ESTATE WINERY

30480 71 Street (Black Sage Road), BC
250-498-1040; www.deserthills.ca
Open all year.

Year founded:	2003
Annual production:	8000 cases
Signature wine:	Syrah Select (C$$$)
Premium wine:	Zinfandel (C$$$)
Value wine:	Unoaked Chardonnay (C$$)
Estate vineyards:	Toor

The affable Randy Toor and his brother Jesse manage the family wine business with an infectious enthusiasm. The Toor family took an ailing apple orchard on the Black Sage Road, and in 1995 planted 23 acres (9.3 ha) of syrah, merlot, cabernet sauvignon, gamay, malbec, and a little pinot gris.

The Desert Hills wines are cleanly made with focused flavors. The syrah in particular is a robust wine with jammy fruit and spicy edges. The gamay is an unusual variety for the area, and is a pleasurable find for its fruit-sweet, bright, blackberry flavor. The Mirage Bordeaux-style blend is a rich wine with plenty of grip and good fruit.

FAIRVIEW CELLARS

13147 334th Avenue, Oliver, BC
250-498-2211
www.fairviewcellars.ca
Open during the season; restricted hours.

Year founded:	1997
Annual production:	3000 cases
Signature wine:	Cabernet Franc (C$$)
Premium wine:	The Bear Meritage (C$$$)
Value wine:	Sauvignon Blanc (C$$)
Estate vineyards:	Fairview Plateau

Bill Eggert is a one-man band when it comes to running Fairview Cellars. A quietly passionate winegrower, his vineyard is at the extreme northern end of the Golden Mile and has three different soil types. Eggert is best known for his complex red wines, especially his Bordeaux-style blends, made exclusively from grapes grown in his estate vineyard. His initial reputation was won with a merlot–cabernet sauvignon blend that he now calls Madcap Red, but a second cabernet sauvignon–focused blend with added merlot and cabernet franc called The Bear has garnered critical raves. There is also a Two Hoots blend, single-varietal merlot, syrah, and cabernet sauvignon releases, and a succulent sauvignon blanc–sémillon blend.

Fairview wines are wonderfully individualistic, in part reflecting the nature of their creator, and are available in only small quantities (some releases are less than 100 cases). They are absolutely worth the effort to find.

GEHRINGER BROTHERS ESTATE WINERY

Highway 97 at Road 8, Summerland, BC
250-498-3537
www.sunnyosoyoos.com/webpages/gehringer_winery
Open during the season.

Year founded:	1986
Annual production:	4500 cases
Signature wine:	Dry Riesling (C$)
Premium wine:	Eherenfelser Icewine (C$$$ 375 ml)
Value wine:	Cuvée Noir (C$)
Estate vineyards:	Gehringer Brothers, Dry Rock

Brothers Walter and Gordon Gehringer are meticulous in their winemaking, partly because of having been trained in Germany, though at two different wine institutions. The family had the idea of creating a winery in 1973, but took seven years to research climate and location, finally buying a 65-acre (26.3-ha) Okanagan property in 1981.

Initially the winery concentrated on Germanic white varieties and a few hybrids, making them in a clean, off-dry style. As tastes moved to the dry side, the winery followed with drier wines, and, as winters in the Okanagan became less cold, they planted more French varieties, including pinot noir, pinot gris, chardonnay, sauvignon blanc, merlot, cabernet sauvignon, and cabernet franc. Today, the unassuming winery makes a range of clean, bright, fresh-flavored wines at reasonable prices. Gehringer Brothers may not have the marketing élan of some of its flashier neighbors, but its understated style consistently delivers excellent quality and top-notch value.

GRAY MONK ESTATE WINERY

1055 Camp Road, Okanagan Center, BC
1-800-663-4205; www.graymonk.com
Open all year.

Year founded:	1982
Annual production:	70,000 cases
Signature wine:	Estate Series Pinot Gris (C$$)
Premium wine:	Odyssey White Brut (C$$)
Value wine:	Latitude 50 Series White (C$)
Estate vineyards:	Gray Monk

George and Trudy Heiss helped pioneer the fine wine industry of British Columbia, when they began planting grapes north of Kelowna in the early 1970s. Like many at the time, they started out with hybrids, but ripped them up in favor of vines imported from Europe: auxerrois, gewürztraminer, kerner, and pinot gris. The latter grape, known in Austria by the nickname gray monk, became the name of their winery.

Astutely located on east bank slopes with spectacular views of Okanagan Lake, Gray Monk is justifiably known for its clean, aromatic, fully flavored white wines—particularly the Odyssey Pinot Gris made from low-yielding old vines planted in 1976. In addition to the highly popular Latitude 50 blended white, red, and rosé wines (the name describes their location, very far north), winemaker George Heiss Jr. also makes an Odyssey sparkling wine, port-style wine, merlot, and pinot noir.

HESTER CREEK ESTATE WINERY

13163 326th Street, Oliver, BC
250-498-4435; www.hestercreek.com
Open all year.

Year founded:	1983 (then called Divino)
Annual production:	20,000 cases
Signature wine:	Pinot Blanc (C$$)
Premium wine:	Reserve Cabernet Sauvignon (C$$$)
Value wine:	Unoaked Chardonnay (C$)
Estate vineyards:	Hester Creek

Hester Creek is fast becoming a signature winery in the southern Okanagan Valley under current owner Curt Garland. Blessed with an estate vineyard that

LE VIEUX PIN

34070-73rd Street, Black Sage Road, Oliver, BC
250-498-8388; www.levieuxpin.ca
Open all year; limited hours.

Year founded:	2004
Annual production:	3500 cases
Signature wine:	Vaila Pinot Noir Rosé (C$$)
Premium wine:	Apogée Merlot (C$$$$)
Value wine:	Gewürztraminer (C?)
Estate vineyards:	Le Vieux Pin

Le Vieux Pin (the name refers to an old pine tree in the vineyard) is an early, excellent example of the Okanagan Valley's new generation of well-financed, boutique wineries. By focusing on rigorous techniques in the vineyard, including high-density planting, organic low-input practices, dry farming, and very small crop loads, Le Vieux Pin obtains high-quality, intense fruit. In the cellar, strict attention is paid to hand-sorting the fruit, and noninterventionist winemaking brings out the best in the grapes.

Le Vieux Pin's wines are focused and well crafted. The pinot noir wines cover the style gamut, from the dark, rich, masculine Belle, to the spicy, aromatic Émol, and the quietly elegant Périgée. The merlot wines, especially the Apogée, are dense and chocolatey, with plump cherrylike flavors and substantial body. The white wines are delightfully aromatic and full of fruit.

MISSION HILL FAMILY ESTATE WINERY

1730 Mission Hill Road, West Kelowna, BC
250-768-7611; www.missionhillwinery.com
Open all year.

Year founded:	1981
Annual production:	100,000 cases
Signature wine:	Oculus (C$$$$)
Premium wine:	Oculus (C$$$$)
Value wine:	Five Vineyards Chardonnay (C$)
Estate vineyards:	Mission Hill Road, Naramata Bench, Black Sage Bench, Osoyoos, Lakeshore

There are few more impressive winery estates than Mission Hill. Resplendent on the side of Mount Boucherie, Mission Hill stands as a beacon for the entire British Columbia wine industry. It was planned that way. Owner Anthony von Mandl purchased the winery with a vision of refashioning both it and the province's wine world as a whole. Under the direction of winemaker John Simes, the winery today produces a portfolio of superbly made wines that express the power, grace, and diversity of Okanagan Valley grapes.

At the top of the Mission Hill's lineup is the Legacy Series, comprised of the opulent Oculus, a classically silky Bordeaux-style blend; the remarkably rich, fruity Quatrain red blend; and Perpetua, a perfectly balanced, rich, concentrated chardonnay. Below these wines is a foundation of tiered products that deliver a wine for every taste and budget. Supporting the Mission Hill wines is an amazing culinary program, and a visitor experience made impressive as much by the wines as the unparalleled architecture and grandeur of the winery grounds.

NK'MIP CELLARS

1400 Rancher Creek Road, Osoyoos, BC
250-495-2985; www.nkmipcellars.com
Open during the season.

Year founded:	2002
Annual production:	18,000 cases
Signature wine:	Qwam Qwmt Syrah (C$$$)
Premium wine:	Qwam Qwmt Riesling Icewine (C$$$$ 375ml)
Value wine:	Chardonnay (C$$)
Estate vineyards:	Inkameep

Nk'Mip Cellars (pronounced in-ka-meep) is the first aboriginal-owned and operated winery in North America. Part of the Osoyoos Indian Band's long-term plan, which includes the adjoining Spirit Ridge Vineyard Resort & Spa, the winery takes advantage of its long-developed vineyards. Winemaker Randy Picton crafts excellent, bright, fresh pinot blanc, riesling, and chardonnay in a separate White Fermentation Room, and his reds in a Red Fermentation Room. Wines are moved by gravity to ensure gentle treatment.

The top-of-the-line wines are labeled Qwam Qwmt (translated as achieving excellence), and excellent they are. The syrah is powerful yet elegant; the merlot is firm, and packed with sweet fruitiness; the Meritage is silky and harmonious; and the pinot noir wines are among the best in the province. The beautiful tasting room is airy and offers great views. Stay at the resort next door, enjoy the gourmet restaurant, and savor the Nk'Mip wines.

New vines, in milk cartons for protection, await planting between older, more widely spaced vines, in the Okanagan Valley.

POPLAR GROVE WINERY

1060 Poplar Grove Road, Penticton, BC
250-493-9463; www.poplargrove.ca
Open all year; limited hours.

Year founded:	1995
Annual production:	15,000 cases
Signature wine:	The Legacy (C$$)
Premium wine:	The Legacy (C$$)
Value wine:	Chardonnay (C$$)
Estate vineyards:	Poplar Grove

Ian Sutherland has been the driving force behind Poplar Grove, ever striving to learn more about winemaking (vacations are often taken working at wineries in other regions) and driving Poplar Grove to become a cult winery thanks to a reputation for flawless winemaking and marketing savvy.

The Legacy is a benchmark blend of merlot, cabernet franc, cabernet sauvignon, and malbec aged for two years in barrel and then 18 months more in

Quails' Gate winemaker, Grant Stanley.

bottle. Such holding back of wines is unusual, but typical of Poplar Grove's commitment to quality. The other wines are treated just as specially. The merlot is full of ripe fruit framed by clean acidity; the cabernet franc is fabulous, possibly the finest in the province. All of Poplar Grove's wines are excellent. A new winery and tasting room facility also make Poplar Grove a landmark winery to visit.

QUAILS' GATE

3303 Boucherie Road, Kelowna, BC
250-769-4451; www.quailsgate.com
Open all year.

Year founded:	1989
Annual production:	55,000 cases
Signature wine:	Old Vines Foch Reserve (C$$$)
Premium wine:	Stewart Family Reserve Pinot Noir (C$$$)
Value wine:	Quails' Gate Rosé (C$)
Estate vineyards:	Quails' Gate

Perched beautifully overlooking Okanagan Lake on the side of Mount Boucherie, Quails' Gate's vineyard offers an enviable destination for visitors. In the tasting room, tucked into a charming wood and stone building, it is difficult to know where to start. I'd head for the Stewart Family Reserve wines, especially the pinot noir. Winemaker Grant Stanley specializes in the variety and arguably makes the best in the province. But don't overlook the chardonnay, a barrel-fermented, full malolactic version that offers plush polish and flavor.

Quails' Gate wines also include a remarkable Old Vines Marechal Foch Reserve, one of the best riesling wines in British Columbia, and an extensive line of well-crafted Okanagan Valley wines including pinot noir, merlot, cabernet sauvignon, chenin blanc, and gewürztraminer. The entire wine tasting and touring experience at Quails' Gate is appealing and educational, and includes the fine dining offerings of the Old Vines Restaurant. This winery is a not-to-be-missed Okanagan Valley experience.

ROAD 13 VINEYARDS

13140 316A Avenue (Road 13), Oliver, BC
250-498-8330; www.road13vineyards.com
Open during the season.

Year founded:	1998
Annual production:	15,000 cases
Signature wine:	Jackpot Pinot Noir (C$$$)
Premium wine:	Fifth Element (C$$$)
Value wine:	Honest John's White (C$$)
Estate vineyards:	Home, Castle, Rock Pile

Pam and Mick Luckhurst purchased the former Golden Mile Cellars, complete with its castlelike winery building and tasting room, in 2003 without significant wine experience of their own. They were fast learners. They hired winemaker Mike Bartier, later changed the winery's name to Road 13 (the old name for their road), and focused on growing the best fruit they could. In short order, they became known for crafting excellent wines.

It is hard to say what wine is Road 13's best. I am partial to the pinot noir wines: the Road 13 bottling is highly balanced and finely made, and the Jackpot Pinot Noir is full of focused cherry flavors accented with admirable spice notes. The Old Vines Chenin Blanc is a rare treat and worth seeking out, while both the Fifth Element (a blend of the five standard red Bordeaux varieties) and the Jackpot Syrah are well executed, delightfully balanced, big-style red wines.

In early 2010, the winery announced the abandonment of some popular varietal wines—including their best-selling merlot—in favor of a new emphasis on blended wines that they feel better reflect the Okanagan Valley wine character.

SANDHILL

1125 Richter Street, Kelowna, BC
250-762-9144; www.sandhillwines.ca
Open during the season.

Year founded:	1997
Annual production:	29,000 cases
Signature wine:	Sandhill Small Lots wines (C$$–$$$)
Premium wine:	Small Lots Syrah (C$$$)
Value wine:	White Label Pinot Gris (C$$)
Estate vineyards:	Sandhill

Sandhill has its roots in Calona Vineyards, the oldest winery in the Okanagan Valley, but is for practical purposes a separate label. Winemaker Howard Soon is an icon in British Columbia enology, and crafts impeccable premium wines from the Sandhill Estate Vineyard and selected, carefully farmed Okanagan Valley vineyards.

Of particular note is Soon's Small Lots Program (generally no larger than 400 cases) all made from single vineyards. The program includes a unique sangiovese, plus unusual single-variety renditions of petit verdot, malbec, barbera, and viognier. Also made are three superb blends, called one, two, and three. The rest of Sandhill's wines are more available, easily approachable, and excellent examples of what great winemaking can do when confronted with greatly grown grapes.

SEE YA LATER RANCH

2575 Green Lake Road, Okanagan Falls, BC
250-497-8267; www.sylranch.com
Open all year.

Year founded:	1995
Annual production:	25,000 cases
Signature wine:	See Ya Later Riesling (C$)
Premium wine:	Ping (C$$)
Value wine:	Jimmy My Pal (C$$)
Estate vineyards:	Hawthorne Mountain

The original plantings for Hawthorne Mountain Vineyards, now 101 acres (40.8 ha), were in 1960, and have long been a center of wine production under the ownership of Harry McWatters and later Vincor. The quirky label design (featuring a winged dog) refers to an individualistic, long-gone owner of the ranch and his compassion for dogs.

See Ya Later Ranch wines include a classic gewürztraminer, clean riesling, bright pinot noir, fresh pinot gris, and an excellent ehrenfelser. Also made is the prized Ping, a big, bold Bordeaux-style blend that delivers black cherry fruit and vanilla framed by firm tannins. The See Ya Later Ranch tasting room is located in a restored heritage stone house dating back to the early 1900s.

See Ya Later Ranch Vineyard has sweeping views of the Okanagan Valley.

SUMAC RIDGE ESTATE WINERY

17403 Highway 97N, Summerland, BC
250-494-0451; www.sumacridge.com
Open all year.

Year founded:	1979
Annual production:	110,000 cases
Signature wine:	Pinnacle (C$$$$)
Premium wine:	Pinot Blanc Icewine (C$$$$ 375 ml)
Value wine:	Private Reserve Rosé (C$)
Estate vineyards:	Sumac Ridge, Black Sage

Harry McWatters founded what is now British Columbia's oldest estate winery in 1979, and went on to become perhaps the most influential individual in the growth and development of the Okanagan Valley's wine community. Sumac Ridge sold its first vinifera wines in 1981; created the first British Columbia–grown chardonnay in 1983; released the first of what is now one of the province's best-selling sparkling wines, Steller's Jay Brut, in 1989; was named Top Winery of the Year by the *Globe & Mail* in 1999; released its Pinnacle red blend in 1997; and in 2001, Sumac Ridge Chardonnay is named Wine of the Year at the All-Canada Wine Competition. Sumac Ridge's impact on the British Columbia wine industry has been inestimable.

Today, Sumac Ridge's superb line of sparkling wines, which also includes the Sparkling Pinnacle, and a unique sparkling shiraz, may be its most popular products. The chardonnays (Private Reserve, Black Sage Vineyard, and Unoaked), Bordeaux varietals from Black Sage Vineyard, and the Pinnacle red and white blends are excellent as well. Sumac Ridge's gewürztraminer is a solid standby.

SUMMERHILL PYRAMID WINERY

4870 Chute Lake Road, Kelowna, BC
250-764-8000; www.summerhill.bc.ca
Open all year; limited hours.

Year founded:	1991
Annual production:	30,000 cases
Signature wine:	Cipes Brut Nonvintage (C$$)
Premium wine:	Platinum Series Zweigelt Icewine (C$$$$+)
Value wine:	Pinot Gris (C$)
Estate vineyards:	Summerhill, Banberry

There is no missing Summerhill Pyramid Winery: just look for the big white pyramid. No kidding. Owner Stephen Cipes, a former New York city property developer turned winery owner, has erected a geometrically precise pyramid building that uses no ferrous metal and has no electricity in the chamber, all for the purpose of aging wine.

Summerhill organically farms about 50 acres (20.3 ha) of estate vines to produce a wide range of popular wines, the best known of which may be their sparkling wines. Experienced British Columbian winemaker Eric von Krosigk crafts a Brut, Blanc de Noir, Pinot Noir Brut, and a sparkling wine that uses icewine as the dosage. Also made are four delicious icewines and a variety of red and white wines at reasonable prices. Despite the seemingly offbeat spiritualism, Cipes and von Krosigk are serious about their organics and their wines, and orchestrate a distinctive wine tasting experience.

TANTALUS VINEYARDS

1670 Dehart Road, Kelowna, BC
250-764-0078; www.tantalus.ca
Open by appointment only.

Year founded:	2004
Annual production:	2000 cases
Signature wine:	Old Vines Riesling (C$$)
Premium wine:	Riesling Icewine (C$$$$)
Value wine:	Riesling (C$$)
Estate vineyards:	Dehart Road

Tantalus Vineyards makes spectacularly dry, acidic, crisp, fresh, steely, and fruity riesling wines—some of the most intriguing in North America—as well as enticing pinot noir wines composed of an international blend of German and French clones. The estate vineyard, managed by Warwick Shaw and now finishing a transition to organics, was planted in 1978 and is the sole source for the Tanatlus label.

Tantalus makes the most of its fruit, producing wines with piercing flavors and memorable style. Jane Hatch has the perhaps easy job of marketing these perennially sold out, sought-after wines. Tantalus also makes a rare, succulent riesling icewine from hearty, over-20-year-old vines. All Tantalus wines are spectacular, as is the winery and tasting room, the province's first LEED-certified winery.

TINHORN CREEK VINEYARDS

32830 Tinhorn Creek Road, Oliver, BC
250-498-3743; www.tinhorn.com
Open all year.

Year founded:	1994
Annual production:	37,000 cases
Signature wine:	Oldfield Series Merlot (C$$)
Premium wine:	Oldfield Series Syrah (C$$$)
Value wine:	Tinhorn Creek Pinot Gris (C$$)
Estate vineyards:	Tinhorn Creek, Fischer, Diamondback

With significant estate vineyards on both the Golden Mile and Black Sage Road, Tinhorn Creek can draw upon superb fruit for its wines. Chairman and owner Kenn Oldfield and winemaker Sandra Oldfield give the beautiful winery and vineyards a distinctly personal, family feel, which follows through in their supple, accessible, generous wines. A leader in sustainability and the survivability of wildlife, including participating in an endangered snake protection program, Tinhorn Creek takes stewardship as seriously as its winemaking.

The Oldfield Series is the winery's reserve tier, the wines being held longer in the bottle for additional character. The lush, beautiful merlot is complemented by a crisp, clean, complex blend of multiple white varieties called 2Bench White. There are also an Oldfield Series 2Bench Red, syrah, and pinot noir, the latter held in barrel and bottle for three years. All Tinhorn Creek wines are superbly made and very well priced, allowing the wine lover to enjoy tastes of many different south Okanagan Valley varieties.

WORKING HORSE WINERY, VINEYARDS, AND FARM

5266 Coldham Road, Peachland, BC
250-448-5007; www.workinghorsewinery.com
Open by appointment only.

Year founded:	2008
Annual production:	1200 cases
Signature wine:	Rare Breed White (C$$)
Premium wine:	Tilman Ice Riesling (C$$$$+ 375 ml)
Value wine:	Rare Breed White (C$$ 375 ml)
Estate vineyards:	Working Horse

Tilman Hainle and Sara Norman have a vision for their 22 acres (8.9 ha) as a modern working example of sustainable heritage farming. Tilman planted his first vines here in 1973, which is also where he and his father made the first commercial icewine in North America. Today these vines are sustainably grown, hand-picked, and hand-sorted for small quantities of intense wine, on a farm whose commitment to sustainability may be unmatched anywhere else in the province.

This winery is a working vineyard and farm, growing additional organic herbs and vegetables, and offering farm-stay accommodations. A team of rare

At Tinhorn Creek Vineyards, Kenn Oldfield is chairman and owner, and Sandra Oldfield is winemaker and owner.

Suffolk draft horses, an endangered heritage breed, add to the biodynamic and sustainable focus. And the wines are beautiful. The Tilman Ice Riesling is fantastically intense and balanced, and early releases of very small-production estate pinot noir and rosé show impressive promise.

Similkameen Valley Wine Country

The next valley to the west of the Okanagan Valley, the Similkameen Valley, parallels the southern part of the Okanagan Valley and reaches west following the course of the Similkameen River. The growing number of small vineyards and wineries here are clustered around the towns of Keremeos and Cawston.

This high-elevation, semiarid land is similar in geologic makeup to the Okanagan Valley, with the notable difference that there is no large body of water to moderate temperatures. The Similkameen River may have some effects on closely located vineyards, but generally it has little impact on viticulture in the valley. Influences on grape growing in this appellation are the steep sides of the valley and the relative proximity to masses of heat-retaining rock. Air movement is high in the valley, but also is extra warm, and the warmth can get trapped in the valley depression and not dissipate at night. The air movement tends to reduce diseases and pests, but the trapped valley warmth can also create an ovenlike effect that can bring sustained high daytime temperatures above 100°F (37.7°C).

Growing degree days average 2480 (1360), so the area can ripen a wide array of grapes. Merlot, in particular, does well here, as do pinot gris, pinot noir, chardonnay, and cabernet franc. Hybrid grapes are also popular. Most vineyards are small, under 20 acres (8 ha), and many of the valley's wineries supplement their fruit with purchases of Okanagan Valley grapes.

Soils are mixed glacial deposits, well drained, with gravelly textures, and in some sites contain more clay and organic matter than generally found in the Oka-

SIMILKAMEEN VALLEY WINE COUNTRY AT A GLANCE

Year established: 2005
Number of wineries: 12
Approximate vineyard acreage:
    580 acres (232 ha)
Predominant soil types: mixed gravelly glacial
    deposits with some clay loam
Vineyard growing degree days: 2480 (1360)

Most important grape varieties
merlot, chardonnay pinot noir,
pinot gris, pinot blanc, cabernet franc

nagan Valley. Certain sites can be extremely rocky, which is appealing to vintners both because of the general lack of nutrients and heat retention provided by the rocks, and also because of the perceived similarity to certain famous French vineyards.

Agriculture in the Similkameen Valley goes back to the nineteenth century, and grapes have been cultivated here since the 1950s. The area does have viticultural challenges. The combination of wind and heat can rapidly dry vines, and irrigation is critical especially at the end of the season when vines are the most stressed. There are frost risks, and though the winters in the Similkameen Valley are colder than in the Okanagan Valley, the Similkameen's early reputation for killing grapevines in the winter probably had more to do with inadequate viticultural knowledge than any inherent detraction in the climate.

In recent years, adventurous winegrowers have expanded their stake in the area, and new vineyards and wineries are bringing fresh attention to the Similkameen. Growth is partly because of the high repute earned by a few boutique labels in the valley, and partly because of the bargain land prices in contrast to the trendy, expensive Okanagan Valley.

WINERIES AND WINES TO SAMPLE

HERDER WINERY & VINEYARDS

2582 Upper Bench Road, Keremeos, BC
250-499-5595; www.herder.ca
Open during the season; limited hours.

Year founded:	2002
Annual production:	2500–3000 cases
Signature wine:	Josephine (C$$$)
Premium wine:	Josephine (C$$$)
Value wine:	Pinot Gris (C$$)
Estate vineyards:	Herder

Lawrence and Sharon Herder's new winery and tasting room sets a high standard of elegance for Similkameen wineries. Sited against an impressive rock crag, the winery—with guesthouse, pool, and four-hole golf course—and associated vineyard have commanding views. And the wine is great, too.

Herder received his wine training in California, and in the Similkameen he has the *terroir* to produce the big red wines he likes. Herder uses fruit from both the Okanagan and Similkameen Valleys to produce an excellent Bordeaux-style blend called Josephine, a spicy and concentrated merlot, and cabernet franc sourced from Osoyoos. For whites, a tank-made pinot gris, chardonnay, and a snappy blend round out recent releases.

Vancouver Island Wine Country

Vancouver Island is the largest island on the west coast of North America, made up of about 12,400 square mi (32,134 km2) of land, of which a small fraction is suitable for vineyards. The landmass runs on a northwesterly angle, with the southern tip dipping below the 49th parallel, so from many places on the southern part of the island, a glance due east will have you looking at Washington state, not British Columbia.

The island is a formidable geologic formation, with the Vancouver Island Ranges taking up the bulk of its mass. These mountains, which reach above

VANCOUVER ISLAND WINE COUNTRY AT A GLANCE

Year established: 2005
Number of wineries: 25
Approximate vineyard acres: 100
Predominant soil types: mixed clay and silty
    loam with some gravel
Vineyard growing degree days:
    1600–1700 (871–926)

Most important grape varieties
pinot gris, pinot noir, gewürztraminer, pinot blanc, gamay, merlot, ortega, siegerrebe, madeleine angevine, müller-thurgau, bacchus, kerner, maréchal foch

7000 ft. (2133 m), are the British Columbia rain-barrier equivalent to the Olympic Mountains in Washington and to the Coast Range in Oregon. The west side of Vancouver Island is incredibly wet: storms off the Pacific Ocean batter against these mountains, dropping prodigious precipitation, as much as 261 in. (665 cm) in a year. The eastern side of the island receives a more reasonable amount of rainfall, averaging 39 in. (993 mm) in the town of Duncan, near the location of most of the island's vineyards. The majority of the rain falls during the winter months.

Surprisingly, the southeast side of the island is classified as a Mediterranean climate, and is one of the mildest in Canada. The Pacific Ocean moderates temperatures throughout the year, but also the island is near warm ocean currents that help deliver sunny, balmy days during the growing season, aided by the seasonal buildup of continental high-pressure systems that keep storms at bay. Daytime summer temperatures of the wine countries average around 68°F (20°C), and can reach as high as 78°F (25.5°C). While this weather is comfortable for humans, it is cool for vinifera; growing degree days average be-

tween 1600 and 1700 (871–926). Winters are mild as well, with a growing season that ranges from 170 to 200 days.

But every year on the island is different. The low levels of heat accumulation leave little wiggle room for winegrowers if weather doesn't cooperate. This climate is marginal for vinifera grapes, and only the earliest ripening varieties can provide a measure of ripening reliability. A cool season such as 2008, for example, can hinder full maturation of grapes in even the optimally sited vineyard.

Most of the island's vineyards and wineries are located in the Cowichan Valley near the town of Duncan, the area south of Cowichan Bay, and on the middle sections of the Saanich Peninsula. Here, the hills and slopes are close enough to the water to have reduced frost risk, the summers are dry enough for most vineyards to irrigate, and sufficient warmth is available for early ripening varieties. Soils in the area are mixed, overlaying both volcanic basalts and granites. Generally high in mineral content, the soils have some clay, gravel, and silts, and are generally fairly fertile.

Many of the island's wineries today hedge their bets by buying Okanagan Valley grapes to supplement what they grow on their own vineyards. Some of the more popular island-grown vinifera varieties include pinot gris, pinot noir, gewürztraminer, pinot blanc, gamay, some merlot, and even a Hungarian grape called agria used more for blending than as a stand-alone variety. Of more importance here are the hybrid grapes, and cross-bred varieties which have been developed especially for cooler climates. Widely planted varieties include ortega, siegerrebe, madeleine angevine, müller-thurgau, bacchus, kerner, and maréchal foch. Experimental plantings of other varieties is also popular as island growers seek to discover what will flourish best in their climate, including the seemingly unlikely cousins cabernet sauvignon and cabernet franc.

Harvesting grapes by hand at Venturi-Schulze Vineyards.

(*opposite*) Netting vines helps protect the plants from birds.

WINERIES AND WINES TO SAMPLE

ALDERLEA VINEYARDS

1751 Stamps Road, Duncan, BC
250-746-7122
Open by appointment only.

Year founded:	1998
Annual production:	2000 cases
Signature wine:	Clarinet (C$$)
Premium wine:	Pinot Noir Reserve (C$$$)
Value wine:	Pinot Gris (C$$)
Estate vineyards:	Alderlea

Roger Dosman began planting his south-sloping 10-acre (4-ha) vineyard outside of Duncan in 1994 and has been fine-tuning it ever since. Decisive in his approach to winegrowing, if a variety doesn't meet his standards, out it goes. Consequently, what remains has proved its worth, which can be tasted in the small amounts of well-made wine that Alderlea releases each year. Dosman uses only island-grown fruit, feeling that the wines he makes are distinctive of the locale where they are grown.

Pinot noir is a specialty, though a prized maréchal foch (given the proprietary name of Clarinet) is grown as well. For whites, pinot gris, a blend of auxerrois and chardonnay, and—most unusually for Vancouver Island—a viognier are also made. Alderlea's wines, whether red or white, show great fruit clarity, with bright, fresh flavors.

AVERILL CREEK VINEYARD

6552 North Road, Duncan, BC
250-709-9986; www.averillcreek.ca
Open during the season.

Year founded:	2005
Annual production:	4000 cases
Signature wine:	Averill Creek Pinot Noir (C$$)
Premium wine:	Averill Creek Pinot Noir (C$$)
Value wine:	Somenos Rosé (C$$)
Estate vineyards:	Averill Creek

Former physician Andy Johnston began planting his vineyard on the southeast slope of Mount Prevost in 2002, and now has 10 acres (4 ha) in full production. His focus is pinot noir (with cousin pinot gris also planted), and unlike most other wineries on the island, he eschews the growing of hybrid grapes.

To support the pinot program, Averill Creek's attractive winery building is designed on a gravity-flow system, so that no pumping or excessive handling need take place between the vineyard and the barrels. Johnston is a firm believer in handling pinot noir gently, and early Averill Creek releases have shown strong quality. The winery also produces a fine barrel-aged pinot gris, a lighter bodied tank-fermented pinot gris, some estate merlot, and a gewürztraminer.

BLUE GROUSE ESTATE WINERY

4365 Blue Grouse Road, Duncan, BC
250-743-3834; www.bluegrousevineyards.com
Open during the season; restricted hours.

Year founded:	1989
Annual production:	2000 cases
Signature wine:	Pinot Gris (C$$)
Premium wine:	Black Muscat (C$$)
Value wine:	Müller-Thurgau (C$$)
Estate vineyards:	Blue Grouse

Hanz Kiltz has been making commercial wine on Vancouver Island since 1993. Today he and his family farm a 31-acre (12.5 ha) vineyard that was originally planted by the pioneer island winegrower John Harper. Kiltz is an island purist, using only fruit from his Cowichan Valley vineyard, which is managed by his wife Evangeline. Son Richard is the German-trained winemaker, and daughter Sandrina is a Vancouver-based sommelier and wine educator.

Blue Grouse produces an excellent, full-bodied pinot gris, plus well-made bacchus, siegerrebe, ortega, and müller-thurgau. For reds, the pinot noir is superbly crafted and a ringer for some Oregon pinots. Blue Grouse was the first on the island to plant gamay noir, and it is the only winery making a distinctive off-dry red wine they call Black Muscat.

VENTURI-SCHULZE VINEYARDS

4235 Vineyard Road, Cobble Hill, BC
250-743-5630; www.venturischulze.com
Open by appointment only.

Year founded:	1993
Annual production:	2500 cases
Signature wine:	Venturi-Schulze Vineyards Pinot Noir (C$$$)
Premium wine:	Venturi-Schulze Vineyards Pinot Noir Reserve (C$$$$)
Value wine:	Bianco di Collina (C$$)
Estate vineyards:	Venturi-Schulze

Giordano Venturi and Marilyn Schulze, along with winemaking daughter Michelle Schulze, have firmly established themselves in the top ranks of Canadian vintners by combining a purist's dedication to meticulous growing, a scientist's focus on data and knowledge, and an artist's creative expression.

Using exclusively estate, own-rooted vines, Venturi-Schulze makes amazingly delicious, fresh, vibrant wines that showcase how good Vancouver Island wine can be. The Venturi-Schulze Vineyards Pinot Noir (and the rarely made Reserve) are first-rate, the sparkling wines (white, rosé, and red) are crisp and fresh, and a range of dry, minerally, and aromatic whites deliver character-rich tastes. One good example is the Bianco di Collina, a blend of three hybrid grapes, that is aromatic, crisp and dry, with a tasteful combination of fruit and herb flavors. The noted Brandenburg No. 3 is an exceptional dessert wine made in part from juice simmered over an open wood fire.

Always distinctive in approach, Venturi-Schulze spares no cost in its organic vineyard, crown-caps (like a beer bottle) its sparkling wines and many of its still wines, blends with artful abandon, and names its wines with unusual flair. It even makes a traditional aceto balsamico vinegar, one of a few in North America. Venturi-Schulze's wines are expensive, sell out rapidly, and have leagues of devoted fans.

Enjoying a glass of wine at Blue Grouse Estate Winery.

Gulf Islands Wine Country

Many of the Gulf Islands, the islands in the southern Strait of Georgia that hug the eastern shore of massive Vancouver Island, are home to a growing community of tenacious wineries exploring the outer fringes of North American viticulture. With a climate generally considered to be cool Mediterranean, the islands offer promising, though in many ways challenging, prospects for fine winegrowing.

From Hornby and Denman Islands in the northwest to Saturna Island in the southeast, this 100-mile (160-km) arc of islands lies within the Georgia Basin ecosystem which also includes the Puget Sound. These islands were formed by deformation and thrust of bedrock that is primarily sedimentary—sandstone, siltstone, shale, and conglomerate—though some granites and schist rocks appear on Salt Spring Island.

Approximately 12,000 years ago, the retreat of the glaciers left behind a mantle of till on the islands, which has since been eroded by wind and water action. In many places in the Gulf Islands, there are large portions of bare bedrock, while on benches, valleys, and in low-lying land there are thin soils of textures that vary from fine to coarse. Generally, all of the soils on the islands are well draining, sandy or gravelly loams, and historically have supported agriculture where there was enough open land for cultivation and water for irrigation.

The rain barrier of the Olympic Mountains to the south and the interior mountains of Vancouver Island to the west create a dry corridor in the Gulf Islands that poses one of the key challenges for vintners. The islands in general average between 31 and 47 in. (800–1200 mm) annual precipitation, with Saturna Island being somewhat drier at 23 to 31 in. (600–800 mm). But 80 percent of this precipitation falls between October and April, leaving the heart of the growing season extremely dry; some vineyards get as little as 2 in. (50 mm) of rain in the summer. The well-drained soils do not retain nearly enough of the winter's moisture to support vinifera vines

GULF ISLANDS WINE COUNTRY AT A GLANCE

Year established: 2005
Number of wineries: 8
Approximate vineyard acreage:
   100 acres (40 ha)
Predominant soil types:
   Thin gravelly and sandy loams
Vineyard growing degree days:
   1292-1652 (700-900)

Most important grape varieties
pinot noir, pinot gris, gewürztraminer, pinot blanc, ehrenfelser, marechal foch, ortega, and zweigelt

through the entire growing season, which at nearly 200 days is one of the longest in Canada. Irrigation must be supplied either by groundwater wells, which are restricted or can be saline-infected, or by ponds and reservoirs.

The growing season may be dry, but it is also cool, with summer temperatures moderated by the surrounding ocean. Mean July minimum temperatures on the islands range from 51.8°F to 59°F (11°C to 15°C), and the mean maximum varies from 69.8°F to 77°F (21°C to 25°C). Individual vineyards can differ substantially from the climatic norm of the region, with some reporting summer temperatures commonly reaching 86°F (30°C) and above. Heat accumulation in this climate is long and slow, with growing degree days averaging 1292–1652 (700–900). The cool viticultural climate of the islands poses the biggest winegrowing challenge: getting grapes fully ripe. Site selection is a vital variable, and the smartest

Vineyards and wineries on British Columbia's Gulf Islands enjoy spectacular scenery while they grapple with challenging growing conditions to produce delightful wines.

Because of the rain shadow of the Vancouver Island Ranges, Gulf Island vineyards can be quite dry.

The influence of marine air on the vineyards of the Gulf Islands makes sites like Morning Bay Vineyards on Pender Island good for cool-climate grapes.

(*opposite*) The winegrowing spirit in the Gulf Islands is at once adventuresome and whimsical.

vintners have chosen vineyard sites that offer good southern exposure or are located near rock masses that can help retain heat. Other viticultural tricks of the trade are often employed to help ensure maximum fruit development, including grafting to rootstocks that encourage earlier ripening and tenting vines with plastic sheeting in the spring to create an artificial greenhouse effect that adds heat units.

Of prime importance is matching grape varieties to the climate. Early ripening grapes such as pinot noir, pinot gris, gewürztraminer, some pinot blanc, and even a bit of chardonnay are island mainstays. Also widely planted are crosses and hybrid grapes specifically designed to ripen in a cool climate. Among the most popular are ehrenfelser, maréchal foch, ortega, and zweigelt. Many of the Gulf Island wineries supplement their small estate vineyards with grapes purchased from the Okanagan Valley, which accounts for some otherwise improbable wines from the Gulf Islands, such as Bordeaux-style blends.

While the Gulf Islands have long been known for their productive agriculture—everything from peppers to apples—only since 1998 have wine grapes been part of the region's produce. The first winery was established on Saturna Island, though vineyards had been planted in the islands before then. Today, wineries of various sizes and sophistication can also be found on North Pender, Salt Spring, Thetis, and Hornby Islands, and also Quadra Island, which is technically too far north to be a part of the Gulf Islands but is considered here.

The winegrowing challenges of the Gulf Islands are formidable, and the long-term, sustainable quality of many of the vineyards is yet to be determined. The difficulties of growing wine grapes here, plus the distinctive lifestyle that the islands engender, seem to attract a hardy sort of visionary. These are people who soldier onward in their wine quest, an admirable trait.

WINERIES AND WINES TO SAMPLE

GARRY OAKS WINERY

1880 Fulford-Ganges Road, Salt Spring Island, BC
250-653-4687; www.garryoakswine.com
Open all year; limited hours.

Year founded:	2000
Annual production:	1500 cases
Signature wine:	Garry Oaks Pinot Gris (C$$)
Premium wine:	Zeta (Zweigelt) (C$$)
Value wine:	Blanc de Noir (C$$)
Estate vineyards:	Garry Oaks

Garry Oaks Winery takes its name from the local Oregon white oak, *Quercus garryana*, a hardwood tree indigenous to the Northwest with a range from Oregon to the Gulf Islands, though remaining stands of the trees are rare in British Columbia. Uniquely, Garry Oaks Winery ages its pinot noir wine in barrels made from Garry oak.

In 1999, Marcel Mercier and Elaine Kozak purchased a 100-year old farm and planted 7 acres (2.8 ha) of predominantly pinot noir, pinot gris, gewürztraminer, and zweigelt. The steeply sloped vineyards are organically farmed, and produce excellently balanced, silky pinot noir wines that are worth seeking out. The winery's Classic line includes pinot noir and pinot gris, and the Originals series includes unusual varieties and blends.

SALT SPRING VINEYARDS

151 Lee Road, Salt Spring Island, BC
250-653-9463; www.saltspringvineyards.com
Open during the season; limited hours.

Year founded:	2003
Annual production:	2000 cases
Signature wine:	Millotage (C$$)
Premium wine:	Pinot Noir Reserve (C$$$)
Value wine:	Pinot Gris (C$$)
Estate vineyards:	Salt Spring

Salt Spring Vineyards, winery, and B&B are a charming slice of the island's arty, earth-friendly aesthetic. Fanciful signs with colorful, flowing mermaids guide visitors to the intimate, woodsy, cabinlike winery and tasting room, and the fecund gardens and netted vineyards beckon one to relax on the patio.

Bill and Jan Harkley founded the first winery (by a mere 30-minutes) on popular Salt Spring Island, after they had planted 3 acres (1.2 ha) of estate vineyard to pinot noir, pinot gris, chardonnay, and the French hybrid léon millet. New owners Dev and Joanne McIntyre continue the legacy. Winemaker Paul Troop produces a fine pinot noir, a merlot from purchased Okanagan Valley fruit, and a tasty, unique blend of maréchal foch and léon millet they call Millotage. To obtain these surprisingly good wines, I recommend that you travel to the winery, because its small production is not likely to grow in the near future.

SATURNA ISLAND FAMILY ESTATE WINERY

8 Quarry Road, Saturna Island, BC
250-539-5139; www.saturnavineyards.com
Open all year; limited hours.

Year founded:	1998
Annual production:	10,000 cases
Signature wine:	Pinot Gris (C$)
Premium wine:	Vintner's Select Pinot Noir (C$$)
Value wine:	Chardonnay (C$)
Estate vineyards:	Rebecca, Robyn's, Longfield, Falconridge

Saturna Island Family Estate Winery was the first, and is the largest, of the Gulf Island wineries. With 60 acres (24 ha) of south-facing vines in four vineyards, the oldest dating back to 1995, the winery grows all of its own fruit for its wines. The vineyards abut a huge rock face that collects heat during the day and releases it at night to coddle the grapes.

Swiss-trained winemaker Daniel Lagna, formerly of Mission Hill, produces elegant renditions of Vintner's Select Pinot Noir (appropriately light in style with notes of strawberry), pinot gris (lots of apple, kiwi, and citrus notes with balanced spiciness), chardonnay (fruity, fleshy, and fresh-tasting), and a merlot.

Owner Larry Page has carefully managed his vines, which shows in the wines. The picturesque setting is a popular destination. With a wine shop and bistro, the winery offers tours.

The vineyards of Saturna Island, British Columbia.

271

Fraser Valley Wine Country

The Fraser Valley is a vast floodplain formed by the emptying of the Fraser River as it descends from interior mountains. The valley runs from Hope at its eastern end, generally southwesterly to Abbotsford, and opens widely to the northwest, forming a large delta that also includes the metropolitan area of Vancouver. The Fraser Valley is bounded on the west by the Strait of Georgia.

The Fraser Valley is the breadbasket of British Columbia, an area rich in farms and agriculture. The soils are well-drained silts and clays that are rich in nutrients, having been formed by both glaciation and river deposits. A wide variety of crops, from hazelnuts to wasabi, strawberries, and cabbage, grow easily on these fertile soils, including wine grapes.

Summer weather in the area is warm, sunny, and dry. Average temperatures range from 65°F to 70°F (18.3°C to 21.2°C), with maximums reaching to 80°F (26.6°C). Annual precipitation is plentiful at around 55 in. (1418 mm), but the majority falls in the winter, and the well-drained soils can become dry by the end of summer, so irrigation can be important. Winters are wet and mild, with temperatures only occasionally dipping far below 30°F (−1.1°C). Frost-free days range from 180 to 230, making for a long, cool growing season.

The first substantial planting of wine grapes in the Fraser Valley occurred in the early 1980s, when Claude Violet began establishing a vineyard for the first winery in the area, Domaine de Chaberton. He planted 40 different grape varieties in an attempt to discern over the years what would grow best. In the Fraser Valley today, there are over 200 acres (80.9 ha) of wine grapes under cultivation. The cool season requires early ripening grapes, and among the vinifera varieties, expected ones are grown: pinot noir, pinot gris, pinot blanc, gewürztraminer, chardonnay. Many hybrids and crosses are also extensively grown, including bacchus, siegerrebe, and madeleine sylvaner. The region is also well known for producing fine fruit wines.

FRASER VALLEY WINE COUNTRY AT A GLANCE

Year established: 2005
Number of wineries: 16 (including fruit wineries)
Approximate vineyard acreage: 204 acres (82 ha)
Predominant soil types: rich loams with mixed silts and clay
Vineyard growing degree days: 2480 (1360)

Most important grape varieties
chardonnay pinot noir, pinot gris, pinot blanc, gewürztraminer

One of the economic appeals of having a winery in the Fraser Valley is its close proximity to Vancouver, the largest wine market in Canada's west. Many of the wineries here are geared for wine tourists, and while they are rightfully proud to show off the products of their estate vineyards, often the wineries also purchase fruit from the Okanagan Valley in order to supply some of the more expected, and fashionable, wine varieties that don't prosper in the Fraser Valley.

WINERIES AND WINES TO SAMPLE

DOMAINE DE CHABERTON ESTATE WINERY

1064 - 216 Street, Langley, BC
604-530-1736; www.domainedechaberton.com
Open all year.

Year founded:	1981
Annual production:	40,000 cases
Signature wine:	Pinot Gris (C$$)
Premium wine:	Ortega, Botrytis Affected (C$$$ 375 ml)
Value wine:	Cuvée Rouge (C$)
Estate vineyards:	Domaine de Chaberton

Domaine de Chaberton, the oldest and largest winery in the Fraser Valley, was founded by Claude and Inge Violet, who consciously decided that being located near Vancouver made more sense than being in the Okanagan Valley. And in 1981, when they planted their vineyard, that indeed made sense. The current owners, Hong Kong executive Anthony Cheng and Vancouver businessman Eugene Kwan, continue to make wines from this signature winery, recently adding a new series of bright New World–style wines under the Canoe Cove Wines name.

Big-boned reds, especially the syrah and cabernet sauvignon under the Domaine de Chaberton brand, are very popular, while an attractively priced red blend and fresh whites are also very well made. The winery's Ortega is an intensely sweet wine, the flavors having been concentrated by the naturally occurring botrytis mold that shrivels the skins and adds an intriguing spice. The winery is a popular destination, and the associated Bacchus Bistro is a great place to sample the Domaine's wines with well-prepared food.

British Columbia's wine countries offer visitors breathtaking beauty and high wine quality.

IDAHO

IDAHO'S WINE COUNTRIES AT A GLANCE

Vineyard acreage:	1600 acres (647.5 ha)
Number of wineries:	40
Annual cases produced:	225,000
Economic impact of wine:	$73 million

Most important grape varieties
riesling, chardonnay, cabernet sauvignon, merlot, syrah

Wine countries (AVAs)
Snake River Valley[†]

[†]Shared with Oregon.

Idaho's wine country is windswept and remote, but the climate of the Snake River Valley is conducive to many vinifera varieties. Sawtooth Winery's vineyard is one of Idaho's largest.

WITH A SURFEIT of maverick spirits, spare ground, and stubborn will, Idaho's winegrowers and winemakers are fiercely proud of their vines and wines. Long on ambition, this nascent wine community is building its knowledge and honing its craft in the steady belief that it can be the next great wine country.

Growth in Idaho wine has been strong. From a start in 1975 of just 2 wineries in the state, Idaho became home to 11 wineries by 2002 and 40 wineries in 2009. Wine sales in Idaho grew from $15 million in 2002 to $52 million in 2008. In 2008, there were approximately 62 Idaho wine grape growers supplying the needs of 40 wineries. From 1999 to 2006, the amount of vineyard acreage grew 85.5 percent. By 2008, the wine grape crop was Idaho's second most important fruit in terms of acreage and third most important in terms of dollars, with an annual revenue of approximately $5.7 million. These numbers show great momentum, even if the scale of the industry is still small. The approval of the Snake River Valley AVA in 2007 was taken by many as a stamp of credibility for Idaho, and an encouragement to future expansion. And while the large majority of vineyards and wineries are located within the Snake River Valley, there are scattered adventurous wineries whose homes are elsewhere in Idaho.

But Idaho still has a long row to hoe. The state's modern wine history goes back to 1976, but it is only in recent years that any amount of reliable wine quality and availability has garnered critical accolades, attracted more trained vintners to the state, and started to earn a wider than local market for Idaho wine. As the state matures, more attention is being paid to sharing and advancing winegrowing knowledge, under the growing realization that the key to future success is in raising the overall quality of everyone's wines. But Idaho's wine culture tends more toward an assemblage of individual growers and winemakers rather than a cohesive community. Often self-trained in the viticultural arts and staunch in the pursuit of their own dream, they willingly share knowledge and are building a strong industry. But it is also fair to say that in Idaho, everyone still very much does his or her own wine thing.

This situation makes Idaho an exciting, if sometimes challenging, place for adventurous winegrowers and wine lovers. There is no benchmark grape variety or wine style here that newcomers must master before they gain respectability, as there is, for example, with pinot noir in Oregon's Willamette Valley. There is not yet a signature wine that consumers can identify as Idahoan, in the same way that merlot is associated with Washington. Here every vineyard or winery is free to find out what works best, and there are plenty of like-minded folks to cheer them on. But in such a stimulating and viticulturally free environ-

ment, dangers can lurk. New grapes and new wines can win attention simply because of their newness, not necessarily because they are of intrinsically great quality.

If a winery is proud of its success with pinot noir, for instance, is that because it is one of the few made in the state and therefore shines? Or does the wine truly compete on the same scale used to judge other pinot noir wines grown in the Northwest? It can be hard to tell. Or what does it mean when an Idaho winery, which attracts critical raves for the quality of its wines, doesn't actually use grapes grown in Idaho? How representative of the appellation could such an acclaimed winery really be? These issues are ones Idaho faces as it matures in the wider wine world. Such questions also apply to any part of the Pacific Northwest where committed growers and winemakers are experimenting in a new territory or at the fringes of

climate conditions. These efforts are to be encouraged, even lauded, but they should also be kept in a broader perspective beyond local standards and wine predilections. This is beginning to happen in Idaho.

Vineyard sophistication has advanced to the point where growers are willing to pull out vines bearing varieties that are clearly not successful, and winemakers are honing their skills while homing in on those grapes that make the best wine in Idaho's climate. No longer simply settling for merely acceptable wine, Idaho's winemakers are striving for new standards of quality. New vineyards are being planned that apply the latest climate data and soil

Ste. Chapelle Winery is the largest in Idaho, producing more cases of wine than the rest of the state's producers combined.

The distinctive training arrangement at 3 Horse Ranch Vineyards is an example of Idaho inventiveness.

Sawtooth Winery's vineyards are an important component of Idaho's wine production.

surveys, and winemakers are starting to pare their wines down to those they can focus on making well, rather than trying to have a wine for every taste.

Rhône varieties, for instance, are increasingly planted as it is discovered that they flourish in the right Idaho locations, producing wines of depth that satisfy a growing market. Stubborn attitudes are softening as it is realized that you don't have to grow cabernet sauvignon in order to be successful, especially if the grape can't get fully ripe every year, and that not every white wine has to be made sweet.

The key to broader wine success in Idaho—or anywhere—is improved wine quality. In all the discussions of public policy initiatives to enhance wine country tourism, legislative changes to facilitate more wine sales, and programs to fund regional infrastructure development to encourage wine growth, the concept of wine quality can get lost. The reality is that economic success is driven by sustained wine quality.

It is a simple truth for any emerging wine region: make good wine, and the people will come. Idaho's winemakers are fast learning this. That's why they are beginning to apply organic farming methods to improve the quality of the soil and therefore their fruit; why they are paying more attention to matching grape varieties to site conditions; why they are becoming more rigorous in their grape handling, equipment capabilities, and cellar sanitation.

Trying to describe the character of Idaho's wine culture is like trying to keep water in your cupped hands. Idaho's wine culture is so young and rapidly changing that there is little consistent character yet to hold on to. Washington's wine industry was once that way. So was Oregon's. British Columbia has only recently coalesced into a powerful wine entity. Idaho is on the same exciting wine journey as its neighbors, and savvy wine lovers looking to get in on the ground floor should explore Idaho's fast-developing wine industry.

IDAHO'S WINE GEOGRAPHY

Idaho is generally thought to be a state rich in mountains and poor in agriculture, except for potatoes. While this is not entirely wrong, it discounts the expansive lower lying land of the southern part of the state. This vast basin, known as the Snake River Plain, extends like a sly half smile from the town of Ontario, just over the border in Oregon, down through Boise, Mountain Home, and Twin Falls at the southern bend of the arc. From there, the broad plain turns up toward the northeast through Pocatello and Idaho Falls. Along the upturned western portion of this arc, mostly on the well-drained benches and terraces neighboring the towns of Caldwell and Parma, the majority of Idaho's vineyards are found. There are some small vineyards and a few wineries in the northern panhandle section of Idaho. Usually, these wineries source grapes from nearby Washington, and their total production of Idaho-grown grapes is insignificant, though the quality of their wines can be quite high.

The two most salient facts about Idaho's wine country geography are that it is the highest and the most inland of the Northwest's appellations. Most of Idaho's vineyards are between 2200 and 3000 ft. (670.5–914.1 m) elevation—the highest vineyards in the Northwest—and are roughly 550 mi (885 km) from the Pacific Ocean. This combination of elevation and interior location make for distinctive wine-growing conditions. In keeping with the generally high desert and continental nature of the climate, summers in Idaho's wine country are very warm and dry, winters are very cold, and the growing season is very short—from 125 to 150 days. The climate is more extreme than any other wine country in the Northwest. Summers can see sustained temperatures well above 100°F (37.7°C), while winters can have multiple days below 0°F (−17.7°C). When you average the temperature throughout the year, it comes out to an interesting number: 51.4°F (10.8°C), which is

IDAHO'S WINE PIONEERS

Though Idaho today is not a major wine consuming state, it does have a history of wine production. The state's viticultural history goes well back into the nineteenth century, though frequently made claims that the first vineyards or wineries in the Northwest were in Idaho are not accurate.

As settlers populated the Northwest, it seems someone was always seeking a place to plant grapes, and the valleys and plains of Idaho was as likely as anywhere to harbor grape-growing potential. In Idaho, near Lewiston where the Clearwater and Snake Rivers meet, pioneer planter and French émigré Louis Delsol grew grapes in 1872—though there are indications that a few earlier vineyards may have been planted in the region—and is reported to have made wine in 1875.

In the 1880s, fellow Frenchman Robert Schleicher established in Lewiston what came to be one of the largest vineyards in the Pacific Northwest at the time. With approximately 130 acres (52.6 ha) and multiple vinifera varieties, Schleicher produced copious amounts of well-regarded commercial wine and established a solid bar of viticultural professionalism. One of his 1902 vintage wines came to the favorable attention of George C. Hussman, a viticulturist for the U.S. Department of Agriculture in, of all places, Napa, California. He deemed the wine to be the equal of anything made in Napa at the time. And Schleicher himself predicted a glowing future for winegrowing in Idaho, saying the state offered a "splendid field for intelligent experimentation." as quoted in *The Wine Project* by Ronald Irvine and Walter Clore.

As in all of the country, Prohibition killed Idaho's wine industry. It wasn't until the 1970s that modern winegrowing began anew in Idaho with the establishment of Ste. Chapelle Winery.

just barely above the 50°F (10°C) threshold where vinifera is considered a viable crop.

The winters bring the averages down, not the lack of growing season heat. At elevations typical of where vineyards are planted, the Snake River Valley is considerably warm, with a range between 2603 and 3305 (1428–1818) GDD. At the high extreme, there are more heat units than experienced by any other Northwestern wine country. At the low end, growing season heat in the Snake River Valley is about equivalent to the Yakima Valley. The short growing season and high daytime heat mean that proper site selection is critical for Idaho winegrowers. In a macroclimate that delivers a short, hot season, understanding the mesoclimate of the vineyard is paramount. The slopes and exposures of individual sites dramatically alter the winegrowing potential within the appellation.

The relatively long winter can be vine-killingly cold. Extreme minimums of −32°F (−35°C) have been experienced within the past 25 years in areas where vineyards exist. Even so, since the late 1990s, winter temperatures have generally not approached these levels, with the exception of 2006, when winterkill seriously impacted some vineyards. With proper care, vines have not experienced severe winter stress here in many years.

Another consequence of its interior location is that summers are quite dry. Mean annual precipitation can be 10 in. (254 mm) or less, with July and August experiencing around 0.25 in. (6.3 mm). Irrigation is clearly required for vineyard health, but unlike many other Northwest wine regions, there is currently no significant development pressure threatening water resources, so whether it comes from the Snake River, groundwater, or runoff, there appears to be ample supply.

Sandy soils in the Snake River Valley help encourage vines to put extra energy into fruit ripening.

THE GRAPES AND STYLES OF IDAHO'S WINES

Idaho is still too young, the winegrowing too diverse, and the continuity from vintage to vintage too tenuous to make accurate generalizations about Idaho wine styles. While there is not yet a dominant grape variety, some potential contenders are emerging.

The short, warm summers and cold nights are conducive to many white varieties. Riesling, in particular, has historically been a strong performer and is widely planted in the Snake River Valley. The majority of the state's riesling production goes into inexpensive and easy-drinking, off-dry wines. But because of the Snake River Valley's ability to retain strong acidity in the grapes, dry rieslings, up to now a relative rarity, have great potential in the area. Also promising are late-harvest and even ice wine renditions of riesling. Very dry and cool autumns give growers the opportunity to safely let riesling hang on the vine long after the normal harvest, accumulating sugars and intensity for these luxurious styles of riesling.

Chardonnay, pinot gris, and increasingly viognier take advantage of the region's climate, allowing winemakers to produce wines that emphasize the fresh, crisp fruit flavors of the varietals. Increasingly, Idaho producers are moving away from the thickly textured, oaky, and buttery style of whites, realizing that the region's climate is better suited to allowing these grapes to express their natural, unfettered fruitiness.

Among red grapes, Idaho early chose the traditional Bordeaux varietals, emphasizing cabernet sauvignon and merlot. The key to both these grapes is finding the right site to provide a long enough growing season for the fruit to ripen fully mature character. When this happens, both varieties in the Snake River Valley show good body, full black fruit flavors, and plenty of juicy character. With the region's cold nights, both of the grapes tend to show a lean, nicely tart quality that distinguishes them from the products

A dry growing season and sparse soils make Idaho vines dig deep for nourishment.

Young Idaho grapes not yet at the ripening stage.

of other Northwest growing regions. The best Idaho cabernet and merlot wines are made with less aggressive oak treatment to ensure that the ripe character isn't overshadowed.

Recently, wineries in the Snake River Valley have been producing impressive wines out of traditional Rhône grapes, indicating that perhaps the southern regions of France might prove the best model for Idaho producers. Syrah, in particular, shows great promise, with its delightful combination of fresh plum and blackberry fruit flavors, combined with strong acidity that helps showcase the peppery, earth, and meaty qualities of the grape. The grape seems to like the region's warm growing season, readily developing full fruitiness and varietal character. At the same time, the short season helps prevent over-ripeness that can lead to jammy or dried fruit flavors. Sister white grapes, such as viognier and rousanne, also are showing well, though so far there are only small amounts of these grapes growing in the area,

Two keys to developing signature Idaho grapes will be to find the sites that best match the natural growing cycle of the grapes—always an ongoing process—and then to make the wines in a fashion that lets them show their character best: in other words, making judicious winemaking steps that don't overpower the fruit with too much new oak or that don't use too long an aging time.

For a time it seemed that winegrowers either planted all the expected grape varieties because they thought it was what people wanted to buy, or they made eccentric wines of all types to be new and novel. While that approach is still somewhat true today, a great deal more winegrowing sophistication is apparent in a new crop of excellent wines coming from Idaho. Existing vintners are gaining more experience and applying it to their vines and wines, and newcomers are applying their winegrowing knowledge within the Idaho context.

As more experience is gained and knowledge disseminated throughout the region, the winegrowing composition of the Snake River Valley will continue to evolve. For instance, in the early 1990s the wines from Idaho that garnered the most praise were chardonnays, but today it is the Rhône varieties that are the most talked about. What might it be in another 10 years?

IDAHO'S WINE COUNTRIES

Snake River Valley Wine Country
The Snake River Valley is Idaho's only AVA, and it was greeted with praise and pride when it was announced in 2007. At last, thought most local wine people, Idaho would get the viticultural respect it was due. While such respect should come from wines, not borders, the establishment of the appellation did bring new awareness to Idaho's wine country.

The Snake River Valley is part of the Columbia Basin and was originally formed by geologic processes similar to those of eastern Washington and Oregon. Its borders generally follow the outline of ancient Lake Idaho that formed within today's valley. Two thirds of the appellation are in Idaho and one third in Oregon, but there is no substantial viticulture currently in the Oregon portion, and the Idaho portion encompasses approximately 90 percent of the state's vineyard acreage.

Originally created from periodic volcanic activity, about 12 million years ago extensive faulting caused today's Snake River Valley to sink relative to the surrounding higher elevation mountains, forming the rift depression we see today. Over millions of years, lakes formed in this valley, eventually creating ancient Lake Idaho, which filled the valley up to about 3600 ft. (1100 m) for about 6.5 million years. Lake Idaho eventually drained into Hells Canyon, leaving behind terraces of mixed sediments and gravels. Repeated lava flows smothered these sediments in some places, while windblown loess covered them in other places. Toward the end of the most recent glaciation about 14,500 years ago, ancient Lake Bonneville (of which today's Great Salt Lake is thought to be a rem-

SNAKE RIVER VALLEY WINE COUNTRY AT A GLANCE

Year established: 2007

Number of wineries: 25

Total acreage: 5,350,300 acres (2,165,100 ha)*

Idaho portion acreage:

    3,812,700 acres (1,542,900 ha)

Approximate vineyard acreage:

    1600 acres (648 ha)

Predominant soil type

    very mixed: sandy loam, sedimentary

    gravels, volcanic clay, loess

Vineyard growing degree days:

    2363–3305 (1295–1818)†

Most important grape varieties

syrah, cabernet sauvignon, riesling, merlot, gewürztraminer, chardonnay

*Figures apply to the entire appellation.

† Figures apply to Idaho portion of the appellation only.

nant) flooded into the Snake River Valley, carving the landforms we see today. Backwashes of sediment, benches and terraces of gravel, and slack-water bars are present throughout the valley as remnants of the Bonneville Flood, forming the soils and terrain of today's vineyards.

So complex were these geologic activities that today there is simply no dominant soil type within the appellation. Even the official petition for AVA status stressed that soils were "not a distinguishing factor" for the appellation. Some vineyards are planted on slack-water silts abundant in quartz and feldspar sands, while others are on gravelly ground containing goodly amounts of clay. Some vines are rooted in sandy loam, others in calcareous clays, and still other on sandy loess. Depending on the soil, the origin may be lake sediments, volcanic basalts, or windblown loess, giving winegrowers a range of potential soil characteristics to work with. An interesting thing to watch in coming years will be the increasing sophistication of matching vinifera varieties to these various soils.

Common within the AVA, the soils, regardless of what kind, are generally thin and very well drained, making irrigation management a necessity. The abundance of terraces and benches also means that vineyards have lots of sloped areas, providing water and air drainage.

Idaho's main winegrowing region is distinctly a warm-climate growing zone, despite its high elevation. Heat summations demonstrate that the Snake River Valley shares similar growing season heat with much of Washington's Columbia Valley, so the appellation is suited for similar grape varieties, most of which are currently being grown here.

Winegrower Ron Bitner has been an important force in helping grow the strength of Idaho's wine industry.

WINERIES AND WINES TO SAMPLE

BITNER VINEYARDS

16645 Plum Road, Caldwell, ID
208-899-7642; www.bitnervineyards.com
Open all year; limited hours.

Year founded:	1997
Annual production:	1000 cases
Signature wine:	Reserve Cabernet Sauvignon ($$)
Premium wine:	Cabernet Shiraz ($$$)
Value wine:	Dry Riesling ($)
Estate vineyards:	Bitner

Ron Bitner is one of the most experienced and expert winegrowers in Idaho. His 15 acres (6 ha) of vinifera are the source for the wines of Bitner Vineyards, as well as for some of the wines of Koenig Distillery and Winery; Greg Koenig makes the wines for Bitner Vineyards.

The first blocks of Bitner's riesling and chardonnay were planted in 1981, making them some of the earliest vines in the state. Since then, cabernet sauvignon, merlot, petit verdot, viognier, and shiraz (syrah) have been added. The Bitner Dry Riesling shows how well this grape variety can do in the Snake River Valley, and the Reserve Cabernet Sauvignon is very well made.

CINDER WINES

The Urban Winemakers Cooperative
107 East 44th Street, Garden City, ID
208-433-9813; www.cinderwines.com
Open all year; Saturday only.

Year founded:	2006
Annual production:	1000 cases
Signature wine:	Viognier ($$)
Premium wine:	Syrah ($$)
Value wine:	Dry Rosé ($)
Estate vineyards:	uses purchased fruit

Cinder Wines (the name refers to the volcanic nature of much of the soils in the wine country) is an example of where Idaho wines are going. Bringing a practical education in winemaking from Washington's Chateau Ste. Michelle, Boise-native Melanie Krause became intrigued at the possibilities of Idaho *terroir*. Seeking grapes from Fraser, Williamson, Sawtooth, and other vineyards, Cinder debuted its first wine, a viognier, to rave reviews.

Rounding out the Cinder lineup are a syrah, chardonnay, dry rosé, and a Bordeaux-style blend. The tasty viognier is cleanly made, lean in style, and full of fruit, pointing the way to an impressive future for this small producer.

HELLS CANYON WINERY

18835 Symms Road, Caldwell, ID
208-454-3300; www.hellscanyonwinery.com
Open during the season; limited hours.

Year founded:	1980
Annual production:	3000 cases
Signature wine:	Deer Slayer Syrah ($$)
Premium wine:	Idaho Cabernet Sauvignon Reserve ($$)
Value wine:	Bird Dog White ($)
Estate vineyards:	Hells Canyon, Falcon's Fall

Former chef, now winery owner and winemaker, Steve Robertson saw vineyard potential in the land above the Snake River, and turned it into reality. In 1981, he planted the Hells Canyon Vineyard on the slopes overlooking the Owyhee Mountains. With cabernet sauvignon, chardonnay, cabernet franc, merlot, and syrah grapes to work with, he began achieving critical acclaim for his wines, including a rave notice from Britain's *Decanter* magazine for his 1985 chardonnay.

Today, Robertson produces a range of wines that consistently win state and regional awards. The Hells Canyon Deer Slayer Syrah is a deftly balanced wine that admirably marries spice and fruit. The Reserve merlot and cabernet sauvignon releases also show classic varietal character with an appealing acidic verve.

KOENIG DISTILLERY & WINERY

20928 Grape Lane, Caldwell, ID
208-455-8386; www.koenigdistillery.com
Open all year; limited hours.

Year founded:	1995
Annual production:	3200 cases
Signature wine:	Syrah Three Vineyard Cuvée ($$)
Premium wine:	Cuvée Amelia Reserve Syrah ($$$)
Value wine:	Chardonnay, Bitner Vineyard ($)
Estate vineyards:	Koenig

The Koenig family homesteaded fruit-growing on the Sunny Slope, and even made fruit wine during the Great Depression. Today, brothers Andy and Greg Koenig apply careful vineyard practices and winemaking techniques to the production of single-vineyard and blended wines. Relying on small yields and traditional techniques, Koenig wines represent some of Idaho's best.

Always made in small quantities with a focus on careful winemaking, Koenig's syrah has great power and spice, while its cabernet sauvignon is rich with coffee notes and plenty of structure. Koenig also makes an occasional riesling ice wine, pinot noir, and riesling. Plus, Koenig is also a distillery, making superb single-fruit eau de vie brandies.

Winemaker Greg Koenig of Koenig Distillery & Winery, Idaho.

WHAT CLIMATE CHANGE MIGHT MEAN FOR NORTHWEST WINE

Climate is one of the most important influences on the kinds of wine grapes that can be successfully grown in a region. The potential consequences of climate change is important to Pacific Northwest winegrowers and winemakers, many of whom are already farming on the fringes of climatic suitability for vinifera.

Gregory V. Jones PhD, associate professor of geography at Southern Oregon University in Ashland, has done groundbreaking research on the history of climate change and its possible future impacts on winegrowing. In one study, Jones gathered data on the mean air temperature over the past 50 years from most of the world's prestigious wine regions, including central and eastern Washington and northern and southern Oregon, to see what trends could be discovered. "Out of 27 worldwide locations, we found the vast majority of all regions showed significant growing-season warming, on average, of 2.3°F," says Jones. For the Pacific Northwest, the data showed a smaller, but still significant, 1.8°F rise over the past 50 years.

To explore whether this warming trend might continue, Jones used a widely accepted climate-change model produced by the Hadley Center for Climate Prediction in England. Running the numbers for the next 50 years predicts a continued average temperature rise of 3.6°F in the world's wine regions. Add the predicted rise to the historical rise since 1950, and you get an average growing-season temperature increase over a 100-year period of nearly 6°F for the world's wine regions and somewhere between 4°F and 5°F for the Pacific Northwest.

For southern Oregon and Washington, the predicted warming is a little greater than the average, while for Oregon's Willamette Valley, the temperature rise is predicted to be a little less. If the Pacific Northwest's growing season does continue to warm over the next half century, Jones points out, regional growing conditions will change, with grapevines ripening earlier.

In cooler areas like the Willamette Valley, warming impacts could have some benefits. Additional growing season heat could result in more reliable, higher quality vintages, and warm-climate grape varieties could become more viable in that area, thereby expanding grape-growing possibilities. Additional climatic warmth, however, could also cause cool-adapted vines planted in the warmer parts of the region to struggle, perhaps even limiting the future viability of pinot noir in the region.

In warm to hot areas such as eastern Washington, such climate change could be more challenging. The growing season could lengthen, causing more demand for already limited irrigation. Warmer winters could make vineyards more vulnerable to disease, and the added heat could mean fruit would develop sugar ripeness earlier, without enough time on the vine to develop good acid balance. The hottest parts of Washington's wine countries could become less viable for winegrowing if average temperatures rise high enough.

If Jones's predictions become realized, the Pacific Northwest wine region that could potentially benefit the most from climatic warming is British Columbia's Okanagan Valley. Longer growing seasons and warmer winters could mean more reliable and balanced ripening of a wider variety of grapes. The downside, Jones notes, might be fewer opportunities to make the popular icewine.

Jones thinks such a future for Northwest winegrowing is likely, and he has more data to support this opinion. For instance, he's found that the number of frost-free days in Northwest wine regions has increased strikingly since 1948. There has been a reduction in frost occurrence, longer frost-free periods, and greater heat accumulation in the western U.S. grape-growing regions over the period. Jones's research in Oregon shows an average of about 30 more frost-free days per year since 1948 in all the appellations except the Rogue Valley. His preliminary results for Washington are similar.

There is no question that the prospect of a climate shifting to warmer growing seasons has the Northwest wine community watching temperature trends and wondering how to adapt for the future.

SAWTOOTH WINERY

13750 Surrey Lane, Nampa, ID
208-467-1200; www.sawtoothwinery.com
Open all year; limited hours.

Year founded:	1988
Annual production:	20,000 cases
Signature wine:	Syrah ($$)
Premium wine:	Reserve Gewürztraminer Ice Wine ($$)
Value wine:	Chardonnay ($)
Estate vineyards:	Sawtooth, Skyline

Sawtooth Winery was founded in 1987 as Pintler Cellars, with the planting of a 15-acre (6-ha) vineyard in the Snake River Valley. The Pintler family sold the winery to Corus Brands (now owned by Precept Wine Brands in Washington) in 1998, which changed the name. Today, winemaker Bill Murray uses fruit from some of the largest vineyards in the state to craft what the winery terms Main Line cabernet sauvignon, merlot, and syrah, plus chardonnay, pinot gris, riesling, viognier, and late harvest gewürztraminer. Another product tier, the Reserve offers smaller quantities of select cabernet sauvignon, merlot, syrah, chardonnay, and a gewürztraminer ice wine.

Newly planted vines at Sawtooth Winery.

SNAKE RIVER WINERY

786 W Broad Street, Boise, ID
208-345-9463; www.snakeriverwinery.com
Open all year; limited hours.

Year founded:	2000
Annual production:	4000 cases
Signature wine:	Barbera ($$)
Premium wine:	Reserve Bordeaux Blend ($$)
Value wine:	Riesling ($)
Estate vineyards:	Arena Valley

Scott and Susan DeSeelhorst purchased Arena Valley Vineyard in 1998 and immediately began refurbishing the growing practices to improve fruit quality. By applying more rigorous techniques, including leaf pulling, altering the trellis, and changing the irrigation regimen, they felt they had heartily improved the fruit. In 2000, they built a small winery and made their own wines under the Snake River Winery name.

New plantings of barbera (their first release of this wine was the 2004 vintage), grenache, touriga nacional, and tinto cão add some intriguing varietal possibilities to the winery's lineup of riesling (off-dry and late-harvest), merlot, cabernet sauvignon, and chardonnay (oaked and unoaked). The winery also makes a delicious blend called Syrah Grenache Mourvèdre, an unusual-for-Idaho zweigelt, and a solid Bordeaux-style blend.

STE. CHAPELLE WINERY

19348 Lowell Road, Caldwell, ID
208-453-7843; www.stechapelle.com
Open all year.

Year founded:	1976
Annual production:	150,000 cases
Signature wine:	Winemaker Series Riesling ($)
Premium wine:	Riesling Ice Wine ($$, 375 ml)
Value wine:	Winemaker Series Riesling ($)
Estate vineyards:	uses purchased fruit

Ste. Chapelle is Idaho's largest winery, and is now owned by Ascentia Wine Estates in Healdsburg, California. Founded in 1976, it is also Idaho's oldest modern winery. Riesling was the first wine produced by Ste. Chapelle from Idaho-grown grapes, and today the winery produces large amounts of the variety in a dry, Alsatian style, an off-dry, easy-drinking mode, and in unctuous late-harvest and ice wine formats.

Winemaker Chuck Devlin also produces a select series of wines, including chardonnay, sauvignon blanc, dry gewürztraminer, merlot, syrah, and cabernet sauvignon. Ste. Chapelle's wines are all reasonably priced. Of special note is the rare ice wine: Ste. Chapelle is one of the few places in the Northwest outside of British Columbia that can produce this wine with some regularity.

3 HORSE RANCH VINEYARDS

5900 Pearl Road, Eagle, ID
208-863-6561; www.3horseranchvineyards.com
Open during the season; limited hours.

Year founded:	2003
Annual production:	12,000 cases
Signature wine:	Estate Grown Viognier ($$)
Premium wine:	Cabernet Sauvignon/Merlot ($$)
Value wine:	Reserve Riesling ($)
Estate vineyards:	3 Horse Ranch

In 2003, Gary and Martha Cunningham began planting a vineyard on their ranch following organic principles. Since they lived on the land, they wanted it to be clean, and they felt that organic grapes would make the best wine and the wine most authentically reflective of the site. With a focus on hand-farming, from pruning to harvest, 3 Horse Ranch Vineyards released its first vintage in 2008.

The winery emphasizes Rhône varieties, employing the winemaking skills of Greg Koening (of Koenig Distillery & Winery) to produce roussanne, viognier (and a roussanne-viognier blend), and syrah, plus pinot gris, and merlot, all from estate grapes. The wines of this new Idaho winery indicate a strong future.

Gary Cunningham of 3 Horse Ranch Vineyards, Idaho.

(*right*) Ste. Chapelle wine-maker, Chuck Devlin.

WINE GRAPE VARIETIES GROWN IN THE PACIFIC NORTHWEST

(r) red

(w) white

agria (r)
albariño (w)
aligoté (w)
arneis (w)
auxerrois (w)
bacchus (w)
barbera (r)
cabernet franc (r)
cabernet sauvignon (r)
carmenère (r)
chardonnay (w)
chardonnay musqué (w)
chenin blanc (w)
cinsault (r)
counoise (r)
dolcetto (r)
ehrenfelser (w)
gamay (r)
gamay noir (r)
garnacha (grenache) (r)
gewürztraminer (w)
grenache blanc (w)
grüner veltliner (w)
gutadel (w)

kerner (w)
lemberger (r)
léon millet (r)
madeleine sylvaner (w)
madeline angevine (w)
malbec (r)
maréchal foch (r)
marsanne (w)
merlot (r)
mourvèdre (r)
müller-thurgau (w)
muscat (w)
muscat canelli (w)
muscat ottonel (w)
nebbiolo (r)
ortega (w)
petit sirah (r)
petit verdot (r)
picpoul (w)
pinot beurot (w)
pinot blanc (w)
pinot gris (w)
pinot meunier (r)
pinot noir (r)

primitivo (r)
riesling (w)
roussanne (w)
sangiovese (r)
sauvignon blanc (w)
sémillon (w)
shiraz (r)
siegerrebe (w)
sousão (r)
syrah (r)
tempranillo (r)
tinto cão (r)
touriga nacional (r)
trebbiano (w)
vermentino (w)
viognier (w)
zinfandel (r)
zweigelt (r)

BIBLIOGRAPHY

Agriculture Canada. 1987. Soils of the Gulf Islands of British Columbia. Volume 1: Soils of Saltspring Island. Report 43, British Columbia Soil Survey, Vancouver, British Columbia.

Agriculture Canada. 1988. Soils of the Gulf Islands of British Columbia. Volume 2: Soils of North Pender, South Pender, Prevost, Mayne, Saturna, and Lesser Islands. Report 43, British Columbia Soil Survey, Vancouver, British Columbia.

Allan, Stuart, Aileen R. Buckley, and James E. Meacham. 2001. *Atlas of Oregon*. 2d ed. Ed. William G. Loy. Eugene: University of Oregon Press.

Allen, Lawrence J., and J. Elizabeth Purser. 1977. *The Winemakers of the Pacific Northwest*. Vashon Island, Washington: Harbor House.

Alt, David. 2001. *Glacial Lake Missoula and its Humoungous Floods*. Missoula, Montana: Mountain Press.

Applegate Valley Winery Association. http://www.applegatewinetrail.com/.

Aspler, Tony. 1999. *Vintage Canada: The Complete Reference to Canadian Wines*. 3d ed. Whitby, Ontario, Canada: McGraw-Hill Ryerson.

Aspler, Tony. 2006. *The Wine Atlas of Canada*. Toronto: Random House Canada.

Ball, Trent, and R. J. Folwell. 2003. *Wine Grape Establishment and Production Costs in Washington, 2003*. Pullman: Washington Sate University Cooperative Extension.

BC Adventure. 2009. Physiology of British Columbia: The Okanagan Valley. http://www.bcadventure.com/adventure/frontier/homestead/okan.htm.

Berger, Dan. 2008. The Coolness Factor: Rethinking Where Varietals Grow Best. *AppellationAmerica.com*. http://www.appellationamerica.com/wine-review/607/Cold-Hot-Climates.html.

Bierle, Kristin, D. Holley, and G. Black. *The Economic Impact of the Wine Industry on Idaho's Economy*. Boise, Boise State University Center for Business and Economic Research, December 2008.

Blosser, Susan Sokol. 2006. *At Home in the Vineyard: Cultivating a Winery, an Industry, and a Life*. Berkeley: University of California Press.

Boenisch, Kerry McDaniel. 2004. *Vineyard Memoirs, or "So this is what it's like to plant a vineyard?": Oregon Wine Pioneer Recollections of Living, Grape-Growing and Winemaking in the 1970s*. Dundee, Oregon: CKMB.

Bowen, P. A., C. P. Bogdanoff, B. F. Estergaard, S. G. Marsh, K. B. Usher, C.A.S. Smith, and G. Frank. 2005. Geology and wine 10: Use of geographic information system technology to assess viticulture performance in the Okanagan and Similkameen Valleys, British Columbia. *Geoscience Canada*, 32 (4). http://journals.hil.unb.ca/index.php/GC/article/viewArticle/2718/3167.

Bremmer, Lynn, and John Bremmer. 2008. B.C. Grape Acreage Report, August 15. Mount Kobau Wine Services, Oliver, B.C.

British Columbia Wine Institute. http://www.winebc.com/.

British Columbia Wine Institute. 2008. *2007–2008 Annual Report*. Kelowna: British Columbia Wine Institute.

Busacca, Alan J., and L. D. Meinert. 2003. Wine and geology: The terroir of Washington State. In *Western Cordillera and Adjacent Areas*, Field Guide 4. Ed. Terry W. Swanson. Boulder, Colorado: The Geological Society of America, 69–85.

Carlson, Brad. 2007. The New Napa Valley? Idaho wine region receives national grape-growing designation. *Idaho Business Review*. April 30. http://www.idahobusiness.net/archive.htm/2007/04/30/The-New-Napa-Valley-Idaho-wine-region-receives-national-grapegrowing-designation.

Carson, Bob. General Geology of Southeastern Washington. Whitman College, Walla Walla, Washington. http://www.whitman.edu/geology/LocalGeo.html.

Cass, Bruce, and Jancis Robinson, eds. 2000. *The Oxford Companion to the Wines of North America*. New York: Oxford University Press.

Chehalem Mountain Winegrowers. http://www.chehalemmountains.org/.

Chitkowski, Rebecca L., and J. R. Fisher. 2005. Effect of soil type on the establishment of grape phylloxera colonies in the Pacific Northwest. *American Journal of Enology and Viticulture* 56 (3): 207–211.

Clark, Corbet. 1989. *American Wines of the Northwest: A Guide to the Wines of Oregon, Washington, and Idaho*. New York: William Morrow.

Clarke, Oz, and Margaret Rand. 2001. *Oz Clarke's Encyclopedia of Grapes*. London: Websters International.

Columbia Cascade Winery Association. http://www.columbiacascadewines.com/.

Columbia Gorge Wine Growers. http://www.columbiagorgewine.com/.

Columbia River Wine Country. http://www.columbiariverwine.com/.

Columbia Valley Winery Association. http://www.columbiavalleywine.com/.

Danehower, Cole. 1999–2005. *Oregon Wine Report*. 25 vols. Scottsburg, Oregon: Cole Danehower.

Danehower, Cole. 2002. Ken Wright: Pursuing the pure expression of pinot noir. *Oregon Wine Report* 9: 18–21.

Danehower, Cole. 2004. It's getting hot out here! *Northwest Palate*, March/April: 22–23.

Danehower, Cole. 2006. Oregon's Emerging Pinot-Scape: Winemakers Define Success on Their Own Terms. *SFGate.com*. http://www.sfgate.com/.

Danehower, Cole. 2007. Snake River Valley appellation a first for Idaho. *AppellationAmerica.com*. April 19. http://wine.appellationamerica.com/wine-review/374/New-AVA-in-Idaho.html.

Dawson, Lawrence. 1992. Are Idaho wines influenced by altitude? *Wines & Vines*. April 1992. http://findarticles.com/p/articles/mi_m3488/is_n4_v73/ai_121156909/.

Day, J. H., L. Farstad, and G. G. Laird. 1959. *Soil Survey of Southeast Vancouver Island and Gulf Islands, British Columbia*. Report 6, British Columbia Soil Survey. Research Branch, Canada Department of Agriculture in cooperation with University of British Columbia and British Columbia Department of Agriculture, Ottawa.

Dundee Hills Winegrowers Association. http://www.dundeehills.org/.

Eola–Amity Hills AVA. http://www.eolaamityhills.com/content/index.php.

Fattig, Paul. 2008. Veni, vidi, viticulture: Grower came to the Rogue Valley and saw the land for vineyards. But will they conquer the region's agricultural future? *Mail Tribune*, July 13. http://www.mailtribune.com/apps/pbcs.dll/article?AID=/20080713/NEWS/807130321&template=printart.

Fraser Valley Wineries Association. http://www.fvwa.ca/.

Fritz, Marlene. 2000. *Vintage Idaho*. 2000. Moscow: University of Idaho. http://info.ag.uidaho.eduy/magazine/summer_2000/vintage.html.

Full Glass Research. 2005. *The Economic Impact of the Wine and Wine Grape Industries on the Oregon Economy*. http://www.fullglassresearch.com/fgrpress.htm

Gillerman, Virginia S., D. Wilkins, K. Shellie, and R. Bitner. 2006. Geology and wine II: *Terroir* of the western Snake River plain, Idaho, USA. *Geoscience Canada* 33 (1): 37–48.

Goode, Jamie. 2005. *The Science of Wine: From Vine to Glass*. Berkeley: University of California Press.

Greenough, John D., L. M. Mallory-Greenough, and B. J. Fryer. 2005. Geology and wine 9: Regional trace element fingerprinting of Canadian wines. *Geoscience Canada* 32 (4). http://journals.hil.unb.ca/index.php/GC/article/viewArticle/2712/3155.

Gregutt, Paul. 2004. Washington's rising riesling reputation. *The Seattle Times*, August 11. http:/'seattletimes.nwsource.com/cgi-bin/PrintStory.pl?slug=winecolumn11&date=20040811.

Gregutt, Paul. 2007. *Washington Wines & Wineries: The Essential Guide*. Berkeley: University of California Press.

Gregutt, Paul. 2009. Wineries in Idaho's Snake River Valley are finally making a mark. *The Seattle Times*: March 9. http://seattletimes.nwsource.com/cgi-bin/PrintStory.pl?document_id=793191&zsection_id=2004078393&slug-pacificpadviser01&date=20090301.

Gregutt, Paul. 2009. Yakima Valley wineries see a fruit-full future. *The Seattle Times*: March 29. http://seattlketimes.nwsource.com/cgi-bin/PrintStory.pl?documenty_id=...923702&zsection_id=2004078393&slug=pacificpadvidser 29&date=20090329.

Grogan, Peter. 2008. Winemaking in Washington state. *The Telegraph*, September 19. http://www.telegraph.co.uk/core/Content/displayPrintable.jhtml;j...VCBQ0IV0?xml=/wine/2008/09/19/wine-pacific119.xml&site=10&page=0.

Haeger, John Winthrop. 2004. *North American Pinot Noir*. Berkeley: University of California Press.

Haeger, John Winthrop. 2008. *Pacific Pinot Noir: A Comprehensive Winery Guide for Consumers and Connoisseurs*. Berkeley: University of California Press.

Hall, Lisa Shara. 2000. The Continued Strength of Alsatian Varietals in Oregon. *Wine Business Monthly*. http://www.winebusiness.com/html/PrinterVersion.cfm?dataId=2257..

Hall, Lisa Shara. 2001. *Wines of the Pacific Northwest: A Contemporary Guide to the Wines of Washington & Oregon*. London: Mitchell Beazley.

Hall, Lisa Shara. 2008. Oregon Harvest Report. *Wine Business Monthly*. http://www.winebusiness.com/news/?go=getArticle&dataId=59635. October 27.

Harbertson. James F. 2009. Introduction to Winemaking. Part 1: Overview of Winemaking & Determining Ripeness. Presentation slides, Washington State University Extension. Downloaded in February at ext.nrs.wsu.edu/Video/Wine/doc/harbertson1.ppt.

Hellman, Edward W., ed. 2003. *Oregon Viticulture*. Corvallis: Oregon State University Press.

Hinkel, Joanne. 2001. High desert vineyard. *AmericanProfile.com*. December 16, 2001. http://www.americanprofile.com/heroes/articel/1797,html?printable=true.

Horse Heaven Hills Wine Growers. http://www.horseheavenhillswinegrowers.org/index.html.

Idaho Business Review. 2009. Study: Wine industry contributed $73 million to Idaho economy in 2008. *Idaho Business Review*. April 10. http://www.idahobusiness.net/print.htm/2009/04/10/Study-Wine-industry-contributed-73-million-to-Idaho-economy-in-2008.

Idaho Grape Growers and Wine Production Commission. http://www.idahowines.org/.

Irvine, Ronald, and Walter J. Clore. 1997. *The Wine Project: Washington State's Winemaking History*. Vashon Island, Washington: Sketch Publications.

Jackson, Philip L., and A. Jon Kimerling, eds. 2003. *Atlas of the Pacific Northwest*. Corvallis: Oregon State University Press.

Johnson, Hugh., and Jancis Robinson. 2001. *The World Atlas of Wine*. London: Mitchell Beazley.

Jones, Gregory V. 2003. Umpqua Valley AVA: A GPS and GIS Vineyard Mapping and Analysis of Varietal, Climate, Landscape, and Management Characteristics. Southern Oregon University Geography Department, Ashland, Oregon, in cooperation with the Umpqua Valley Chapter of the Oregon Winegrowers' Association and the Oregon Wine Advisory Board.

Jones, Gregory V., N. Snead, and P. Nelson. 2004. Geology and Wine 8. Modeling viticultural landscapes: A GIS analysis of the *terroir* potential of the Umpqua Valley of Oregon. *Geoscience Canada* 31 (4): 167–178.

Juillerat, Lee. N.d. Idaho, the Pacific Northwest's Oldest Wine-Producing Region. *Visit Idaho*. http://hubpages.com/hub/The=Grapes-in-Idaho-Produce-Devine-Wine.

Julian, James W., Clark F. Seavert, Patricia A. Skinkis, Philip VanBuskirk, and Steve Castagnoli. 2008. *Vineyard Economics: Establishing and Producing Pinot Noir Wine Grapes in Western Oregon*. Oregon State University Extension Service EM 8969-E, Corvallis, Oregon. August.

Kaiser, C., P. Skinkis, and M. Olmstead. N.d. *Protecting Grapevines from Winter Injury*. Pacific Northwest Extension Publication, Oregon State University, Corvallis.

Kelley, C. C., and R. H. Spilsbury. 1949. *Soil Survey of the Okanagan and Similkameen Valleys, British Columbia*. Report 3, British Columbia Survey. The British Columbia Department of Agriculture in Cooperation with Experimental Farms Service, Dominion Department of Agriculture, Ottowa.

Kirk, Ruth, and Richard D. Daugherty. 2007. *Archaeology in Washington*. Seattle: University of Washington Press.

Lake Chelan Wine Valley. http://www.lakechelanwine-valley.com/.

Lavin, Kate. 2008. Oregon's umbrella for sustainability. *Wines & Vines*. May 14, 2008. http://www.winesandvines.com/sections/printout_article.cfm?article=headline&content=55540.

Levy, Ken. 2003. Idaho adds vineyards, awards to wine legacy. *Capital Press*. June 27.

Lien, Jana. 2008. Rolling fields of grapes? *Wine Press Northwest*. June 15. http://www.winepressnow.com/summer08/story/2060.html.

Locati, Joe J. 1978. *The Horticulture Heritage of Walla Walla County 1818–1977*. Walla Walla, Washington: Joe J. Locati.

Lukacs, Paul. 2000. *American Vintage: The Rise of American Wine*. New York: Houghton Mifflin.

Margalit, Yair. 1997. *Concepts in Wine Chemistry*. Ed. James D. Crum. San Francisco: The Wine Appreciation Guild.

Mayfield, Robert. N.d. Washington vs. Oregon: Distinguishing the Northwest's Two Unique Wine Regions. *The Wine News*. http://www.thewinenews.com/augsep01/feat.html.

McGourty, Glenn T. 2008. Growers transition to organic. *Wines & Vines*. July. http://www.winesandvines.com/template.cfm?section=features&content=56565.

Meinert, Lawrence D., and A. J. Busacca. 2000. Geology and Wine 3: *Terroirs* of the Walla Walla Valley appellation, southeastern Washington State, USA. *Geoscience Canada* 27 (4): 149–171.

Miglavs, Janis. 2008. *Oregon: The Taste of Wine*. Portland, Oregon: Graphic Arts Books.

Mihalovich, Michele. 2008. Growing Grapes by the Moon. *Daily Tidings*. June 20. http://archive.dailytidings.com/2008/0620/stories/0620_wine.php.

Miles, S. D. *Oregon 1986 Vineyard Acreage*. Extension Service, Oregon State University, Corvallis.

Miller, George R. 2002. *Pacific Northwest Weather*. Portland, Oregon: Frank Amato Publications.

Minskoff, Alan. 2009. Fraser Winery—Boise's First. *NewWest.Net*. March 6. http://www.newwest.net/main/print/24071.

Mitham, Peter. 2008. Freezing, drying, learning: Willamette wineries get creative to salvage a wet harvest. *Wines & Vines* (January): 26–32.

Moore, George W. 2002. Geology of Vineyards in the Willamette Valley, Oregon. September 16. http://cmug.com/chintimp/willamette.vineyards.htm.

Naramata Bench Wineries. http://www.naramatabench.com/wineries.aspx.

Narasin, Ben. 2008. Oregon's Willamette Valley: Islands of *terroir*. *Sommelier Journal* (December). http://www.sommelierjournal.com/articles/article.aspx?year=2008&month=12&articlenum=64.

Nagel, C. W., M. Atallah, G. H. Carter, and W. J. Clore. 1972. Evaluation of wine grapes grown in Washington. *American Journal of Enology and Viticulture* 23 (1): 14–17.

National Agricultural Statistics Service. 2008. *2007 Oregon Vineyard and Winery Report*. USDA, NASS, Oregon Field Office, Portland, Oregon.

National Agricultural Statistics Service. 2009. *2008 Oregon Vineyard and Winery Report*. USDA, NASS, Oregon Field Office, Portland, Oregon.

National Climate Data and Information Archive. 2000. Canadian Climate Normals 1971–2000, Naramata, British Columbia. http://www.climate.weatheroffice.ec.gc.ca/.

National Climate Data and Information Archive. 2000. Canadian Climate Normals 1971–2000, Osoyoos West, British Columbia. http://www.climate.weatheroffice.ec.gc.ca/.

Northwest Fisheries Science Center. 2000. Environment History and Features of Puget Sound. November. http://www.nwfsc.noaa.gov/publications/techmemos/tm44/environment.htm.

Olmstead, Mercy, K. Williams, and M. Keller. 2006. *Canopy Management for Pacific Northwest Vineyards*. Washington State University Extension, Pullman.

Oregon Pinot Camp. 2008. The Oregon pinot noir story; Soil into wine; Oregon pinot noir style & vintages; Oregon pinot noir challenge & opportunity; Oregon's cool whites. Unpublished. Portland, Oregon.

Oregon Wine Advisory Board. 1993. *OSU Wine Grape Research Progress Reports, 1992–1993*. Agriculture Experiment Station, Oregon State University Special Report 926, Corvallis.

Oregon Wine Board. http://www.oregonwine.org/Home/.

Parker, Rev. Samuel A. 1838. *Journal of an Exploring Tour Beyond the Rocky Mountians, Under the Direction of the A. B. C. F. M. Performed in the Years 1835, '36, and '37.* Ithaca, New York: Rev. Samuel A. Parker. Downloaded via http://books.google.com/.

Patton, Kristi. 2009. Similkameen Valley Emerging as Wine Region. BCLocalNews.com. http://www.bclocalnews.com/okanagan_similkameen/pentictonwesternnews/lifestyles/42631587.html. April 8.

Perdue, Andy. 2003. *The Northwest Wine Guide: A Buyer's Handbook.* Seattle: Sasquatch Books.

Peterson-Nedry, Judy, and Robert M. Reynolds. 1998. *Oregon Wine Country.* Portland, Oregon: Graphic Arts Center.

Phillips, Rod. 2000. *A Short History of Wine.* New York: HarperCollins.

Phylloxera Task Force at Oregon State University. 1995. *Phylloxera: Strategies for Management in Oregon's Vineyards.* Oregon State University Extension Service EC 1463 (November), Corvallis.

Pinney, Thomas. 2005. *A History of Wine in America: From Prohibition to the Present.* Berkeley: University of California Press.

Pintarich, Paul. 1997. *The Boys Up North: Dick Erath and the Early Oregon Winemakers.* Portland, Oregon: Wyatt Group.

Prial, Frank. 1991. Wine: Oregon's Gold Coast. *New York Times.* August 25. http://www.nytimes.com/1991/08/25/magazine/wine-oregon-s-gold-coast.html.

Prial, Frank J. 1998. Wine Talk: How Long Can Oregon Stay Low Key? *New York Times.* February 4. http://www.nytimes.com/1998/02/04/dining/wine-talk-how-long-can-oregon-stay-low-key.html.

Puget Sound Wine Growers. http://pugetsoundwine.org/default.aspx.

Rattlesnake Hills Wine Trail. http://www.rattlesnakehills.com/

Robinson, Jancis. 1996. *Jancis Robinson's Guide to Wine Grapes.* Oxford, England: Oxford University Press.

Robinson, Jancis, ed. 2006. *The Oxford Companion to Wine.* Oxford, England: Oxford University Press.

Roed, Murray A. 2009. Geological History of Okanagan Valley and Origin of Lake Okanagan, British Columbia. http://www.geoscapes.ca/pov/okhistory4.html.

Scates, Shelby. 1987. Underdog Washington wines enjoy sweet taste of success. *Seattle Post-Intelligencer*, March 31. http://seattlepi.nwsource.com/archives/1987/8701080512.asp.

Scholz, Gary. 2008. Scholz: Behind the scenes of Idaho's wine industry. *IdahoStatesman.com.* May 13. http://www.idahostatesman.com/life/v-print/story/377821.html.

Schreiner, John. 2001. *Icewine: The Complete Story.* Toronto: Warwick Publishing.

Schreiner, John. 2004. *The Wineries of British Columbia.* North Vancouver, British Columbia: Whitecap Books.

Schreiner, John. 2007. A wine industry takes flight. *Canadian Wine Annual*: 49–101.

Shaw, David. 2005. A proper noir mystery. *The Los Angeles Times*, May 4. http://articles.latimes.com/2005/may/04/food/fo-matters4.

Shellie, Krista C. 2007. Viticultural performance of red and white wine grape cultivars in southwestern Idaho. *HortTechnology* (October–December): 595–603.

Simon, Pat. 2000. *Wine-Tasters' Logic.* London: Faber & Faber.

Snake River Valley Wine Region. http://www.snakerivervalleywine.org/

Southern Oregon Wineries Association. http://www.sorwa.org/

Swinchatt, Jonathan. 2006. The evolution of *terroir. The World of Fine Wine* (13): 95–100.

Umpqua Valley Wineries. http://www.umpquavalleywineries.org/.

University of Idaho College of Agricultural and Life Sciences, Sandpoint R&E Center. Grape Cultivars for the Inland Northwest & Intermountain West. http://www.ag.uidaho.edu/sandpoint/grapes.htm.

U.S. Department of Agriculture. 2006. Bellpine Series. http://www2.ftw.nrcs.usda.gov/osd/dat/B/BELLPINE.html.

U.S. Department of Agriculture. 2006. Jory Series. http://www2.ftw.nrcs.usda.gov/osd/dat/J/JORY.html.

U.S. Department of Agriculture. 2006. NEKIA Series. http://www2.ftw.nrcs.usda.gov/osd/dat/N/Nekia.html.

U.S. Department of Agriculture. 2006. Washington Vineyard Acreage Report. National Agricultural Statistics Service, Washington, DC.

U.S. Department of Agriculture. 2006. Willakenzie Series. http://www2.ftw.nrcs.usda.gov/osd/dat/W/WILLAKENZIE.html.

U.S. Department of the Treasury, Alcohol and Tobacco Tax and Trade Bureau. 2000. Applegate Valley Viticultural Area (99R-112P). *Federal Register* 65 (241), December 14, Rules and Regulations, 78096–78099.

U.S. Department of the Treasury, Alcohol and Tobacco Tax and Trade Bureau. 2004. Establishment of the Dundee Hills Viticultural Area (2002R-218P). *Federal Register* 69 (229), November 30, Rules and Regulations, 69524–69527.

U.S. Department of the Treasury, Alcohol and Tobacco Tax and Trade Bureau. 2004. Establishment of the Southern Oregon Viticultural Area (2002R-338P). *Federal Register* 69 (235), December 8, Rules and Regulations, 70889–70893.

U.S. Department of the Treasury, Alcohol and Tobacco Tax and Trade Bureau. 2005. Establishment of the McMinnville Viticultural Area (2002R-217P). *Federal Register* 70 (11), January 18, Rules and Regulations, 2801–2805.

U.S. Department of the Treasury, Alcohol and Tobacco Tax and Trade Bureau. 2005. Establishment of the Red Hill Douglas County, Oregon Viticultural Area (2001R-88P). *Federal Register* 70 (198), October 14, Rules and Regulations, 59996–60002.

U.S. Department of the Treasury, Alcohol and Tobacco Tax and Trade Bureau. 2005. Establishment of the Ribbon Ridge Viticultural Area (2002R-215P). *Federal Register* 70 (104), June 1, Rules and Regulations, 31342–31345.

U.S. Department of the Treasury, Alcohol and Tobacco Tax and Trade Bureau. 2006. Establishment of the Chehalem Mountains Viticultural Area (2002R-214P). *Federal Register* 71 (227), November 27, Rules and Regulations, 68458–68463.

U.S. Department of the Treasury, Alcohol and Tobacco Tax and Trade Bureau. 2006. Establishment of the Eola–Amity Hills Viticultural Area (2005R-216P). *Federal Register* 71 (136), July 17, Rules and Regulations, 40400–40404.

U.S. Department of the Treasury, Alcohol and Tobacco Tax and Trade Bureau. 2007. Establishment of the Snake River Valley Viticultural Area (2005R-463P). *Federal Register* 72 (46), March 9, Rules and Regulations, 10598–10603.

Wagner, Cindy, and Karin Hanna, eds. 2000. *BC Wine Country: The Book.* Kelowna, British Columbia: Blue Moose Publications.

Waldin, Monty. *Biodynamic Wines.* 2004. London: Mitchell Beazley.

Walla Walla Valley Wine Alliance. 2003. http://www.wallawallawine.com/.

Washington State University, College of Agricultural, Human, & Natural Resource Sciences. 2003. *Crop Profile for Wine Grapes in Washington.* Pullman, Washington.

Washington Wine Commission. http://www.washingtonwine.org/.

Willamette Valley Wineries. http://www.willamettewines.com/.

Wine Islands Vintner's Association. http://www.wineislands.ca/.

Wines Northwest. Idaho wineries, wines and wine country. http://www.winesnw.com/idhome.html.

Wine Yakima Valley. http://www.wineyakimavalley.org/.

Winkler, A. J., James A. Cook, W. M. Kliewer, and Lloyd A. Lider. 1974. *General Viticulture.* Berkeley: University of California Press.

Winter, John D. N.d. *Geology of the Walla Walla Area.* Whitman Collage. Presentation slides downloaded March 2009; www.whitman.edu/geology/winter/WW%20and%20wine.ppt.

Wittneben, U. 1986. *Soils of the Okanagan and Similkameen Valleys.* MOE Technical Report 18; Report 52, British Columbia Soil Survey. B.C. Ministry of Environment, Victoria.

Woodall, Stacie, P. Wandschneider, J. Foltz, and R. G. Taylor. 2002. Valuing Idaho wineries with a travel cost model. In *Western Agricultural Economics Association, 2002 Annual Meeting*, Los Angeles. Department of Agricultural Economics and Rural Sociology, University of Idaho, Moscow.

Woodinville Wine Country. http://www.woodinvillewinecountry.com/.

Yamhill–Carlton District AVA. http://www.yamhillcarltondistrict.com/index.php.

INDEX